H
.oo

D1119018

Timing and Turnout

Timing and Turnout

*How Off-Cycle Elections Favor
Organized Groups*

SARAH F. ANZIA

THE UNIVERSITY OF CHICAGO PRESS   CHICAGO AND LONDON

SARAH F. ANZIA is assistant professor of public policy at the Goldman School of Public
Policy at the University of California, Berkeley.

The University of Chicago Press, Chicago 60637
The University of Chicago Press, Ltd., London
© 2014 by The University of Chicago
All rights reserved. Published 2014.
Printed in the United States of America
23 22 21 20 19 18 17 16 15 14   1 2 3 4 5

ISBN-13: 978-0-226-08678-1 (cloth)
ISBN-13: 978-0-226-08681-1 (paper)
ISBN-13: 978-0-226-08695-8 (e-book)
DOI: 10.7208/chicago/9780226086958.001.0001

Library of Congress Cataloging-in-Publication Data

Anzia, Sarah F., author.
  Timing and turnout : how off-cycle elections favor organized groups / Sarah F. Anzia.
    pages cm
  Includes bibliographical references and index.
  ISBN 978-0-226-08678-1 (cloth : alk. paper) — ISBN 978-0-226-08681-1 (pbk. : alk.
paper) — ISBN 978-0-226-08695-8 (e-book) 1. Elections—United States. 2. Voter turnout—
United States. I. Title.
  JK1965.A69 2013
  324.973—dc23

                                                                              2013022421

♾ This paper meets the requirements of ANSI/NISO Z39.48-1992 (Permanence of Paper).

TO JOSH

Contents

List of Illustrations   ix

Acknowledgments   xi

CHAPTER 1.   Timing and Turnout: The Basics   1

CHAPTER 2.   A Theory of Election Timing   16

CHAPTER 3.   Partisan Power Play: Election Timing Politics in the
Nineteenth Century   37

CHAPTER 4.   Interest Groups and Election Timing Choice in the
Twenty-First Century   81

CHAPTER 5.   Estimating the Effect of Off-Cycle Election Timing: School
Board Elections   126

CHAPTER 6.   "What Election?" Timing, Turnout, and Policy in California
Cities   167

CHAPTER 7.   Implications for Democracy, Representation, and
Institutional Stability   200

Appendixes   217

Notes   235

Index   269

Illustrations

FIGURES

FIGURE 3.1 Turnout in national, state, and city elections, New York City, 1859–76 53

FIGURE 3.2 Voter turnout and vote share for Democrats in New York City elections, 1860s 55

FIGURE 4.1 Election timing bills by state, 2001–11 92

FIGURE 4.2. Types of elections affected by consolidation proposals 94

FIGURE 4.3. States with school board election consolidation bills, 2001–11 112

FIGURE 4.4. Sponsorship of bills proposing school board election consolidation 113

FIGURE 4.5. Proportion voting for on-cycle school board elections 115

FIGURE 4.6. Proportion voting for on-cycle school board elections, clearest cases 117

FIGURE 4.7. Sponsorship of consolidation bills, excluding state and school board bills 121

FIGURE 5.1. Voter turnout in Minnesota school board elections 140

FIGURE 5.2. Marginal effect of a five-percentage-point decrease in turnout 143

FIGURE 5.3. Treatment and control school districts, House Bill 1 153

FIGURE 5.4. Pretreatment attributes of treatment and control districts 155

FIGURE 6.1. California municipal election timing by county, 2008 174

FIGURE 6.2. Firefighter and police officer compensation by city election timing 187

TABLES

TABLE 1.1. A snapshot of state and local election timing in the United
            States 8

TABLE 2.1. Election timing and vote shares of competing groups 30

TABLE 3.1. Votes cast in San Francisco during on-cycle and off-cycle
            elections, 1856–69 60

TABLE 3.2. Municipal election timing in 1940 and 1986, by state 75

TABLE 4.1. Citizens' election timing preferences by party and
            ideology 88

TABLE 4.2. Legislative progress of election consolidation bills 97

TABLE 4.3. State partisanship and the legislative progress of nonschool
            election consolidation bills 122

TABLE 5.1. The Eight-State Test of the effect of election timing 133

TABLE 5.2. The Eight-State Test and partisanship, union strength, and
            competition 138

TABLE 5.3. The Minnesota Test of the effect of election timing and
            turnout 142

TABLE 5.4. The Texas Test of the effect of election timing on
            turnout 154

TABLE 5.5. The Texas Test of the effect of on-cycle elections,
            matching 157

TABLE 5.6. The Texas Test, district fixed effects regression 161

TABLE 6.1. Voter turnout and election timing in city council
            elections 178

TABLE 6.2. City election timing and firefighter compensation, basic
            model 189

TABLE 6.3. City election timing and firefighter compensation, with
            controls 190

TABLE 6.4. City election timing and police officer compensation 193

TABLE 6.5. Election timing and city finance 196

Acknowledgments

I have benefited from the guidance and support of many people as I have worked on this project. First and foremost, I am deeply indebted to my mentor and good friend Terry Moe. Not only did he encourage me to develop this project in the first place, but he also read multiple drafts of all the chapters, gave me feedback on the material I presented at workshops and conferences, and always had insightful comments and suggestions for how to improve the book. He has been a steady source of encouragement and inspiration, even when I encountered significant roadblocks. I have benefited in countless ways from his warmth and generosity. I am extremely grateful.

This project would not have become what it is without the support and feedback of a few key individuals. Special thanks to William Howell, who gave me incredibly helpful, thoughtful comments on the manuscript and who has been tremendously encouraging and supportive of the project. Thanks also to Chris Berry for getting me started down this path: it was through working as a research assistant for Chris at the University of Chicago and having several conversations with him about the timing of special district elections that I first started thinking about election timing as a research topic. I also owe a big thank you to Jonathan Rodden, who has read multiple drafts of these chapters and has given me many ideas on how to improve, extend, and frame my work. His support and guidance have been indispensable. I am also extremely fortunate to have had the help of Mike Tomz over the last few years. My conversations with Mike have helped me organize and clarify my ideas as well as improve my empirical work. Thanks, Mike, for all of the time and energy you have put into reading and critiquing my research. It has also been a pleasure to work with Morris Fiorina, whose big-picture comments on some of my earliest drafts of these chapters considerably shaped the trajectory of the project. I am indebted to Dave Brady for his unwavering support and enthusiasm and his reminders of the importance of studying "big" questions. Thanks to Jessica Trounstine for her detailed comments on the manuscript, for her many suggestions of different ways to test the theory, and for sharing data. And to Molly Jackman, thank you for your friendship and for all of the advice you have given me on this project—especially in the spring of 2009 when we brainstormed for hours on end and you helped me straighten out my thinking.

This project also benefited from the advice, feedback, and support of a number of other people, including Josephine Andrews, Richard Bensel, Mike Binder, Carles Boix, Henry Brady, Isa Chaves, David Daniels, Kyle Dropp, John Ellwood, Sean Farhang, Jim Fearon, John Ferejohn, Tammy Frisby, Sean Gailmard, Justin Grimmer, Bobby Gulotty, Steve Haber, Scott Handler, Laurel Harbridge, Danielle Harlan, Saul Jackman, Simon Jackman, Karen Jusko, Vlad Kogan, Thad Kousser, Keith Krehbiel, Ruth Kricheli, Diqing Lou, Beatriz Magaloni, Neil Malhotra, Colin McCubbins, Victor Menaldo, Jeff Milyo, Clayton Nall, Maggie Peters, Ken Schultz, Gary Segura, Jas Sekhon, Paul Sniderman, Rachel Stein, Jonathan Wand, Amber Wichowsky, and Gerry Wright. Thanks to the Hayek Fund for Scholars donors and review committee for providing funding to purchase the 1986 ICMA dataset. I am also indebted to John Tryneski at the University of Chicago Press for his enthusiasm about the book, for his insights, and for selecting two fantastic reviewers who gave me incredibly helpful feedback on the manuscript. Many thanks also to Rodney Powell, who was very helpful with the technical aspects of the manuscript preparation, and to Tiffany Li, Kevin McNellis, and Anna Scodel for their research assistance.

Parts of chapter 5 were previously published in "Election Timing and the Electoral Influence of Interest Groups," by Sarah F. Anzia, *Journal of Politics* 73, no. 2 (2011): 412–27, Copyright © 2011 Southern Political Science Association. These parts of the chapter are reprinted with the permission of Cambridge University Press. Other parts of chapter 5 were previously published in "The Election Timing Effect: Evidence from a Policy Intervention in Texas," by Sarah F. Anzia, *Quarterly Journal of Political Science* 7, no. 3 (2012): 209–48. Parts of chapter 3 were previously published in "Partisan Power Play: The Origins of Local Election Timing as an American Political Institution," by Sarah F. Anzia, *Studies in American*

Political Development 26, no. 1 (2012): 24-49, © Cambridge University Press. These parts of the chapter are reprinted with permission.

I am especially grateful for my family and friends who have been supportive of me as I have worked on this project, even when that work has come at the expense of my time with them. My parents, Joan and Dan, and my sisters, Carolyn and Maura, have been loving and understanding throughout. Thanks to Jill, David, Jimmy, Louis, Sandy, Lauren, Lijie, and Alexi for the many forms of support you have provided in the last few years. Special thanks to Bill McCready for encouraging me to apply to graduate school many years ago. My love and thanks to my daughter, Emma, for lighting up my life and giving me the proper perspective. And to Josh, my husband, words cannot express how grateful I am to have your love and support. Thank you for your endless patience, for your consistently good advice, and for being there for me in the good times and the tough times.

CHAPTER ONE

Timing and Turnout

The Basics

When it comes to voter turnout rates in industrialized democracies, the United States is at the bottom of the list. About 55 to 60% of eligible American voters participate in US presidential elections, compared to turnout rates of 91% in Belgium, 90% in Italy, 86% in Sweden, and 81% in Australia. Some of the gap between the United States and other democracies can be explained by unusual voter registration requirements in the United States and compulsory voting laws in countries like Belgium and Australia, but nonetheless, the differences are striking. In fact, the sole industrialized democracy whose turnout rates in national elections regularly fall below that of the United States is Switzerland, and with its average turnout rate of 54%, it is not far behind.[1]

Moreover, turnout rates of 55 to 60% are by no means *typical* of elections in the United States; those figures describe American voter participation at its highest. Turnout in midterm congressional elections runs closer to 35%, and participation rates in national primary elections are lower still. Of course, American government is much more than just its national government. According to the preliminary counts of the 2012 Census of Governments, there are 89,055 individual governments in the United States, most of which are *local* governments like counties, cities, townships, school districts, and the like.[2] And in local government elections, voter turnout rates of 20%, 10%, or even lower are common. Thus in comparison to the turnout levels of most elections conducted in the United States, the 55 to 60% turnout rates of presidential elections are actually quite high.[3]

However, citing average turnout statistics by the type of government in the United States masks an enormous amount of variation across govern-ments. Consider, for example, two cities in the San Francisco Bay Area: Palo Alto and Berkeley. Palo Alto, the municipality adjacent to Stan-ford University, has a considerably smaller, older, and wealthier popula-tion than Berkeley, and so based on what scholars have established about the correlates of political participation,[4] many would guess that Palo Alto municipal elections would have higher turnout rates than Berkeley mu-nicipal elections. But in fact the opposite is true. In 2008, a full 65% of Berkeley registered voters cast a vote in their city election, whereas the following year, only 38% of Palo Alto registered voters participated in their city races. Those elections were not anomalous. In 2002 and 2006, Berkeley city races had participation rates of 57% and 59%, respectively, while Palo Alto turnout was a mere 38% in 2007.[5]

Why the large turnout gap between the two cities—and in the unex-pected direction? The explanation is actually quite simple: Berkeley's city elections are held in November of even-numbered years, concurrently with presidential elections, gubernatorial elections, and congressional elections, whereas Palo Alto's city elections have historically been held in November of the odd-numbered years, concurrent only with local school board elections.[6] Anyone skeptical of this explanation for the turnout gap need only look at turnout rates in some of the ballot measure elections that have been held in Palo Alto in November of even-numbered years: In November 2008, a full 82% of Palo Alto registered voters cast a vote for or against local Measure N—a measure dealing with library improve-ments. In 2002, 56% voted in Palo Alto ballot measure races.[7] Thus within Palo Alto, turnout was 18 percentage points higher in city elections con-current with gubernatorial and congressional elections than in the odd-numbered years, and it was a whopping 44 percentage points higher when city elections were concurrent with a presidential election.

The case of Palo Alto versus Berkeley illustrates a pattern that is al-ready familiar to some political scientists: that is, the *timing* of elections affects voter turnout. In a study of California cities, for example, Zoltan Hajnal, Paul Lewis, and Hugh Louch found that turnout in off-cycle city elections averaged 36 percentage points lower than in city elections held during presidential elections.[8] Similarly, using a sample of fifty-seven cities across the country, Curtis Wood estimated that off-cycle election timing dampened city election turnout by an average of 29 percentage points.[9] Analyzing a sample of elections in thirty-eight large cities over twenty-five years, Neal Caren also found that turnout was significantly lower in cities that did not hold elections at the same time as presidential elections, by about 27 percentage points.[10] Not only are these effects large, but they also dwarf the effects of other institutional variables these scholars examine. As Hajnal concluded, "election timing is the most important factor in explaining local voter turnout."[11] Wood summarized his findings similarly, saying, "the single largest predictor of voter turnout is holding city elections concurrently with national and state elections."[12] Clearly, turnout in municipal elections hinges greatly on whether they are held on the same day as national elections.

This is not purely a municipal election phenomenon. Using a national sample of school districts, Frederick Hess estimated an 18-percentage-point turnout gap between school board elections held during state and national elections and school board elections held on other days.[13] Nor is it limited to local government. Gubernatorial elections attract the most voters when they are held concurrently with presidential elections and the fewest voters when they are held in the odd-numbered years.[14] Midterm congressional election turnout averages 13 percentage points lower than turnout in presidential-year congressional elections.[15] In general, voter turnout in the United States varies predictably with whether elections of one type are bundled with—or separated from—elections that attract greater participation.

Given that election timing is so consequential for voter turnout, one would think the electoral calendar would be a major focus of research among political scientists. After all, it is a political institution, and the study of political institutions is at the very heart of the discipline.[16] And yet the topic of election timing in the United States barely shows up in the literature on institutions. The most basic questions remain pretty much unexplored: Who decides when elections will be held, and how are those decisions made? Does the timing of elections matter for more than just voter turnout? Does election timing affect election outcomes, or public policy? These are fundamental questions about the operation and substance of American democracy, and yet the extant literature offers little in the way of answers.

This book is an attempt to make some headway. It focuses on the causes and consequences of election timing, by which I mean whether or not elections of one type (for example, city elections) are concurrent with elections of another type (for example, presidential elections). My main argument is that the timing of elections has great potential to affect not only how *many* people vote but also *who* votes, which candidates win, and to whom elected officials respond in designing public policy. Specifically, I argue that shifting from on-cycle to off-cycle election timing has the effect of increasing the electoral presence of *the organized*, for two main reasons: First, those who have a large stake in an election outcome turn out to vote at high rates regardless of when that election is held, and many of the individuals with the greatest stake in election outcomes are members of organized groups. Second, off-cycle election timing enhances the effectiveness of organized groups' mobilization efforts, since each additional mobilized supporter goes further toward tipping the election outcome when turnout is low. In general, the members and mobilized supporters of organized groups should make up a greater proportion of the active electorate in off-cycle elections than in on-cycle elections.

This change in the composition of the electorate that results from a shift in election timing has great potential to shape election outcomes and policy making, and in some political contexts, it's relatively easy to see how. In particular, when organized interest groups seek policies with concentrated benefits and distributed costs, and when they face relatively little organized competition, they should be more successful in electing their preferred candidates and securing favorable policies when elections are held off-cycle rather than on-cycle. However, even when organized groups compete over policy, and even when voters on both sides of an issue are equally motivated to turn out, election timing can still tip the balance of power in favor of one group or its rival, with potential to change the outcome. The choice of election timing is therefore a consequential one, and not just for voter turnout but also for election results and the substance of public policy.

A Snapshot of Election Timing in the United States

Before I can move forward with an evaluation of the causes and consequences of election timing, a very basic problem must be resolved. That is, aside from national elections and a few studies that have examined samples of local governments, we do not even have basic information on when elections are held in most American governments. There is no single source that provides such information, and the laws governing election timing vary tremendously by state. Thus creating a sketch of when different types of elections are held across the United States requires researching each state one by one. Considering that the rules governing election timing in many states are quite complex, collecting that kind of information is a nontrivial task.

Take the state of New Jersey as an example. The schedule of elections in New Jersey is so complex that it makes one wonder whether it should be called a "schedule" at all. Its state-level elections are held in November of odd-numbered years, separate from US presidential and congressional elections. Elections for the state's twenty-one counties and any of its 566 municipal governments that hold partisan elections are held annually in November, but most of its municipalities that have nonpartisan elections hold their regular elections on the second Tuesday in May. School district elections, on the other hand, have historically been held on the third Tuesday in April.[17] Fire district commissioners are elected on an entirely separate day: the third Saturday in February. The dates of most other special district elections are so elusive that groups of citizens have actually banded together to try to figure out when governments like sanitation districts elect their representatives.[18] So, in addition to national Election Day, which refers to the Tuesday after the first Monday of November of even-numbered years, New Jersey voters are asked to go to the polls in the odd-numbered years, in the winter, on a couple of dates in the spring, and in many cases during the summer too. This does not even account for primary elections or special elections, which add to the list of voters' responsibilities.

New Jersey therefore has something that looks more like a steady stream of elections every year than a single Election Day once every two years. And in some other states, the rules governing election timing are even harder to follow. For example, some states give local governments discretion to hold elections whenever they want. Other states give local governments a menu of election dates from which they can choose. There are even some states that establish a uniform election day for a particular type of government but then carve out exceptions for certain places. The thought of trying to keep track and make sense of all these rules is quite daunting. And yet at the same time, it is difficult to ask questions about how election timing matters, or why elections are held when they are, if we don't actually *know* when elections are held. So as a necessary preliminary step, I set out to collect some basic information on the rules governing election timing in each of the fifty states.

First off, it is important to note that there are many different types of elections in the United States: regular elections, primary elections, runoff elections, special elections to fill vacancies, ballot measure elections, tax and bond elections, charter or constitutional elections, recall elections, and so on. To make the task at hand manageable, I focus on the timing of regular elections for government officials. I also exclude nonschool special districts from my search, since determining when special districts hold elections is prohibitively difficult for many states.[19] I used a variety of resources to assemble the information, including state statutes and constitutions, information provided by the offices of secretaries of state, reports compiled by state municipal leagues and state school board associations, and many phone and e-mail communications with government officials and associations of local governments.

The final product of the data collection effort is a snapshot of state and local election timing in the United States as of January 2012, which I summarize in table 1.1. Since government is structured differently in each state, I group the information in the table into four categories: the rules governing state elections, county elections, municipal elections, and school district elections. For each category in each state, I document the month of the regular elections as well as whether those elections are held in even-numbered years, odd-numbered years, or annually. In many states, this is straightforward, since all of the elections within each of the four categories are held on the same day. As I alluded to above, however, oftentimes the election timing rules for a certain category of government cannot be summarized so simply. There might be subtypes of governments within a particular category that hold elections at different times. For example, within the municipal government category, villages might be required to hold elections on one day and cities on another. Alternatively, individual governments within a category might have discretion to choose from among a menu of established election dates. In table 1.1, I label all such cases as having "Multiple schedules." I also distinguish between cases with "Multiple schedules" and cases in which governments in a given category have broad latitude to choose whatever election date they please with very few restrictions. For the latter cases, I indicate that election timing for the category "Varies." Where necessary, the table notes document detail on individual cells of the table.

Even with all of these simplifications, the information in table 1.1 is a lot to process. In a way, this is testament to just how complex the American electoral calendar really is. But ultimately, my interest in this book is in whether elections for governments like states, cities, and school districts are held on the same day as other elections or not. Therefore, to summarize the information about election concurrence in each state, I have used a bold font if at least some elections of that type of government in that state are held at times other than November of even-numbered years. The cells left in a normal font are those for which all elections in that category and state are held concurrently with congressional and presidential elections.[20]

It is the bold font that really highlights the patterns of election scheduling in the United States. At the level of state government, there are only five states that hold some or all of their regular elections in the odd-numbered years: Kentucky, Louisiana, Mississippi, New Jersey, and Virginia. The rest of the states hold elections concurrently with national elections. While November of even-numbered years is also the modal choice for county elections, there are several states that hold county elections at other times. In California and Tennessee, regular county elections are concurrent with statewide primaries. In Louisiana, Mississippi, Pennsylvania, and Virginia, county elections are in November of the odd-numbered years. Two states—New Jersey and New York—hold county elections annually in November (with some exceptions), and in Wisconsin, there are both nonpartisan county elections in April and partisan county elections in November. Alaska's boroughs, which are similar to counties, hold elections annually in October. Thus even at the county level, there is quite a bit of variation in when regular elections are held.

But the variation really takes off when we move to municipal elections. For municipal government, elections in November of even-numbered years are the exception rather than the norm, a schedule used by only five of the fifty states: Arkansas, Kentucky, Nebraska, Oregon, and Rhode Island. In several states, some municipal elections are held concurrently with national general elections while others are held off-cycle, either because individual governments have a choice over their election scheduling or because certain types of municipalities have on-cycle elections and others have off-cycle elections. In North Dakota, municipal elections are concurrent with the state's primary elections, and in South Dakota, it is permitted but not required for municipalities to hold elections during the statewide primary. In many states, however, *all* municipal elections are held on days other than national general or primary elections. Thus the rules for municipal elections in most states are quite different from the rules for state and county elections. Across the United States, municipal elections tend to be held on days other than national elections.

It is much the same for school districts: the dominant rule is one of separation of school board elections from national elections. In total, eighteen states have a uniform school board election date that does *not*

TABLE I.I **A snapshot of state and local election timing in the United States**

State	State Elections	County Elections	Municipal Elections	School Elections
AL	November / Even	November / Even	**August / Even**	**Varies**[1]
AK	November / Even	**October / All**[2]	**October / All**[3]	**Varies**
AZ	November / Even	November / Even	**Multiple schedules**	November / Even
AR	November / Even	November / Even	November / Even	**September / All**
CA	November / Even	**June / Even**	**Multiple schedules**[4]	**Multiple schedules**
CO	November / Even	November / Even	**Multiple schedules**	**November / Odd**
CT	November / Even	N/A	**Multiple schedules**	**Multiple schedules**
DE	November / Even	November / Even	**Varies**	**May / All**
FL	November / Even	November / Even	**Varies**	November / Even
GA	November / Even	November / Even	**November / Odd**	**Multiple schedules**[5]
HI	November / Even	November / Even	N/A	N/A
ID	November / Even	November / Even	**November / Odd**	**May / Odd**
IL	November / Even	November / Even	**April / Odd**[6]	**April / Odd**
IN	November / Even	November / Even	**November / Odd**	November / Even
IA	November / Even	November / Even	**November / Odd**	**September / Odd**
KS	November / Even	November / Even	**April / Odd**	**April / Odd**
KY	**November / All**[7]	November / Even	November / Even	November / Even[8]
LA	**November / Odd**	**November / Odd**[9]	**Multiple schedules**	November / Even[10]
ME	November / Even	November / Even	**Varies**	**Varies**
MD	November / Even	November / Even	**Varies**	November / Even
MA	November / Even	November / Even	**Varies**[11]	**Varies**[12]
MI	November / Even	November / Even	**Multiple schedules**	November / Even
MN	November / Even	November / Even	**Multiple schedules**	**Multiple schedules**
MS	**November / Odd**	**November / Odd**	**June / Odd**[13]	**Multiple schedules**[14]
MO	November / Even	November / Even	**April / All**	**April / All**[15]
MT	November / Even	November / Even	**November / Odd**	**May / All**
NE	November / Even	November / Even	November / Even[16]	November / Even[17]
NV	November / Even	November / Even	**Multiple schedules**	November / Even
NH	November / Even	November / Even	**Varies**[18]	**Varies**
NJ	**November / Odd**	**November / All**	**Multiple schedules**	**Multiple schedules**
NM	November / Even	November / Even	**March / Even**[19]	**February / Odd**
NY	November / Even	**November / All**[20]	**Varies**[21]	**May / All**[22]
NC	November / Even	November / Even	**November / Odd**[23]	**Varies**[24]
ND	November / Even	November / Even	**June / Even**	**Varies**
OH	November / Even	November / Even	**November / Odd**	**November / Odd**
OK	November / Even	November / Even	**April / Odd**[25]	**February / All**
OR	November / Even	November / Even	November / Even	**May / Odd**
PA	November / Even	**November / Odd**	**November / Odd**	**November / Odd**
RI	November / Even	N/A	November / Even[26]	November / Even[27]
SC	November / Even	November / Even	**Varies**	**Varies**
SD	November / Even	November / Even	**Varies**[28]	**Varies**[29]
TN	November / Even	**August / Even**	**Varies**	**Varies**[30]
TX	November / Even	November / Even	**Multiple schedules**	**Multiple schedules**
UT	November / Even	November / Even	**November / Odd**	November / Even
VT	November / Even	November / Even	**March / All**	**Varies**[31]
VA	**November / Odd**	**November / Odd**	**Multiple schedules**	**Multiple schedules**
WA	November / Even	November / Even	**November / Odd**	**November / Odd**
WV	November / Even	November / Even	**Varies**[32]	**May / Even**
WI	November / Even	**Multiple schedules**	**April / All**	**April / All**
WY	November / Even	November / Even	**Multiple schedules**	November / Even

TABLE I.I *continued*

Notes:

1. County school boards are elected in November of even years; city school boards that are elected hold elections at various times throughout the year.
2. Alaska has boroughs rather than counties.
3. Anchorage holds its elections in April.
4. Charter cities can choose their election dates.
5. County school board elections are held during state general or primary elections; municipal school board elections are in November of odd years or during primaries.
6. Chicago holds elections in February of even years.
7. Statewide offices are elected in odd years; legislative offices are elected in even years.
8. Independent school districts that embrace a fifth class city can hold elections in May.
9. Orleans Parish is an exception.
10. Municipal school districts do not necessarily have to hold their elections concurrently with national elections.
11. Town elections are held on various dates in the spring; most city elections are in November of odd years.
12. Municipal school committee elections are during their parent municipalities' elections; districtwide regional school elections are in November of even years.
13. Municipalities with special charters can hold elections at other times.
14. County school districts hold elections in November of even years; municipal school districts hold elections on the first Saturday in March.
15. Urban school districts have biennial elections in April of even years.
16. Omaha and Lincoln hold elections in May of odd years.
17. A few districts hold school elections during statewide primaries or in odd years.
18. Town elections can be on three different dates; village elections are anytime between January 1 and May 1; most city elections are in November of odd years.
19. Four cities hold elections at other times, only one of which is in November of even years (Los Alamos).
20. Different counties have different schedules. All are in November, but some are annual, some are biennial in odd years, and some are biennial in even years.
21. Cities and towns hold elections in November of even years, odd years, or both. Village elections are on the third Tuesday in March but can change to other dates.
22. Albany and the "Big Five" (New York City, Yonkers, Syracuse, Rochester, and Buffalo) are exceptions.
23. Municipalities with nonpartisan elections and runoffs hold general elections on the fourth Tuesday before the November odd-year date.
24. The default date is the date of the statewide primary, but local laws can override that policy.
25. Some charter cities hold elections at other times.
26. Central Falls, Woonsocket, and Jamestown are exceptions; they hold elections in November of odd years.
27. Woonsocket holds elections in November of odd years.
28. The default date is in April of every year, but municipalities can also consolidate with school district elections or the statewide primary in June.
29. Elections must be between the second Tuesday in April and third Tuesday in June of each year, or combined with municipal elections or the statewide primary.
30. County school boards hold elections during the statewide primary in August; municipal school boards choose their own election dates.
31. The annual town school district meeting is usually the date of the town meeting, but the date can be changed to anytime between February 1 and July 15.
32. Most municipal elections are in June of odd years.

coincide with national Election Day. In an additional nineteen states, school board elections take place on a variety of dates throughout the year. Of those, fourteen have *some* school board elections in November of even-numbered years, whereas the other five have *all* off-cycle school board elections. Compared to municipal elections, a larger number of states now require school board elections to be held in November of even-numbered years, but those states—Arizona, Florida, Indiana, Kentucky, Louisiana, Maryland, Michigan, Nebraska, Nevada, Rhode Island,

Utah, and Wyoming—are still well in the minority. As of 2012 the national trend is one of off-cycle school board elections.

By simply summarizing the timing of regular elections for four categories of government in each state, table 1.1 sheds light on just how fragmented the American election schedule is—and I haven't even taken into account primary elections, runoff elections, special elections, ballot measure elections, and the like, all of which can be held on days other than those documented in the table. The picture of American election scheduling that emerges is both fascinating and puzzling, and it points to a number of important, unanswered questions: Why are most local elections held on different days than state and national elections, especially if voter turnout is so much lower in off-cycle local elections? Has it always been this way, or is the fragmentation of the American electoral calendar a relatively recent phenomenon? What are the *consequences* of separating state or local elections from national elections? These are the questions that motivate this book. In the end, I cannot possibly explain each and every election timing rule in every state as well as its evolution over time. But I do provide a general theoretical framework for thinking about election timing and test it in several different political contexts, laying a foundation for more research on election timing in the future.

Preview of the Book

In the next chapter, I start by developing a theory of election timing, and then in chapters 3 through 6, I test that theoretical framework using two different approaches. First, in chapters 3 and 4 I examine the politics of election timing choice. That analysis, even if it were purely descriptive, would be an important contribution to the literature, since as I said earlier, precious little existing research seeks to explain why American elections are held when they are. But more importantly, chapters 3 and 4 present the first tests of the theoretical framework. If changes to election timing affect the distribution of political power among organized groups in predictable ways, as I argue, then we should expect those groups to be active in debates over the scheduling of elections—and the nature of their activity should be predictable as well. Moreover, if the organized groups that care about election timing are important to the officials who make decisions about the election schedule, then I can also use the theory to predict the stances those decision makers will take on election timing issues.

In chapter 3 I test the theory by examining the politics of city election timing choice in the nineteenth century. By digging into the histories of three large American cities and tracing what happened to their election schedules between the 1840s and the dawn of the Progressive Era, I find that the election timing of these large American cities changed frequently—a trend that has not been discussed in the literature on American political development. I also find that even before the Civil War, voter turnout was much lower in off-cycle local elections than in on-cycle local elections. Most importantly, my analysis makes it clear that political parties—the organized groups who competed for local offices in New York, San Francisco, and Philadelphia in the nineteenth century— consistently tried to manipulate the timing of elections to their advantage.

The political environment is very different today, and yet the dynamics of election timing politics are much the same. In chapter 4, I analyze a dataset of state legislative bills introduced between 2001 and 2011 that proposed changes to the election timing of various governments throughout the United States. As in chapter 3, I use the theoretical framework to predict which organized groups should prefer off-cycle elections to on-cycle elections, and then I investigate whether those groups testify in favor of or in opposition to the changes proposed in state legislatures. In addition, because the groups that would be affected by proposed election timing changes are important to state legislators' reelection interests, I also test predictions about state legislators' positions on election timing bills. Ultimately, I find that the politics of election timing choice in state legislatures today involves a struggle among groups for electoral influence, just as the theoretical framework would predict.

Beginning with chapter 5, I turn the question around and estimate the *effects* of election timing on organized groups' success in securing favorable policies. As in any study of a political institution's effects, concerns about the endogeneity of election timing are a central focus—and my findings from chapters 3 and 4 indicate that such concerns are well warranted. In chapters 5 and 6, then, I use the lessons gleaned from the first two empirical chapters to inform my tests of election timing's effects. The goal is to craft a set of empirical designs that account for and eliminate the likely sources of bias, yielding clean, causal estimates of the effects of election timing on policy outcomes.

In chapter 5, I apply the theory to the context of local school board elections in nine US states. School board elections are a particularly useful test bed for the theory for several reasons. Most importantly, in school

board elections, one particular interest group tends to be more motivated and better organized than any of its competition: teachers and their
unions. Moreover, teacher unions across the country share many of the
same policy goals, which simplifies the task of identifying a dependent
variable. Notably, one of the main goals of teacher unions is to secure
higher compensation for teachers. And since the board members who
are elected in school district elections largely determine teacher compensation, we can expect compensation to fluctuate within and across districts depending on how influential teachers are in those elections. Consequently, if off-cycle elections allow teachers to have greater influence than
on-cycle elections, school board members in districts with off-cycle elections should better compensate teachers than board members in comparable districts with on-cycle elections.

In chapter 6, I move the empirical analysis beyond school board elections and examine whether the timing of city government elections matters for the degree to which organized interest groups influence city election outcomes. Just as teacher unions are typically the dominant force in
school board elections, municipal employees—especially when they are
organized into unions—are often the most powerful force in city elections
in the United States. Municipal employees rely on city government officials for their salaries and benefits, and, therefore, they have an unusually
large stake in city election outcomes. Furthermore, municipal employees
are highly organized in unions throughout much of the country, and they
have the financial and organizational wherewithal to mobilize and persuade voters. In chapter 6 I test whether off-cycle city election timing con-
fers an advantage on municipal employee unions in California cities by
examining various public finance outcomes.

In the final chapter, I step back from the details of the empirical analysis to reflect on what these findings mean for American democracy. Here
we have an electoral institution that effectively deters a *third* of the electorate from going to the polls. This is a massive effect. To put it into context, moving local elections from off-cycle to the same day as presidential elections is *three times* more effective at increasing turnout than the
most effective mode of mobilization—face-to-face canvassing—that Alan
Gerber and Donald Green found in one of their first get-out-the-vote experiments.[21] So, based on what we learn from the empirical chapters of
the book, is it good or bad that local elections tend to be held separately
from state and national elections? Is having a steady stream of elections
throughout the year preferable to having one or two elections bienni-

ally? There are no straightforward answers to these questions, and as with many issues, where one stands depends on where one sits. But given the trade-offs involved in the choice of election timing—trade-offs that come into focus in this book—it is important to consider how different election schedules affect the quality of the democratic process in the United States.

In the end, election timing deserves more attention than I can dedicate to it in a single book. My hope is that this investigation of an important yet understudied electoral institution will spark a literature dedicated to it—dedicated to learning about the effects election timing has on other outcomes and for other groups, governments, countries, and time periods than the ones I examine here.

The Bigger Picture

The conclusions I draw in this book, however, are not limited to the particular institution of election timing. By shedding light on questions such as what makes institutions stable and what causes them to change, my findings also carry important lessons for the study of political institutions more generally. In addition, they suggest that we should reevaluate the conventional wisdom about who benefits from decreases in voter turnout—and why. Most importantly, and related to the book's implications for political institutions and turnout bias, my findings suggest that *organized groups* play a far greater role in American politics than one would think based solely on a review of the recent American politics literature.

This final point is worth emphasizing, since the next chapter presents a theory that puts organized groups center stage. Put bluntly, most of today's research in American politics does not focus on organized groups; instead, it adopts the individual voter as the unit of analysis. Consider some of the most prevalent styles of studies carried out the last few years: Quite popular, for example, is the use of survey experiments to probe how individual voters react to stimuli. As another example, congressional scholars have taken to using new large-N surveys to evaluate whether members of the US Congress represent the policy preferences of the median voters in their districts. There have also been a number of field experiments evaluating the effectiveness of mobilization treatments on individuals' propensity to turn out. These are valuable research agendas, but they all analyze politics in terms of individual voters, or individual voters aggregated into districts.

That is not to say that there is *no* current research on the political activities and effectiveness of organized groups in American politics—just that it is not as central to the discipline as it once was. Forty to fifty years ago, groups were *the* focus for scholars like Robert Dahl, David Truman, Theodore Lowi, Mancur Olson, and E. E. Schattschneider.[22] Central to the research agenda of the pluralists and pluralist revisionists were questions about how government responds to pressure from interest groups, whether or not public policy is biased by the political activities of interest groups, how and why interest groups form, and how interest groups are related to political parties as organizations. These were important research questions with major implications for our understanding of how American government operates. Yet in recent decades the focus on the role of organized groups in the political process has largely faded.

Despite the direction that American politics research has taken, however, it would be hard to argue that organized groups aren't important in American politics. By appearances, at least, they seem to be hugely important. Interest groups contribute enormous sums of money to candidates and committees, they lobby elected officials, they work to shape rule making in government agencies, they endorse and sometimes even recruit candidates, they mobilize voters—put simply, they are an integral part of the American political process. Recognizing this, some political scientists have begun to urge American politics scholars to once again make organized groups a central part of their research agenda.[23] The theory and findings of this book contribute to that effort. As I show in the chapters to follow, an individual-centric view of American politics cannot explain why elections are held when they are. It is only through an understanding of what *organized groups* have at stake in the timing of elections that one can begin to understand the full consequences of shifts in election timing for politics and policy.

But while the pluralists were right to emphasize the importance of groups, my conclusions in this book are not as rosy as theirs. Both Dahl's *Who Governs?* and Schattschneider's *The Semisovereign People*, for example, express concern about the potential for interest groups to bias the way in which elected officials represent citizens. However, both also conclude that interest groups' ability to capture government is tempered by policy makers' needs to cater to majorities in elections. As Dahl recognizes, though, the degree to which the electoral process actually reduces the likelihood of private interests becoming public policy is contingent on rates of voter participation.[24] What of elections in which 10% of the eligible electorate votes—and not just because of a one-time fluke, but because long-standing electoral rules consistently suppress voter participation? Perhaps those kinds of elections are not the tempering force that Dahl and Schattschneider envisioned. Moreover, if the electoral process obstructs an interest group's ability to secure its private interests in public policy, then that group has strong incentive to try to shape the electoral process so as to reduce voter participation and maximize its own influence. Off-cycle election timing is one reliable way of doing just that. And, as I show in the pages to follow, political parties cannot be counted on to be the solution.

These implications for political institutions, voter turnout, and organized groups aside, my hope is that at a minimum, the theory and empirical results I present in this book advance our knowledge and understanding of an important electoral institution that has heretofore been studied very little. But mine most certainly will not be the final word on the matter. Really, this book is only the beginning. Elections are, after all, a cornerstone of democratic government. Few would question that *how* elections are carried out can be incredibly important for who wins, who loses, and who controls government. And if something as seemingly trivial as the order of names on a ballot can impact election outcomes,[25] it seems obvious that *when* elections are held should matter—potentially quite a bit. What I argue in this book is that the timing of elections *does* matter. It matters not only for how many people vote but also for the composition of the electorate. Because of this, it has enormous potential to tip the balance of power in elections, affecting both the outcomes of elections and the design of public policy.

CHAPTER TWO

A Theory of Election Timing

Some of the facts laid out in the previous chapter present something of a puzzle: Political observers regularly lament that voter turnout in the United States is low. And if turnout is low in national elections, it is far lower in most local elections. Empirically, the most important predictor of voter turnout in local elections is the *timing* of elections—meaning whether they are held on the same day as other elections or on entirely different days. Yet in mapping out when elections are held in the United States, I discovered that 88% of the states hold some or all of their municipal elections off-cycle, and that 74% of the states hold some or all of their school board elections off-cycle. Why is this so? And should we be concerned that so many governments in the United States hold off-cycle elections when it has been shown that participation would dramatically increase if those elections were simply rescheduled to coincide with national Election Day?

Surprisingly, few scholars have investigated these questions. It is worth noting, however, that they are closely related to a question that *has* been the topic of considerable debate: Does it matter that turnout is so low in so many American elections? For those who believe that increasing voter participation is a desirable end in itself, the answer is unambiguously yes.[1] Others, however, might wonder whether low turnout makes a difference to how well the eligible electorate is represented. On that topic, the evidence is mixed. Many political scientists have found that the policy preferences of nonvoters are similar to the preferences of voters, which suggests that smaller electorates represent the eligible electorate reasonably well.[2] However, as Zoltan Hajnal and Jessica Trounstine explain, almost all of the studies that draw such a conclusion examine voters and nonvoters in *national* elections—when turnout is at its highest.[3] As turnout drops from 55% to

30% or even 15% of voters, the potential for skew in the electorate grows. And as of now, we simply do not know much about how election timing affects election outcomes, policy making, and political representation.

In this chapter, I develop a theoretical framework for considering how shifts in election timing affect the composition of the electorate. While previous scholars have examined the impact of off-cycle election timing on the representation of minority voters at the polls,[4] or the proportion of "yes" voters who turn out to vote in tax and bond referenda,[5] my focus here is different: I consider how the timing of elections matters for the electoral influence of *the organized*. The main argument I make is quite simple—so simple that the thrust of it is captured in an observation made by local politics scholar Charles Adrian over fifty years ago:

> The major danger in a light vote lies in the fact that highly organized groups, whether of the nature of old-fashioned city machines or of special interest groups of any type, will thereby be able to control the government, for the lighter the vote the easier it is for such groups to win. They have a solid nucleus of dependable voters. A small turnout does not result in the same percentage distribution of the vote among the various segments of the population as would be found in a large turnout.[6]

Now, this was a comment made in passing. Moreover, Adrian did not mention election timing, nor did he elaborate on the idea or test it empirically. Even so, his years of observing city politics led him to suspect that the power of the organized is enhanced by low voter turnout. My goal in this chapter is to draw the connection between election timing—a political institution that is rarely discussed—and the political influence of the organized—a topic that is of interest to anyone who cares about how government represents its citizens.

In the first part of the chapter, I argue that off-cycle election timing increases the presence of organized interest groups at the polls. My focus is on two different dynamics that play a part in increasing the electoral presence of interest groups as voter turnout decreases—one driven by different incentives among individuals in the eligible voter population, and one driven by the political activity of the groups themselves. The conclusion I draw from this initial discussion is straightforward: I expect that the members and mobilized supporters of organized interest groups make up a greater proportion of the active electorate in off-cycle elections than in on-cycle elections.

In the second part of the chapter, I argue that the timing of elections, through its effects on turnout and the composition of the electorate, has great potential to shape election outcomes and public policy. I start by considering a specific type of electoral context—one that is probably common in the United States—and show that when an interest group faces little organized competition and seeks a policy with concentrated benefits and distributed costs, it should have greater success in securing the policy it favors when elections are held off-cycle rather than on-cycle. The same is true in contexts where multiple interest groups are active but do not compete directly with one another: officials elected in off-cycle elections should make policy more favorable to those groups than officials elected in on-cycle elections. Making predictions about how election timing affects interest groups' fortunes is more difficult when two or more groups work at cross-purposes, but even in those more complicated cases, the theoretical framework still serves as a useful guide. For even when groups compete, election timing can tip the balance of power in favor of one group or its rival, with potential to change the outcome.

The final section of the chapter broadens the definition of "organized group" and explains how the theoretical framework applies to political parties. While parties usually have a broader array of goals than interest groups, both types of groups are political organizations that actively participate in the electoral process, and because of that key similarity, election timing should affect parties in much the same way that it affects interest groups. Moreover, in today's political environment, the electoral fortunes of political parties are inextricably linked to the electoral fortunes of interest groups. Thus if election timing tips the balance of power among interest groups, that should have consequences for political parties as well.

Election Timing and the Composition of the Electorate

In their classic study of voter participation in the United States, Steven Rosenstone and John Mark Hansen evaluate two broad categories of reasons for why people turn out to vote in elections—or not. The first set of explanations relates to the characteristics of individuals, such as their resources and their sense of political efficacy, that factor into people's decisions about whether or not to vote. The second set relates to the influence of group mobilization on voting behavior. Notably, the researchers find that the individual-level factors as well as group mobilization are important for explaining patterns of voter turnout in the United States.[7]

My argument is that both of these factors are also important for explaining how off-cycle election timing increases the importance of organized interest groups in elections. To understand how individual-level incentives play a part in changing the composition of the electorate when election timing is changed, consider two well-established empirical patterns: The first—which I highlighted by comparing Palo Alto and Berkeley in the last chapter—is the connection between election timing and voter turnout. As John Aldrich has explained, more voters are drawn to the polls in national and statewide elections than in local elections, and so voter turnout in local elections should be higher when those elections are combined with national or statewide elections rather than held separately.[8] The second is that, all else equal, citizens who have a large stake in an election outcome are more likely to vote in that election than citizens who have less at stake.[9] As an example of this, Rosenstone and Hansen find that people who care about the election outcome and people who strongly prefer one candidate to the other are more likely to vote than citizens who care less.[10]

With these two patterns in mind, how would we expect the composition of the electorate to change when elections are moved to off-cycle? Notably, the people with a large stake in the election can be expected to participate at high rates *regardless* of when the election is held, even if overall turnout is lower in an off-cycle election. The decrease in turnout that accompanies the shift to off-cycle election timing likely comes disproportionately from those who have less at stake. And if voter turnout decreases unevenly across the electorate in this fashion as a result of a change to electoral timing, then the individuals with a large stake in the election cast a greater proportion of the ballots in an off-cycle election than in an on-cycle election.

A number of researchers have noted this tendency for "stakeholders" to make up a greater proportion of the electorate in off-cycle elections, even if existing research has not drawn out the implications for organized groups. For example, work by William Fischel as well as Eric Oliver argues that homeowners with a stake in maintaining high property values tend to be overrepresented in off-cycle, low-turnout local elections.[11] Separately, Stephanie Dunne, W. Robert Reed, and James Wilbanks theorize that the individuals who want school bonds to pass have more at stake in school bond elections than individuals who would prefer the bonds to fail, and so the proportion of "yes" voters is greater when bond elections are held off-cycle.[12] Marc Meredith provides a more nuanced picture, one in which agenda-setters who want school bonds to pass strategically schedule the bond elections on-cycle or off-cycle depending on which electorate will be more favorable to passage.[13] Terry Moe explains that in school elections generally, off-cycle election scheduling increases the proportion of teachers and school employees who turn out to the polls.[14] And Christopher Berry suggests that off-cycle election timing helps special district officials inflate their budgets, since "high demanders" turn out at disproportionately high rates when special district elections are held at odd times.[15]

To say that individuals with a large stake in elections have a greater presence in off-cycle elections than in on-cycle elections is therefore relatively uncontroversial. One implication of this pattern that has *not* been discussed in existing research, however, is that often the individuals who have the largest stake in election outcomes are members of interest groups.[16] Consider Dunne, Reed, and Wilbanks's and Meredith's study cases of school bond referenda, or Moe's example of school board elections: the school employees who have such a large stake in the election outcome are usually members of public sector unions, which are among the most powerful interest groups in American politics today.[17] The same is true of other government employees in city, county, and state elections. Senior citizens have a large stake in protecting Medicare, Medicaid, and Social Security and therefore have strong reasons to be politically active, but they also tend to be members of the politically powerful AARP. Likewise, in local politics, real estate developers have interests in securing favorable land use decisions, and they also tend to be part of politically active developers' associations. Put simply, the stake individuals have in politics is likely to be positively correlated with membership in politically active organized groups.

Data from the 2006 Social Capital Community Survey (SCCS) generally support this claim.[18] While it is difficult to evaluate exactly how much a given individual has at stake in a particular election, his or her interest in politics can serve as a rough proxy.[19] And the SCCS data show that individuals who report being "very interested" in politics and national affairs are significantly more likely to be members of groups than individuals who report being either "not at all interested" or "only slightly interested." Take neighborhood associations, for example—groups that tend to be active in local politics: 28% of people who are very interested in politics participate in neighborhood associations, whereas only 13% of people who are slightly or not at all interested do. The same goes for professional, trade, farm, and business associations: 31% of the very interested participate, while only 12% of the slightly to not interested participate. Similar patterns hold for labor unions, charity and social welfare organizations, and religious groups: the politically interested are far more likely to participate in these types of groups than those who see themselves as having less of a stake in politics. And unsurprisingly, 21% of the very politically interested are members of public interest groups, political action groups, political clubs, or party committees, whereas only 3% of those with little to no interest in politics do.

My point is simply that by increasing the relative presence of stakeholders at the polls, off-cycle election timing also has the side effect of increasing the importance of organized interest groups in elections.[20] In Adrian's words, these groups "have a solid nucleus of dependable voters."[21] Therefore, we should expect their members and supporters to turn out at high rates even when elections are held off-cycle.

This individual-level effect is only part of the story, however. The organized groups that have a stake in an election do not just passively sit around and hope their members and supporters will turn out to vote. Rather, they take an *active* role in mobilizing supporters and persuading likely voters to vote for their preferred candidates. Interest group leaders remind their members to vote, and they encourage them to contact their friends, neighbors, and coworkers. They operate phone banks, go door to door, and send out mailings to remind their supporters to participate. They can also make it easier for supporters to vote by reminding them of their polling places or by giving them rides to the polls. For individuals who might feel as though they do not know enough about the election to cast a ballot, interest groups can provide information about the election and the issues at stake to encourage those voters to turn out. And of course, many interest groups endorse candidates, which can provide a critical signal to voters as to where candidates stand on the issues. Naturally, groups carry out these activities in an attempt to provide enough supportive votes to tip the election in their favor.

Off-cycle election timing can therefore increase the electoral presence of organized interest groups in another way: by enhancing the effectiveness of their mobilization efforts. In particular, when turnout is low, each additional supportive voter mobilized by a group has a greater impact on the vote share of the candidate or position the group favors. As a result, by mobilizing the same number of voters, the interest group has a greater chance of tipping the election outcome in its favor when the election is off-cycle rather than on-cycle.[22]

A simple example illustrates how this works. Consider an interest group that has the capacity to send an additional five hundred supportive voters to the polls in a city where sixty thousand people are registered to vote. When the city election is held concurrently with a presidential election, absent a group mobilization effort, forty thousand voters turn out to vote. Imagine that 48% of those voters favor the interest group's preferred candidate, and 52% favor the rival candidate. If the interest group mobilizes the extra five hundred supportive voters that it can, those five hundred voters will make up little more than 1% of the total active electorate (500 divided by 40,500). Their mobilization effort raises support for their preferred candidate from 48% to 48.6%, but clearly not enough to give him a majority. In contrast, assume that when the city election is held on an entirely different day, only ten thousand voters participate absent any group mobilization effort. For simplicity's sake, assume that again, 48% of those ten thousand voters prefer the interest group's candidate. Now, if the interest group mobilizes an additional five hundred supportive voters, those five hundred voters make up almost 5% of the active electorate. More importantly, the additional voters put the interest group's preferred candidate over the 50% vote share mark: 5,300 voters in total support the interest group's candidate, compared to the 5,200 votes for the rival candidate. Off-cycle election timing can therefore mean the difference between winning and losing.[23] But regardless of the specifics of a situation, when elections are shifted from on-cycle to off-cycle, interest groups' mobilized votes carry greater weight. And if turnout is low enough, or if the election is close enough, a change from on-cycle to off-cycle election timing can very well mean the difference between an election won and an election lost by an interest group's preferred candidate.

The advantage that accrues to organized groups in off-cycle elections therefore works through two channels. The first, which I call the *individual effect*, occurs even without proactive mobilization by interest groups: as turnout decreases, the individuals who stand to benefit most from the election make up a greater proportion of the electorate. Since many of those with the greatest stake in the election are members of organized interest groups, the individual effect enhances the presence of interest groups at the polls. The individual effect is supplemented by the increased effectiveness of groups' mobilization efforts in off-cycle elections, which I refer to as the *group effect*: because turnout is lower in off-cycle elections, each mobilized voter has a bigger impact on the election outcome when elections are off-cycle. As a result of these two effects together, we should expect a larger proportion of voters to be members and mobilized supporters of interest groups in off-cycle elections than in on-cycle elections.

Election Timing, Election Outcomes, and Public Policy

If off-cycle election timing increases the presence of interest groups in elections, then what are the consequences for election outcomes and policy? This question is more difficult to answer than the one about how off-cycle election timing affects the composition of the electorate, but it is arguably more important. For even if off-cycle election timing increases the proportion of interest group members and their mobilized supporters at the polls, we ultimately want to know whether that matters for how government operates.

Some might be quick to conclude that *of course* it matters. If interest groups play a bigger role in off-cycle elections, then policy should more closely reflect interest group preferences in governments that hold off-cycle elections. Others might point out that most elections feature multiple active interest groups, some of which work at cross-purposes. And if off-cycle election timing increases the electoral presence of all the groups, couldn't the increased strength of one group be canceled out by the increased strength of its rival?

Actually, both of these intuitions are on target. What I argue in this section is that the consequences of off-cycle election timing for election outcomes and policy ultimately depend on the types of policies at stake and the nature of interest group activity. There are many situations in which the increased presence of organized interest groups in off-cycle elections can be expected to produce government that is more responsive to the policy demands of those groups. When groups compete over policy, or where voters on both sides of a policy issue are highly motivated to turn out, making predictions about how election timing affects election outcomes is more difficult. But as I will discuss, even in those more complicated cases, election timing still has great potential to tip the balance of electoral power between rival groups, shaping both election outcomes and public policy.

When it comes to the individual-level effect of a shift to off-cycle election timing, the most straightforward scenario is one in which an interest group seeks a policy with concentrated benefits and diffuse costs (or a policy with concentrated costs and diffuse benefits). In such a case, the individual effect of off-cycle election timing can be expected to work in the group's favor. The logic is simple: The interest group's members stand to reap relatively large direct benefits from the provision of the good, whereas the typical voter in the polity is responsible for but a tiny fraction of the cost. With the benefits of the good distributed so unevenly, and the costs dispersed smoothly, the lowering of turnout in an off-cycle election should not affect proponents and opponents to the same extent. Rather, those who stand to benefit have more at stake than individuals who bear the costs, and so as elections are shifted from on-cycle to off-cycle, turnout should decrease more among opponents than proponents. As a result, the proportion of voters who favor the provision of the good sought by the interest group should be greater in an off-cycle election than in an on-cycle election. And as long as the policy-making process reflects the composition of the active electorate, policies should be more favorable to the interest group's preferences when elections are held off-cycle rather than on-cycle.[24]

In making predictions about how the group effect of a shift to off-cycle election timing shapes election outcomes and policy, the simplest case is a scenario in which a single interest group faces little to no organized competition over the policy it cares about. In such a case, the shift to off-cycle election timing increases the effectiveness of the group's mobilization efforts without also increasing the weight of any opposition group's mobilization efforts. Thus by mobilizing the same number of voters in an off-cycle election as in an on-cycle election, the interest group secures an electorate that is more favorable to its policy position. As a result, policy made by officials elected in off-cycle elections should be more favorable to the interest group than policies made by officials elected in on-cycle elections.

In sum, when an interest group seeks a policy with concentrated benefits and diffuse costs and faces little to no organized competition over that policy, the electorate as a whole should be more favorably disposed toward the group's policy goals in off-cycle elections, and election outcomes and policy should be more favorable to the group as a result. This is hardly a contrived scenario. Actually, I expect that many—if not most—electoral contexts in the United States can be characterized in this way.

For starters, many of the interest groups in the United States organize for economic reasons, and many of the economic benefits sought by such groups have concentrated benefits and diffuse costs. Consider the policies sought by some of the classic examples of economic interest groups in the United States:[25] Organized labor groups seek better wages and benefits for union members. Farm groups might pursue subsidies for milk producers. Business associations generally push for lower corporate tax rates. These policies are inherently distributive in nature, and there is good reason to think the individuals affiliated with such groups would be more motivated to participate in elections affecting those policies than the dispersed group of individuals whose responsibility it is to pay for them. The individual effect of off-cycle election timing should therefore generally work to the advantage of such interest groups.

Furthermore, as James Q. Wilson has argued, it is precisely the policy areas where benefits are concentrated and costs are distributed where one is likely to find highly organized beneficiaries facing little to no organized competition. The same is true when a policy has concentrated costs and distributed benefits: those who stand to pay the costs tend to be more motivated and better organized than the beneficiaries.[26] Certain policy areas—the ones in which the individual effect of off-cycle election timing creates advantages for organized interest groups—are also conducive to lopsided organizational strength. Put simply, the cases where the individual effect tips election outcomes in favor of organized interest groups also tend to be the cases where the group effect does as well.

Actually, it is probably quite common for organized interest groups to face relatively little competition over the policies that are most important to them. A business association seeking a tax break for a company considering a move into a city may well face no organized opposition to that tax break. Likewise, a firefighters' union seeking higher compensation and shorter work hours for local firefighters usually does not confront an anti-firefighter group. The elections these groups are involved in might feature other groups active on *different* policy issues, but that does not change the fact that the business association and the firefighters' union face no direct competition over the particular issues they care about. Therefore, even if there are multiple interest groups active in politics, if each interest group is politically active on a different issue dimension, more than one group can benefit from off-cycle elections.

It is also important to keep in mind that the modal election in the United States is a local election, and while we know far less about local elections than we do about presidential or congressional elections, the little research that has been done suggests that they tend to feature a small number of organized groups.[27] And if there is a positive relation-ship between the number of groups active in an election and the chances that any given group will face direct organized competition to its policy demands, the interest groups that *are* active in local elections might face little organized opposition.

My point is simply that many interest groups *do* seek benefits for which gains are concentrated among their members and costs are dis-persed among the broader public. It is probably also quite common for interest groups to face little organized competition over their primary policy goals. For such groups, both the individual and group effects of off-cycle election timing can be expected to work in their favor. As a result, policy should more closely reflect their preferences when elections are held off-cycle.

Of course, not all interest groups seek policies with concentrated bene-fits and distributed costs. If the policy issue at stake is one where voters on both sides are highly motivated to participate, the individual-level effect of off-cycle election timing might result in little to no change to election outcomes. If, for example, an organized group seeks implementation of an abstinence-only sex education program in the local schools, and that issue is the dominant one in a local school board election, there might not be much asymmetry in the decrease in turnout that comes with off-cycle election timing, since strong opponents of abstinence-only policies might be just as motivated to turn out as strong proponents. It is even possible that *on*-cycle electorates could be more favorable to a group's policy posi-tion.[28] For example, in an environment where pro-choice voters are more highly motivated to participate than pro-life voters, a pro-life group might actually fare better when turnout is high.

Moreover, while the presence of multiple interest groups does not nec-essarily change the fundamental dynamic at play, there are certainly cases of organized groups that work at cross-purposes. Clearly, if two interest groups compete with each other on a single policy dimension, it is not possible for a change to off-cycle election timing to benefit both of them. Rather, a shift to off-cycle election timing and the subsequent lowering of voter turnout would increase the effectiveness of *both* groups' mobiliza-tion efforts, the effects of which could offset each other.

Importantly, however, even when groups prioritize issues on which both sides are highly motivated to participate, and even when two or more groups work at cross-purposes, shifts in election timing have great potential to tip the balance of power between them. The United States is full of examples of competing groups trying to manipulate election timing in order to gain a competitive edge. In West Virginia in 2010, when the question was whether the special election to succeed former governor Joe Manchin would be held in November of 2011 or 2012, groups like the West Virginia Education Association, the state AFL-CIO, and the West Virginia Citizen Action Group all lined up to support the off-cycle special election.[29] In the small coastal city of Half Moon Bay, California, in 2010, the environmentalist faction that had recently lost control of city government sought to shift city elections to November of even-numbered years in expectation that higher turnout rates would help them win future elections against the more prodevelopment faction.[30] So when voters on both sides of an issue are highly motivated, or when organized groups compete against each other, usually the question is not *whether* timing affects election outcomes but rather *who* benefits from off-cycle election scheduling and by *how much*. As before, both the individual and group effects are important to consider in making predictions.

Starting with the individual effect, in the most general sense, an organized group benefits from off-cycle election timing if its members and supporters are more likely to weather the overall decrease in voter turnout than the eligible voters who oppose the group's policy goals. We can therefore think of voters in a particular electoral context as being one of two types: *Consistent Voters* are those who vote in the election regardless of when it is held, and *Presidential Voters* only vote in the election when it is held on the same day as a presidential election.[31] If the percentage of Consistent Voters that prefer a certain candidate or policy is greater than the percentage among Presidential Voters, then the group favoring that candidate or policy will fare better in an off-cycle election. If, however, Presidential Voters are more amenable to the candidate or policy than are Consistent Voters, the group will fare better when elections are held concurrently with presidential elections.

The group effect can also be generalized beyond cases of interest groups that face little to no organized competition. When two groups compete with each other over policy or candidates, the primary factor that determines which group benefits from the group effect of off-cycle election timing is the groups' relative *organizational capacity*. By organizational capacity, I mean the resources a group has at its disposal to mobilize and persuade voters, including financial resources, a membership base that can be tapped for phone banks or door-to-door canvassing, a network of volunteers that can help with sending out mailings, and more.

Of two competing groups, the one with greater organizational capacity can mobilize a larger number of voters in support of its candidate or position. Therefore, in off-cycle elections, the weight of both groups' mobilization activities is enhanced, but it is the group with greater organizational capacity that wins more vote share in an off-cycle election than in an on-cycle election.[32]

It is also important to note that the individual effect and the group effect can move in opposite directions. In discussing the case of a single interest group seeking a distributive policy, I argued that *both* the individual and group effects help the group to secure a more favorable electorate. However, in some contexts, off-cycle election timing might be a boon for a group on the individual dimension but a disadvantage on the group dimension. To draw conclusions about how a particular group will fare in off-cycle or on-cycle elections, one has to determine what the net impact of the two election timing effects will be.

A simple example is useful for illustrating how these two dimensions operate. Consider a scenario in which two organized groups, the Developers and the Environmentalists, are at odds over what should be done with a vacant plot of land in their city. The land-use decision will ultimately be made by the city's mayor, so for the upcoming election, each group nominates a mayoral candidate friendly to its position. Both groups seek to maximize the vote share received by their preferred candidate. The question we want to answer is this: Which group's candidate secures greater vote share when city elections are held off-cycle rather than on the same day as a presidential election?

If the Developers have greater organizational resources at their disposal than the Environmentalists, then in terms of their capacity to mobilize voters, the Developers stand to win greater vote share in an off-cycle election than in an on-cycle election. However, separating the election from a presidential election also demobilizes voters whose interests lie primarily in the highly visible presidential race. Assume that the proportion of voters who favor the Environmentalists over the Developers is greater among Presidential Voters than among Consistent Voters. Clearly, in that case, the Environmentalists stand to win greater vote share in on-cycle elections than in off-cycle elections, since both the individual effect and the group effect of off-cycle election timing work in the Developers' favor. Specifically, the Developers' candidate does better in off-cycle city elections both because Presidential Voters do not vote and because the Developers can dominate the smaller electorate by mobilizing more supportive voters. The Environmentalists' candidate, on the other hand, performs better in an on-cycle environment in which the Presidential Voters participate and in which the superior mobilization ability of the Developers has a more muted effect on the candidates' vote shares.

In contrast, if the Developers are the dominant organizational force in the polity and command a larger percentage of support from Presidential Voters than from Consistent Voters, the Developers' preferences over the election schedule are mixed. The Developers favor off-cycle election timing if they anticipate that they can win greater vote share by controlling the small, off-cycle electorate and closing the floodgates to Presidential Voters. However, if the margin of support for the Developers is significantly greater among Presidential Voters than among Consistent Voters, the Developers' candidate could win a larger percentage of the vote in an on-cycle election. This is a situation in which the two effects of off-cycle election timing pull in opposite directions. The net impact of election timing on the candidates' vote shares therefore depends on which of the two countervailing forces is stronger.

Table 2.1 summarizes the predictions for which election schedule brings greater success to the Developers' preferred candidate on the basis of these two considerations. The vertical dimension characterizes the preferences of Presidential Voters relative to Consistent Voters, and the horizontal dimension depicts the strength of the Developers' organizational capacity relative to that of the Environmentalists. In the middle category, where the groups are equally well organized and their candidates are equally favored by Presidential Voters and Consistent Voters, the Developers' candidate does equally well under on-cycle and off-cycle elections. Wherever the Developers are either weaker than or equal to the Environmentalists in organizational capacity but are more favored by Presidential Voters than by Consistent Voters, the Developers fare better under on-cycle elections. In cases where the Developers are stronger than or equal to the Environmentalists in organizational capacity but are less favored by Presidential Voters than by Consistent Voters, the Developers' candidate wins more vote share in off-cycle elections. When the Developers' candidate's vote share among Presidential Voters is equal to his vote share among Consistent Voters, he does better under on-cycle elections when the Developers are organizationally weaker and off-cycle elections when the Developers are organizationally stronger. In the top left and bottom right corners, the net effect of off-cycle election timing depends on which of the two countervailing forces is stronger.

TABLE 2.1 **Election timing and vote shares of competing groups: Condition that yields greater vote share for the Developers' candidate**

	The Developers have stronger organization	The Developers and Environmentalists are equal in organizational capacity	The Developers have weaker organization
% of Presidential Voters that favor the Developers' candidate is **greater than** the % among Consistent Voters	Depends on vote shares under each condition	On-cycle	On-cycle
% of Presidential Voters that favor the Developers' candidate is **the same as** the % among Consistent Voters	Off-cycle	No difference	On-cycle
% of Presidential Voters that favor the Developers' candidate is **smaller than** the % among Consistent Voters	Off-cycle	Off-cycle	Depends on vote shares under each condition

In principle, this three-by-three matrix can be used to make predictions about which of two groups working at cross-purposes should win greater vote share in an off-cycle election than in an on-cycle election. To do so, one would have to estimate the level of support for each group among Presidential Voters and Consistent Voters (absent mobilization efforts by either group), the relative organizational capacity of the groups, and, if those two factors work in opposite directions, what the combination of the two implies in terms of vote share. By carrying out such an exercise, one could locate a given context within one of the nine cells of table 2.1.

Admittedly, measuring these things can be difficult. Moreover, I have made an important simplifying assumption—that groups seek to maximize vote share—that might not actually hold. It could be, for example, that groups mobilize as a many voters in an election as is necessary to win with some degree of certainty, in which case mobilizing voters to bring their candidates' vote share from 70 to 75% would be unnecessary—or even wasteful. Considering that groups have to use precious resources to mobilize supporters, this is a realistic possibility. What this means is that a group's mobilization effort could be endogenous to election timing. If, for example, the individual effect of off-cycle election timing works in favor of the group, the group may not need to mobilize as many voters in an off-cycle election as in an on-cycle election in order to secure a reasonably comfortable victory margin. In that case, the similarity of the group's vote share in off-cycle and on-cycle elections would mask the fact that the group could have performed much better in the off-cycle election if it had mobilized to its full capacity.

These concerns are of the empirical sort, however. To be sure, the parameters may be difficult to measure, and because of this, making precise predictions about the effect of election timing on election outcomes can be challenging. However, the advantage of this general theoretical framework is that it allows me to account for the effects of election timing in a broad set of electoral contexts. Moreover, it encompasses the type of case in which the prediction is straightforward—the case in which a single group is dominant in organizational capacity and has greater support from Consistent Voters than from Presidential Voters. My view is that on balance, the advantage of the scope of the theory outweighs the disadvantage of the difficulty of testing it in certain environments. After all, political observers seem to think that election timing makes a difference in a wide variety of contexts: state elections, national elections, elections in which multiple groups compete with one another, and contexts where interest groups seek policies for ideological or cultural reasons. This theoretical framework provides a way of evaluating the impact of election timing on election outcomes in all such environments.

One final note about the framework: While table 2.1 suggests that we should be able to identify the *direction* of the election timing effect on election outcomes, the *size* of the effect might also be of interest. First, the size of the effect should be proportionate to the size of the turnout decrease that occurs in moving from an on-cycle to an off-cycle election. For example, a 5-percentage-point drop in turnout should affect a group's electoral fortunes only slightly, whereas a 30-percentage-point drop stands to make a big difference. Thus the differences between midterm and presidential-year US congressional electorates may not be as substantial as the differences between the electorates of municipal elections held in the spring of odd-numbered years and municipal elections held in November of even-numbered years. Even across governments of the same type, or within governments over time, the effect of election timing on interest group influence should vary with the size of the turnout gap.

Two other factors can be expected to affect the size of the election timing effect. First, the size of the individual effect should depend on the size of the difference between the preferences of Presidential Voters and Consistent Voters. All else equal, the greater the support gap between the two groups of voters, the greater should be the individual effect of off-cycle election timing. Second, if two competing groups are relatively well matched in organizational capacity, but one group has a slight edge, a change in election timing might not make a large difference to election outcomes. However, if one group is vastly better resourced than its competitor, the size of the group effect should be large. In the limit, a situation in which one group is very strong organizationally and its competitor is very weak approximates the case of an interest group facing no competition.

Let us step back for a moment to assess what we have gained in this second stage of theoretical development. At the start of this section, I had given a theoretical justification for why organized interest groups should have greater presence at the polls in off-cycle elections than in on-cycle elections, but I had not yet established what this meant for election outcomes and policy. I therefore began this section by developing expectations about the effects of election timing for election outcomes and policy in a particular type of situation—one in which an interest group seeks a policy with concentrated benefits and distributed costs and faces little to no organized competition. The prediction in that case was straightforward: election outcomes and policy should be more favorable to the interest group when elections are held off-cycle rather than on-cycle. From there, I added complexity. What if voters on both sides of an issue are highly motivated to participate in elections? What if an interest group faces direct competition from another organized group? The result was the development of a general framework for thinking about how changes to election timing can tip the balance of power in elections. In that framework, the consequences of election timing for election outcomes are contingent on specific features of the electoral environment.

Political Parties in the Theoretical Framework

Up to this point, my discussion of the effects of election timing has focused on interest groups, but election timing should also affect the fortunes of another type of organized group: political parties. At a minimum, anecdotal evidence suggests that political party leaders care a great deal about when elections are held, what that means for voter turnout, and what timing decisions imply for the success of their candidates and initiatives. In California in 2011, for example, Democrats passed a measure that would require all voter-generated initiatives to be held in November of even-numbered years rather than during spring primaries. Under the belief that the statewide primary electorate in California is more conservative than the November general electorate, Republican leaders called the move a "blatant power grab" by Democrats and public sector unions, one of the Democrats' most important interest group constituencies.[33] Because the theoretical framework allows me to consider how competing groups fare under different election timing regimes, it can be applied to political party competition as well as interest group competition.

To be sure, political parties are different from interest groups in certain ways. Interest groups are simply groups of people with shared interests that pursue their goals through the political process.[34] Whether they are narrow or broad in purpose and size, their primary political goal is to influence policy. Political parties, on the other hand, are more difficult to define.[35] Because parties serve as umbrella-like organizations that represent and promote a whole host of policy positions, they tend to be broader in scale and scope than interest groups.[36] Political parties also serve a number of different functions in politics. They nominate candidates for public office, they mobilize voters in support of those candidates in elections, they organize the activities of the legislative and executive branches of government, and they serve as a sort of glue between voters and their government. Because of this multifunctionality, it can be quite difficult to characterize political parties' goals.[37]

That said, political parties undeniably play an important role in the electoral process in the United States and are similar to interest groups in a few critical ways. As I described above, interest groups pursue their policy goals by both working to elect candidates who are friendly to those goals and lobbying elected officials—lobbying that is usually backed by a promise of support or threat of retaliation in elections, either implicitly or explicitly. Political parties also work to elect their preferred candidates to office by turning out supporters and persuading voters to vote for the candidates they favor. The ultimate ends of political parties as organizations might be more complex than the ends of interest groups—political parties could, for example, care about holding office for patronage as well as policy reasons—but the means to those ends are the same: they have to win elections.

Because a strong performance in elections is important to interest groups and political parties, the election timing framework I described above applies to political parties as well. Since political parties compete with one another in a zero-sum fashion—an office won for one party is an office lost by another—we can simply replace the "Developers" and "Environmentalists" labels of table 2.1 with "Democratic Party" and "Republican Party" to evaluate whether and how off-cycle election timing should shift the balance of electoral power between the two parties. On the vertical dimension, we can ask: Are one party's supporters more motivated to turn out? Do they have more at stake in the election? Most generally, are they more likely to weather a change from on-cycle to off-cycle election timing than the other party? On the horizontal dimension, we can evaluate whether one party is stronger in organizational capacity than the other: Does one party have more financial resources than the other? Does it have a larger volunteer network that it can rely on to turn out voters? By answering these questions and evaluating how they interact with each other, one can make predictions about how changes in election timing will affect the electoral strength of two competing political parties.[38]

In some ways, this treatment of interest groups and political parties as distinct entities is overly simplistic, however, because political parties and interest groups in American politics today are closely interconnected. Certain interest groups, such as the National Rifle Association and the US Chamber of Commerce, consistently align with the Republican Party, whereas others, like the American Federation of State, County and Municipal Employees and the National Education Association, are close allies of the Democratic Party. Furthermore, today's political parties are organizationally weak relative to what they were in the nineteenth century, and they are actually dependent on interest groups in the electoral arena. Few would question that campaign spending by the US Chamber of Commerce is important to Republicans' electoral strength. Likewise, Democrats depend on labor groups to carry out door-to-door canvassing, phone banks, and endorsements on behalf of Democratic candidates. The relationship between interest groups and political parties today is so strong that it is hard to think about their electoral and policy fortunes as separate matters.

It is therefore important to recognize that what is good for the interest groups that are part of a political party's constituency is also good for the political party itself (and, in a two-party system, bad for the rival party). Regardless of whether a political party's goals are electoral or policy oriented, a change in election timing that strengthens an interest group's influence will also likely help the political party that depends on that interest group. Consider a Republican Party leader who seeks solely to maximize the number of votes Republican candidates receive in elections: he gains an advantage from a change in election timing that enhances the influence of interest groups aligned with the Republican Party more so than interest groups aligned with the Democratic Party. Likewise, if that party leader's goals are policy oriented, and a supportive interest group is more successful in electing candidates who will respond to its policy demands in off-cycle elections, the party leader also reaps policy benefits from off-cycle elections. Regardless of whether political party leaders are motivated to win elections or to move policy (or, as is likely, both), because of the interconnectedness of parties and interest groups in American politics today, shifts in election timing have potential to simultaneously affect both interest groups' and political parties' fortunes.

The theoretical framework is therefore highly relevant for political parties as well as organized interest groups. Political parties are electorally active organizations, and we can simply replace the group labels in table 2.1 with the names of political parties to predict how changes in election timing will shape their electoral success. But it is equally important to recognize that in today's political environment, changes that tip the balance of power among interest groups also have consequences for political parties. Parties, after all, depend on interest groups for electoral support. Thus changes that affect interest groups' electoral strength trickle up to political parties.

Looking Ahead

Fundamentally, the manipulation of election timing is about the manipulation of voter turnout. More importantly, it is about reducing turnout among some segments of the electorate more than others. What a shift to off-cycle election timing accomplishes is a change in the composition of the electorate—a change that increases the importance of organized groups in the electoral process.

For interest groups that face little direct organized competition and seek policies that are distributive in nature, I expect to see two patterns:

First, I expect those interest groups to be more successful in their endeavor to elect representatives who will be friendly to their policy goals in off-cycle elections than in on-cycle elections. As a result, I expect officials elected in off-cycle elections to make policy that is more favorable to those groups than officials elected in on-cycle elections. In addition, since those interest groups benefit from off-cycle election scheduling, I expect they actively work to protect off-cycle election scheduling and face relatively weak opposition in doing so.

But it is also important to stress that even in elections where many groups are active, off-cycle election timing can enhance the influence of multiple groups simultaneously, as long as the groups do not work at cross-purposes. And in contexts where multiple groups compete in a zero-sum fashion, or where the issues sought by the groups are nondistributive, changes to election timing still have great potential to tip the balance of power, depending on the specifics of the electoral context. This applies just as much to political parties competing for control of government and policy making as it does to interest groups pursuing favorable policy. And in the modern era, the fortunes of political parties and interest groups are so closely intertwined that I fully expect political parties to play a role in debates over election scheduling. In the chapters to follow, we will learn a great deal about what this means for the politics of election timing choice and for policy outcomes in different types of governments.

CHAPTER THREE

Partisan Power Play

Election Timing Politics in the Nineteenth Century

The United States was not born with its current electoral calendar. In the early years of the republic, there was tremendous variation in when states held their general elections for governors, state legislatures, and members of the US House of Representatives. Even presidential elections were held on different days in different states. To know what cities and towns did prior to the 1830s, one would have to consult individual city and state records, but it is generally believed they held elections on days other than state and national elections because their voting requirements were different.[1]

Over the course of the nineteenth and early twentieth centuries, however, the American electoral calendar evolved. Fairly early in the nineteenth century, the day of presidential elections was made uniform across states. One by one, between the 1840s and the early twentieth century, most state elections were shifted to November so that they coincided with what became the national Election Day. Far less is known about how the timing of local elections has changed over the years, but somehow, political decisions have resulted in a dizzying array of election dates for counties, cities, towns, school districts, and special districts in which off-cycle scheduling remains the norm.

This chapter begins to investigate why elections in the United States are held when they are. Why are some elections—such as congressional elections, most state elections, and some local elections—conducted according to the same schedule as US presidential elections, whereas other elections are held separately from national and most state races? What explains the variation in election timing across governments and within governments over time? These are important questions to answer, for three reasons.

The first has to do with methodological challenges to testing the theory presented in the last chapter. Because it is highly unlikely that any governmental official would be willing to randomly assign governments on-cycle and off-cycle election schedules, empirical tests of the effects of election timing have to rely on observational data. And since the variation in election timing we observe in the world is almost certainly nonrandom, one has to know something about the process that generated that variation in order to design an empirical analysis that estimates causal relationships. By examining the history of election scheduling and learning about the politics of election timing choice, it becomes possible to conduct a more careful and informed analysis of election timing's effects.

But this reasoning treats the question of why elections are held when they are as a means to the end of estimating causal effects rather than, as is more appropriate, a question worthy of study on its own. The theory, no doubt, leads to predictions about the *effects* of election timing: under certain conditions, changes to election timing tip the balance of power among organized groups. But because of those effects, the theory also implies that groups that benefit from a certain election schedule should actively advocate for its implementation. Likewise, groups that have an advantage under the status quo election schedule should try to keep that schedule in place. As a general rule, fights over policy are inherited by institutional choice.[2] As William Riker writes, "One can expect that losers on a series of decisions under a particular set of rules will attempt (often successfully) to change institutions and hence the kind of decisions produced under them."[3] Thus tests of the theory need not be limited to analyses in which some plausibly exogenous variation in election timing is used to predict a measure of group influence. I can also treat election timing as an "endogenous institution" and test whether the groups the theory predicts will benefit from a certain election schedule are actively involved in pursuing it.[4] Of course, whether a change actually occurs as a result of pressure by organized groups will depend on the institutional context within which decisions about election timing are made. Still, investigation of the politics of election timing choice not only provides a backdrop for the study of election timing's effects but also, in itself, can constitute a test of the theory.

Even if I set aside the theory for a moment, the data on American election scheduling that I described in chapter 1 cry out for explanation.

Why did the United States eventually converge on a near-uniform date for presidential, congressional, and state elections? Why did some states, like New Jersey and Virginia, retain odd-year state elections? Why are the vast majority of city and school district elections held on days other than national Election Day? Given the known consequences of election timing for political participation, these questions are well worth investigating—in their own right.

This chapter begins that investigation. My focus is on the history and politics of election timing choice in American local governments—the level of government where off-cycle election timing is most prevalent today.

Literature and Motivation

Few scholars have attempted to explain why local elections in the United States are scheduled when they are—in particular, why so many of them are held on days other than state and national elections. On the one hand, there has been some important work on the strategic scheduling of referenda. Stephanie Dunne, W. Robert Reed, and James Wilbanks, for example, take on the question of why so many school bond elections are held off-cycle, and they argue that local education officials strategically schedule them that way to maximize the proportion of "yes" voters at the polls.[5] Marc Meredith, on the other hand, explains that agenda-setters schedule bond elections in conjunction with national elections if high turnout electorates are more likely to approve them.[6] Similarly, in a historical study, Steven Erie shows that public utility interests in early twentieth-century Los Angeles successfully used off-cycle municipal bond elections to carry out a state-based development strategy.[7] In all of these studies, the basic premise is that the timing of elections can be manipulated to produce an electorate that is more favorable to a particular policy goal.

But most referenda are, by definition, one-shot deals: a need or desire for an election arises, and political officials have to decide when that election will be held. The flexibility of referenda scheduling in the United States is therefore akin to decisions about national election timing in parliamentary democracies, in which the prime minister has authority to choose the date of the next election and can do so in a way that maximizes the probability of his party's success.[8] In the United States, however, the dates of general elections for government officials are stickier.

City officials cannot simply choose the date of the next regular election based on what day will produce the friendliest electorate. Rather, changing regular election dates requires changing state or local laws or—even more difficult—state or local constitutions. While the choice of regular election dates should be thought of as endogenous to political outcomes, the choice is not quite as endogenous as, say, the choice of national election dates in parliamentary systems or decisions about when to hold referenda in the United States.

Aside from referenda, how can we begin to understand why regular elections in the United States are held when they are? The relevant literature on this topic is quite thin. The work that does exist can be divided into two camps of contributions. In the first camp are arguments that scheduling nonpresidential elections (whether they be legislative elections, state elections, or local elections) at the same time as presidential elections works in favor of political parties that compete in presidential elections. For example, Gary Cox suggests that the number of parties competing for seats in a national legislature will be more likely to mirror the number of parties seeking the presidency when the legislative elections are held concurrently with presidential elections.[9] Gabriel Negretto makes a similar argument, asserting that when dominant and large political parties are in control of constitutional conventions, those conventions will be more likely to implement concurrent presidential and legislative elections, since concurrent elections make it harder for smaller parties and third parties to be competitive.[10] Philip Ethington advances a related idea in his study of San Francisco politics in the nineteenth century, arguing that holding the city's elections at the same time as state and national elections strengthened the hand of the major parties in local elections and worked to the detriment of local parties and third parties.[11] Examining national elections in the United States, Erik Engstrom and Samuel Kernell show that the presidential coattail effect on House races in the nineteenth and early twentieth centuries was greater in states where presidential and House elections were held on the same day.[12]

These arguments may well explain election timing choices in many contexts in the United States. Yet if major political parties always benefit from elections concurrent with elections for the national executive, then why are most local elections today held off-cycle? That question is usually answered in a different way—with reference to the unique trajectory of American history: The conventional wisdom is that the standard for off-cycle local elections originated during the Progressive Era, the transformative period that lasted roughly from 1894 to 1917. That was the period in which municipal reformers first gathered at a national level, formed the National Municipal League, and began promoting institutions like non-partisan elections, commission and council-manager government, direct primaries, and at-large elections. Off-cycle election timing is sometimes discussed as one of the reforms they promoted.

It is well understood that the main motivation of the Progressive municipal reformers was to weaken the major political parties, undermine the spoils system, and undercut the political machines that dominated many large American cities during the second half of the nineteenth century. However, the general question of *why* the Progressives wanted to weaken the political parties and the urban machines is still debated today. Were they truly after "good government," or were they simply trying to increase their own chances of controlling it, perhaps, as some argue, by undermining the electoral presence of immigrants and the lower classes that supported machine candidates?[13] When it came to election timing specifically, what did the Progressives think that nonconcurrent local elections would accomplish?

The Progressive rhetoric on the importance of separating local from state and national elections went something like this:

> There is no reason why general politics should enter at all into the contest for city offices. . . . There are no questions of policy dependent upon the position of parties, and there is every reason why the people should vote at the city elections with entire independence of party affiliations. But so long as the city canvass is mixed up with that which is dominated by party feeling it will be impossible to prevent party nominations and their support, in a great measure, on party grounds. . . . If the city election were held in the Spring and conducted by itself on the merits of candidates and of the questions affecting municipal administration alone there would be a much greater chance of independence in voting and of the success of movements headed by citizens irrespective of party to secure honesty, economy, and efficiency.[14]

According to many of the municipal reformers, the main problem was that voters could not make informed decisions about local candidates when local elections were held at the same time as state and national elections. By separating the elections, city issues would be removed from politics, and voters would be able to judge city candidates on their merits and their proposals for city policy—not based on their affiliations with state and national parties whose platforms had nothing to do with local government administration. As the *New York Times* put it, "We cannot have Democratic pavements, Republican water-works, or National Greenback-Labor parks."[15]

However, some political scientists question whether the Progressives' true motives for promoting electoral reforms like nonconcurrent, nonpartisan, and at-large elections were as noble as their rhetoric made them out to be. In her study of municipal reform in the American Southwest, for example, Amy Bridges argues that nonconcurrent elections and other reform-style institutions were key to the reformers' goal of limiting access to the political process. She writes, "Reform governance worked in part by selectively mobilizing 'wieldy' constituencies from the unwieldy societies of their metropolitan settings."[16] The main goal was not to get voters to think clearly about what makes a good candidate for local government, it was to disenfranchise the people who would not support *their* candidates. According to Bridges, the reform organizations that shaped the institutions of so many local governments in the late nineteenth and early twentieth centuries were driven by the same motive as the political parties they opposed: they wanted to win elections.[17]

Jessica Trounstine makes a similar argument about municipal reformers and their promotion of nonconcurrent city elections in her study of machine and reform cities in the United States. Specifically, Trounstine argues that we should not view the reform versus machine battles of the twentieth century as contests between leaders with "good" and "bad" intentions, since the basic goal of the reformers was the same as the goal of the machines. The reformers wanted to win local elections, and they crafted institutions so as to increase their chances of controlling local government in the future. Like Bridges, Trounstine argues that many of the institutions the reformers promoted were intentionally designed to keep immigrants and the lower classes out of politics—to minimize opposition to the reformers' candidates. Nonconcurrence of local elections was one of the tools they used to restrict voter participation and to ensure that electorates were friendly to their candidates and policy agendas.[18]

The arguments of Bridges and Trounstine with respect to election timing have important commonalities with the arguments of Cox, Negretto, and Ethington. The first is an emphasis on groups' electoral self-interest. Negretto and Ethington assert that political parties choose institutions (including election timing) so as to maximize their probability of winning elections in the future. Bridges and Trounstine argue that even though the reformers claimed to have the best interests of citizens in mind, their organizations operated like political parties in all but the name: they pushed to implement institutions that would help them secure and maintain control of local government. Also, in a way, these two camps both argue that smaller and local parties should prefer off-cycle elections since concurrent subnational elections advantage large major parties. This is explicitly asserted by Negretto and Ethington and, I would argue, implied by the arguments of Bridges and Trounstine. To be sure, the emphasis of the latter camp is on the early twentieth century conflicts between reformers and machines—not small versus large political parties. Still, the urban machines were almost always local organizations of one of the major national political parties, and the reformers' party-like organizations were local in nature. Thus by arguing that the reformers promoted nonconcurrent local elections to increase their chances of winning against the machines, one could argue that an implication is that small, local parties should prefer off-cycle elections whereas large parties should prefer elections concurrent with national elections.

Taken as a whole, this literature is an important starting point for understanding the politics of election timing choice in the United States. However, it leaves us quite a distance from the finish line. The first camp provides a helpful framework but does not explain the specific features of the US electoral calendar. The second camp provides a perspective specific to the United States yet only mentions local election timing in passing, as part of the broader package of reforms the Progressives promoted. If off-cycle local election timing did become standard in the United States as a result of the Progressives' institutional reform efforts, then it is surprising that so little has been written of its history. After all, the histories of nonpartisan elections, at-large elections, commission and council-manager government, and other reform-style institutions are fairly well documented, each the subject of multiple studies. Not so for election timing. To the extent that nonconcurrent election timing is even mentioned in the literature, it gets bundled into discussions of other reform-style institutions. The literature thus gives the impression that off-cycle election timing was born alongside nonpartisan elections and commission government in the early twentieth century, and that these institutional arrangements came as package deals.

The near complete lack of work focusing on the history of election timing in the United States is one good reason to study the subject in more detail. But there is another. Interestingly, off-cycle local election timing was not only important to the National Municipal League, but it was also one of the *very first* reforms the organization promoted. In the league's initial meeting in 1894, the delegates disagreed on many points, but one point of consensus that emerged was that the simultaneous holding of city, state, and national elections worked to the advantage of the machines, since the machines were local organizations of the major national parties. Specifically, they argued that the major parties won city offices easily when the elections were on the same day as state and national elections, purely because of their popularity in state and national politics. The National Municipal League's decision to promote off-cycle city election timing actually preceded by several years its endorsement of nonpartisan ballots and commission government.

Furthermore, delegates of the National Municipal League accused the major political parties of having manipulated city election timing so that it worked to their advantage. Frank J. Goodnow, for example, speculated that the election dates of many large cities had at some point been changed from the spring to the autumn months "at the behest of the parties, which felt that with the two elections at the same time they stood a better chance to get control of the city government because state and city issues would be confused."[19] This suggests that by 1894, city election timing may have already had a history of being manipulated for political gain. If so, then it is a history that remains unexplored: the literature on nineteenth-century city politics rarely discusses changes to city election timing as a politically interesting feature of the landscape, if it discusses them at all.[20] In fact, aside from studies of individual cities, which occasionally mention the dates of city elections, we do not even have basic information about *when* cities held their elections during the nineteenth century. Given that election timing has great potential to affect political outcomes, and that the modern election schedule was the accomplishment of the Progressives, it is important to understand the history of election timing manipulation the Progressives may have been reacting to.

With that said, it is not easy to investigate this history. Collecting information on when local governments held elections over a century ago presents a number of challenges. The earliest comprehensive records of municipal election timing I have discovered in my research are from the late 1930s—many years after the Progressive movement wound to a close. As a starting point I have collected data on the timing of elections for three major American cities—New York, San Francisco, and Philadelphia—for the whole of the nineteenth century. The data collection effort revealed that the election schedules of those three cities were actually altered quite frequently between 1840 and 1900—three to four times in each city.

This discovery alone calls for some reevaluation of the things we think we know and understand about the origins of the modern American election schedule. Since the Progressives were clearly not the first to manipulate election timing, why was city election timing changed so frequently in these three cities during the nineteenth century, and what does that teach us about the importance of linking and delinking local elections from state and national elections? Is it always the case that major national political parties prefer on-cycle local elections? Does advocacy of off-cycle election timing always come from the upper and middle classes? My argument in this chapter is not that existing theories are wrong. It is simply that if we look more closely at state and local politics in the nineteenth century, it becomes evident that we need to use a wider lens when studying election timing as an endogenous institution. On some occasions, election timing change *was* motivated by a desire to disenfranchise certain classes of voters. Sometimes, national parties *did* collude to weaken smaller or local parties. But that is not the exhaustive set of possibilities.

In the analysis that follows, I show that the theoretical framework I developed in the last chapter goes a long way toward explaining why local election timing was changed in certain places at certain times. I demonstrate that even in the nineteenth century, delinking city elections from national and state elections decreased voter turnout in city elections. Because the turnout gap between off-cycle and on-cycle local elections existed even then, there is good reason to think that the composition of the electorate also varied depending on when elections were held. Through a combination of qualitative and quantitative analysis, I then show that the political actors who combined and separated city elections from state and national elections did so with an expectation that they would realize electoral gains from the switch—and that their expectations can be understood within the theoretical framework.

As it turns out, the manipulation of election timing was a regular feature of political party strategy in the nineteenth century, and one that existing work has largely overlooked. At the dawn of mass political party organization, as restrictions on white male suffrage crumbled and party elites sought patronage to build their organizations, election timing manipulation emerged as one way to exert some control over the electorate. By changing the time at which city elections were held, party elites could increase or decrease the number of voters who participated in city elections, potentially tipping the balance of party vote share in their favor.

Moreover, the manipulation of local election timing—while commonly credited to the Progressive reformers—actually has much deeper roots than previously acknowledged. In promoting off-cycle city elections, municipal reformers were using a well-worn political party strategy to increase their chances of winning elections. So as we evaluate the merits of off-cycle local election scheduling today, we should think of it not only in terms of the high-minded rhetoric the municipal reformers espoused, but also as the lasting achievement of strategic politicians who, a hundred years ago, wanted to write the rules to weaken the parties so as to improve their own chances of winning.

Applying the Theoretical Framework to Nineteenth-Century City Politics

In nineteenth-century city politics, there were few interest groups in the way we think of them today, as groups outside government that pursue their policy aims by lobbying elected officials and endorsing and contributing funds to candidates. Rather, the organized groups involved in nineteenth-century city politics were political parties. The major political parties—the Whigs and Democrats during the Second American Party System and the Republicans and Democrats during the Third American Party System—regularly competed in local elections, as did state and national third parties, municipal parties, and factions of the major political parties.

The intensity with which parties campaigned for local office at the time is indicative of how much was at stake in local elections—especially the elections of large cities. For all parties, gaining control of city government was necessary for controlling city policy. But there was even more at stake for the parties that competed in state and national politics. Starting in the 1830s, the major political parties were structured as hierarchies with suborganizations at the state, county, city, district, and precinct levels, and the spoils of office helped party leaders hold those hierarchies together.[21] As urban populations grew throughout the nineteenth century, cities became increasingly important to national political parties as sources of votes and patronage.[22] Thus control of city governments gave the parties patronage they could use to strengthen their larger organizations, which helped them win state and national elections. It is therefore not surprising that they invested heavily in winning local contests.

To consider political parties' motives for tampering with the *timing* of local elections, we can turn to the theoretical framework developed in chapter 2. The participation of the group I referred to as Presidential Voters could affect the parties' vote shares in a way that was likely observable and predictable by party leaders: Most voters at that time had strong ties of loyalty to one or the other of the major national political parties, and those parties actively competed in most local elections. Furthermore, the nineteenth-century balloting system encouraged straight-ticket voting: political parties printed their own ballots on strips of paper that contained only the names of their candidates, and most Americans voted by simply depositing the ballots of their preferred party into boxes at their polling place.[23] It is therefore safe to assume that most Presidential Voters simply voted for the municipal candidates of the same party that commanded their loyalty at the level of state and national politics. If so, then party leaders would be able to roughly approximate the impact of Presidential Voter participation on their vote shares by comparing their shares in off-cycle city elections to their city-level vote shares in state and national elections.[24]

The organizational capacity dimension likely also factored into parties' considerations of whether they would fare better under on-cycle or off-cycle elections. That dimension can depict the balance of organizational power between any two types of parties, whether they are the two major national parties, a dominant party with a centralized machine versus a reform party, two local parties, or some other combination of groups. For example, the major national parties might be relatively balanced in their ability to get out the vote for their respective slates of city candidates, or one party might command a more disciplined army of precinct and ward workers and thus be able to turn out more supporters on city election day. In fact, a defining characteristic of most machines was that they were dominant in organizational capacity relative to opposition parties.[25]

In the nineteenth century, one additional consideration could shape the political parties' preferences over election schedules, and one that was related to organizational capacity. Prior to the wave of antifusion laws that were passed around the turn of the century, it was possible for two or more political parties to unite behind a single slate of candidates.[26] Most often, fusion was a strategy employed by weaker parties to put forward a unified opposition to the dominant party. However, parties' willingness to fuse depended on the timing of the local elections: When elections were held on different days than state and national elections, weaker parties were usually eager to combine their efforts in order to defeat the dominant party. However, when city elections were held on the same day as a presidential or gubernatorial election, parties that fielded candidates in those larger races were reluctant to combine efforts with other parties for fear that sharing a slate of local candidates would undermine their local organization, and thereby their state and national candidates.[27] As a result, on-cycle election timing decreased the likelihood of fusion among opposition parties.

Furthermore, the dominant party benefited from the on-cycle schedule because it reduced the risk of intraparty factionalism. When the presidency or the governorship was at stake, a dominant party faction would think twice before running a candidate against the main dominant party candidate, since the party split might carry over to state and national races. The same could be true of third party efforts as well: a local party whose members were, for example, strongly Republican in state and national races would be reluctant to run a separate slate of candidates in local elections if those elections were held on-cycle. For these reasons, the concurrence of city, state, and national elections had the potential to affect the nature of party competition in local elections—which parties would fuse, which factions would run separate slates of candidates, and which third parties would emerge on the local scene.

These three factors—the two dimensions of the theoretical framework plus a third factor specific to the nineteenth century—account for the conditions under which political parties at the local level might have wanted to change city election timing. However, since the focus of this chapter is to explain why local elections are held when they are, it is important to consider how election timing was actually changed during this period. Notably, it was the *state* government that had the authority to determine the timing of municipal elections. Throughout the nineteenth century, state governments set precise bounds for what city governments could and could not do. Moreover, they did so using special legislation—laws designed to apply to specific localities—rather than by the passage of general laws that applied uniformly to all localities in the state.[28] Therefore, *local* incentives to alter election timing were not sufficient for election timing to be changed during the nineteenth century. In order for city political leaders to secure favorable election timing laws, they had to have the support of the state legislature and governor. And because the fates of state and local elected officials were closely bound together by the strong political parties characteristic of the time, state politicians usually took great interest in which parties had advantage in local elections—and therefore in when local elections were held.

To summarize, I argue that two main factors—the difference in party loyalties among Presidential Voters and Consistent Voters, and the relative organizational capacity of competing parties—were important determinants of local political parties' preferences over city election scheduling. In this particular time period, a third factor, related to the parties' organizational capacity, also played a role: the anticipated effects of election timing for inter- and intraparty coordination. However, these factors alone cannot explain when and why election timing changed, because for the most part, local political party leaders were not the ones ultimately responsible for decisions about local election timing. Instead, local election timing was the prerogative of state government. And so to predict whether a particular alignment of party interests at the local level actually resulted in election timing change, we must also consider a fourth factor: whether the party in control of state government was supportive of the change.

Empirical Analysis

In the empirical analysis that follows, I first simply describe when cities held elections during the nineteenth century. While I would have liked to compile longitudinal election data for a large panel of US cities during the nineteenth century, collecting historical city election data is difficult, and so I adopted the strategy of examining a small number of cities in detail over the whole of the nineteenth century. At the outset, I did not know whether I would actually discover cases in which city election timing was changed, so I chose three cities where I expected it to be most likely that politicians would have tampered with city election timing prior to the Progressive Era. The delegates to the National Municipal League were most concerned about the largest American cities and their machine governments, and New York, San Francisco, and Philadelphia were all among the top ten largest urban places in terms of population in 1890 according to the US Census.[29] Each city also had experience with machines: Tammany Hall Democrats ruled New York, a Republican machine governed Philadelphia, and San Francisco had waves of Democratic hegemony.[30] Within these three cities, I found a total of ten election timing switches between the start of the Second American Party System and the turn of the century: four in New York, three in San Francisco, and three in Philadelphia.

With information on the timing of elections in place, I then set out to test whether the theory can account for both the election timing changes and the phases of continuity in election timing. For each city and time period, I evaluate whether voter turnout was higher in city elections held concurrently with state and national elections than in city elections held on separate days.[31] Then I use the four factors laid out above to explain which local parties stood to benefit from off-cycle elections, which parties stood to benefit from on-cycle elections, which party or parties controlled state government, and whether the combination of these conditions would predict change or stability in the local election schedule.

The qualitative and quantitative data I use to measure the four factors in each city at various points in time come from a variety of sources, including the *Tribune Almanac and Political Register*, San Francisco municipal reports, and historical newspapers such as the *New York Times*, the *San Francisco Chronicle*, and the *Philadelphia Inquirer*. A complete list of sources can be found in appendix A. While the secondary literature on nineteenth-century local politics and machines does not discuss election timing changes specifically,[32] city election timing was often changed at the same time that other city institutions were altered, and some of those latter institutional changes *are* discussed in the literature. To understand the context of these institutional changes, I rely heavily on existing work by Amy Bridges, Steven Erie, Philip Ethington, and Peter McCaffery.[33] For specifics on election timing decisions, I also probed newspapers and, where available and applicable, legislative journals and constitutional convention proceedings.[34]

The analytical narratives that follow illustrate that decisions about election timing in these cities were highly contentious and hotly partisan. They illustrate that even in the nineteenth century, voter turnout was higher in city elections held concurrently with state and national elections than in city elections held on separate days. And, most importantly, they show that the theory largely explains the local political parties' preferences over election scheduling. To understand whether these local preferences translated into actual changes in the election schedule, we have to take into account the institutional structure within which election timing decisions were made. But the histories of New York, San Francisco, and Philadelphia make it clear that the lower voter turnout that accompanied off-cycle election timing in the nineteenth century altered the balance of group power, such that political parties—and eventually, the Progressives—fought vigorously to implement election schedules that would give them the upper hand.

New York

In the early years of the Second American Party System, when political parties were beginning to organize on a mass scale, New York City elections were held in April, separately from state and national elections, which, in the state of New York, were both held in November. However, in 1850, the city's election schedule changed, and for most of the decade that followed, New York City's elections were held concurrently with state and national elections in November. What caused the change in the city's election schedule, and why did it happen at that particular time?

As a starting point, it is important to explain why the April city election date did *not* change during the 1840s. By that decade, the Whigs and the Democrats both had organized operations in the city, and they competed fiercely for control of city government. Moreover, data collected by Amy Bridges demonstrate that turnout in the spring city elections fell well below citywide turnout in autumn presidential and gubernatorial elections during the early and mid-1840s.[35] Yet in spite of this turnout differential between spring and autumn elections and the heavy competition between the Whigs and Democrats, there was little incentive for either major party to tamper with city election timing. The two parties were fairly evenly matched in terms of organizational capacity.[36] Moreover, there was little difference between the parties' vote shares in the city in April and November.[37] Neither party stood to gain by making city elections concurrent with national elections.

The situation changed in the late 1840s, however. In 1847 and 1848, Whig candidates performed better in New York City in the higher-turnout November elections than in the April elections. Not only did 17% more city voters participate in the November 1848 election than in the April city election seven months earlier, but also the Whig candidate for president that year won 57% of the citywide vote in a three-way race compared to the 48% that had gone to the Whig mayoral candidate in a two-way race in April 1848. The Whigs also commanded large majorities in the state legislature in 1848 and 1849—even within the New York City delegation.[38] For the Whigs, therefore, 1848–49 was a propitious moment for combining the city election with state and national elections in November. The state legislature drafted a series of revisions to the New York City charter in April 1849,[39] which contained the provision that "the election for charter [city] officers shall be held on the day of the general State election, when all charter offices elected by the people shall be chosen."[40] The first on-cycle election in New York City was held in November of 1850, and the Whigs won the mayoralty by a majority of more than four thousand votes out of forty thousand cast. They also sent three (out of four) Whigs to Congress and selected ten (out of twelve) Whig members for the Assembly.[41] In the short run, the higher voter turnout of the November city elections worked to the Whigs' advantage, since their party had a larger margin of support among Presidential Voters than among Consistent Voters.[42]

However, a mere seven years later, the city's election date was moved back to off-cycle. To understand why, it is important to recognize the dramatic changes in political conditions that took place in New York City (as well as in the state and nation) during the 1850s. Within a few years of the 1850 city election timing switch, the Whigs divided into factions over the slavery issue and ceased to exist as a political party. This disintegration of the Whig Party left the Democratic Party temporarily unobstructed in its effort to organize the New York City electorate, and by the late 1850s, the Democrats commanded an organizational edge in the city and a reliable base of loyal voters, thus marking the beginning of the city's fledgling machine.[43]

Not coincidentally, the 1850s also witnessed the city's first coordinated reform movement, led by a group of businessmen and social notables who protested the city's high tax rates and corrupt officeholders. As a municipal political party fielding candidates for city offices, however, the City Reformers were at a severe disadvantage. Most of its members had attachments to one of the major national parties, and since city elections were held concurrently with state and national elections, many of them were reluctant to stray from the major party tickets to vote for the reform slate in the city. They also lacked the ward and precinct organizations of the Democrats and were opposed to using patronage to build them. As a purely local party, the City Reformers had no way to appeal to the Presidential Voters who came to the polls during on-cycle city elections. The reformers thus faced the stark reality that they could not win unless they coordinated with one of the national parties, which was not likely to hap-

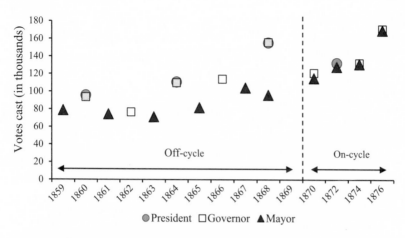

FIGURE 3.1. Turnout in national, state, and city elections, New York City, 1859–76.

pen as long as city elections were held concurrently with gubernatorial or presidential elections.[44]

In an attempt to enhance discipline within its own ranks, enable coordination with other parties, and prevent the participation of Presidential Voters (who, by this time, leaned Democratic), the City Reformers lobbied the state legislature to move city elections back to off-cycle. Their initial effort in 1853 proved unsuccessful in the Whig-dominated legislature,[45] but a few years later, they found a sympathetic audience in the Know Nothing- and Republican-controlled New York legislature, which was devising a new charter for New York City in response to the Democratic mayor's heavily corrupt 1856 reelection campaign.[46] The vote on the new charter, which included a switch to off-cycle city elections, pitted the Know Nothings and Republicans against the Democrats. Every Know Nothing legislator voted in favor of the revised charter, and almost all Republicans—still a new party—voted with the Know Nothings. Every single Democrat voted in opposition.[47] In the first off-cycle city election in December of 1857,[48] the Democratic candidate for mayor won far less in vote share citywide than Democratic candidates for state offices had won one month earlier. Reformers rejoiced in victory when their opposition mayoral candidate was elected, claiming that "the result . . . vindicates the wisdom of the law which changed the time of our municipal election from November to December."[49]

The switch to December elections also had a negative impact on voter turnout in city elections. To illustrate, figure 3.1 shows the number of votes cast in national, state, and city elections in New York City from 1859 to 1876. Throughout the period of off-cycle elections, voter turnout in city elections consistently fell below turnout levels in gubernatorial and presidential elections. In November 1860, over 93,000 New York City residents turned out to vote for president and governor, but only 74,000 people voted for mayor thirteen months later. In 1864–65, about 30,000 more voters participated in the presidential and gubernatorial election than in the mayoral election a year later. By 1868 this gap had widened even further: over 155,000 votes were cast for governor in November, but fewer than 96,000 people voted for mayor a month later. By contrast, when city elections were once again rescheduled to coincide with state and national races in the 1870s, the gap between turnout in local and state elections narrowed substantially. In the November 1874 election, for example, there were 132,000 votes cast for governor and 131,000 cast for mayor. Even in the 1800s, delinking city elections from state and national elections significantly lowered voter turnout.

In the early 1860s, it appears that the lower voter turnout of off-cycle New York City elections worked to the disadvantage of the Democrats. In figure 3.2, I depict the relationship between voter turnout and Democratic vote share by New York City ward in pairs of November and December elections. The horizontal axis in each scatter plot is the percentage change in voter turnout in the ward from the November election to the December election. The vertical axis is the percentage point change in ward-level vote share for Democratic candidates from the November to the December election. In the top left panel, which compares the gubernatorial election of November 1862 to the city election of December 1862,[50] it is clear that in all wards where turnout decreased from November to December, the vote share for the Democratic candidate decreased as well.[51] Moreover, in the wards where turnout dropped the most from the gubernatorial election to the city election, the decrease in vote share for the Democrats was the largest. The top right panel, which compares December 1865 to November 1866, displays a similar pattern. The increase in turnout from December to the following November—an increase of 40%—was associated with a universal increase in vote share for the Democrats, and the wards with the largest increases in turnout also saw the largest increases in votes for the Democrats. Thus in New York City in the early to mid-1860s, the decrease in voter turnout that came with off-cycle city election timing worked against Democratic candidates, and so it is not surprising that the Republican majority in the state legislature kept city election timing as it was.

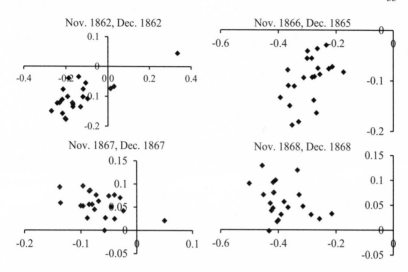

FIGURE 3.2. Voter turnout and vote share for Democrats in New York City elections, 1860s.
Notes: Horizontal axes are the percentage change in turnout from the November election to the December election (e.g., –0.1 = 10% decrease). Vertical axes are the percentage point change in vote share for Democratic candidates from the November election to the December election (e.g., 0.05 = 5 percentage point increase).

It is less clear what to expect of the late 1860s, at which time the organizational prowess of the Democratic Party in New York City reached new heights. Under the famous William Marcy Tweed, "Tammany Hall . . . received a lesson in organization for plunder on a scale undreamed of before."[52] By Erie's account, Tweed "cranked up Tammany's naturalization mill" and registered thousands of immigrants, who then gave their votes to the Democratic candidates for city offices.[53] The Democrats enlarged city payroll to reward these voters, financing the swelling public sector with a massive new program of deficit financing. With such a large change in the organizational capacity of the Democratic Party, it is possible that the lower voter turnout of the city's off-cycle elections began to work in the Democrats' favor.

The bottom left panel of figure 3.2 suggests that was the case. The two elections held in November and December of 1867 featured a reversal of the pattern shown in the top two panels. Turnout still dropped from November to December, but the drop in turnout was associated with a *greater* proportion of votes for Democrats. Moreover, in the wards where turnout dropped the most relative to what it had been in November, the Democratic mayoral candidates received the greatest gains compared to the state Democratic candidate. This trend was repeated in 1868, as shown in the bottom right panel: turnout decreased dramatically from the gubernatorial election of November to the mayoral election of December, and the result was greater vote share for the Democrats.[54] This change in pattern suggests that the strengthening of Democratic organizational capacity helped Democrats fare better in off-cycle elections than they would have in on-cycle elections.

What is puzzling is that in the late 1860s, the Republicans in control of the state legislature did not attempt to move city elections back to on-cycle. The likely explanation is that their incentives to do so were mixed. On the basis of the organizational capacity dimension, off-cycle election timing strengthened Democratic vote share. However, by the late 1860s, more than 60% of New York City voters were loyal Democrats, and so regardless of timing, if the Democrats presented voters with a unified Democratic slate of candidates, they were likely to win in the city. However, the Democratic Party was rife with factionalism during the 1860s, and as long as more than one slate of candidates ran under the label of the Democratic Party, it was not guaranteed that the Tammany Democrats would win. The biggest challenge the Democrats faced during the 1860s was intraparty factionalism, and it was exacerbated by off-cycle election timing. From 1860 to 1874, in every December mayoral race, with the exception of 1868, two or more Democratic organizations put forward separate, competitive candidates. Not only did this split the Democratic vote, but it also gave reformers the opportunity to fuse with one of the anti-Tammany Democratic factions, as they often did during the 1860s. The Democrats' intraparty coordination problems likely explain why reformers and Republicans continued to favor off-cycle city elections into the late 1860s while mainstream Democrats continued to favor on-cycle elections.

Those problems also explain why the city's elections were changed back to on-cycle in 1870. That year, yet another disgruntled group of Democrats calling themselves the Young Democracy mounted an effort to oust Tammany from power.[55] It was also the first year since the mid-1840s that Democrats had control of both chambers of the state legislature and the governorship. In 1870, Tweed proposed a new charter for New York City, and included in the final version of the bill was a provision that the city's elections be moved to November of even-numbered years.[56] The main opposition to the new charter came from the legislators allied with the Young Democracy, who tried to amend the election provision so that city elections would be held in the spring rather than in November.[57] Ultimately, the new charter passed with few opposing votes,[58] and New York City elections were once again moved to the same time as presidential and gubernatorial elections.

In the years following the 1870 election timing switch, reformers came out fully and consistently in favor of off-cycle New York City election timing, even if they recognized the trade-offs inherent in separating city elections from state and national elections. On the one hand, off-cycle elections were good for the reformers because their local organizations had no way to appeal to the Presidential Voters who cast ballots for the major parties in local elections. However, off-cycle election timing also carried disadvantages for the reformers: the Democrats were undeniably better equipped to turn out supportive voters and could more easily overwhelm smaller electorates. An 1875 *New York Times* piece summarized this trade-off nicely:

> It is undoubtedly true that a Spring election would help to familiarize people with the necessity of judging candidates for local office simply with a view to their honesty and capacity, apart altogether from their political affiliations. But there is this obvious danger, that in seeking to destroy the power of the trading ward politicians, the advocates of a Spring election might find themselves working into the hands of that class. The vote at an election held say in April would almost certainly be light, and the people who staid away would be the class whose absence would be a loss to the cause of good government. It requires a great deal of hard work, as our readers may have observed, to get out the better class of voters in this City at any "off" election.[59]

Besides, reformers needed the help of Republicans in the state legislature if they wanted to change local election timing, and throughout the 1870s and 1880s, Republicans were ambivalent about the city election timing issue. Off-cycle elections would have augmented Democratic factionalism, which would have helped the Republicans, but higher voter turnout tended to work in Republicans' favor during the 1870s, and there was no question that the Democrats outmatched the Republicans in organizational capacity.[60] All things considered, Republicans' incentives for changing city election timing were mixed, and their actions during the 1870s and 1880s demonstrated as much. On a couple occasions, Republicans teamed up with reformers to try to change city election timing, but the state's Democratic governors blocked their efforts. In other years, state Republicans were explicitly opposed to reformers' pushes for off-cycle city election timing. To make matters even more complicated, during the 1880s, it was believed that Republicans were complicit in the Democratic machine: reformers complained that Republicans helped Tammany win control of city offices in exchange for either some of the spoils of city government or votes for Republican candidates for state offices.[61] Thus Democrats' desire to suppress factionalism and the ambivalence of the Republican Party toward proposed election timing changes kept the city's concurrent elections in place for a quarter century after 1870.

Reformers finally achieved a permanent transition to off-cycle city elections by amending the state constitution in the mid-1890s. Some critical events contributed to their eventual success: First, ballot reform in the state had somewhat reduced vote- and spoils-trading between Tammany and Republicans, which lessened Republicans' incentives to protect on-cycle elections.[62] Second, a revolt within the Republican Party against the machine tactics of Republican state boss Thomas C. Platt strengthened reform sentiment within the party.[63] Meanwhile, the depression of 1893 and strong national tides swept Republicans into state government and the New York constitutional convention in 1894. During the convention, reformers lobbied the delegates for the separation of municipal elections from state elections,[64] and Republicans—eager to weaken the Democratic machine in New York City as well as the Democratic powerhouses in Brooklyn and Buffalo—agreed to go along with reformers' proposals. They included a provision in the state constitution that city elections—not just in New York City, but also in cities like Albany, Rochester, Syracuse, and Buffalo—would be held off-cycle in November of odd-numbered years.[65]

However, Tammany did not disappear. It suffered a period of decline during the years of Republican control that followed the national realignment of the 1890s, but the Democratic machine reemerged as an organizational powerhouse in 1917, achieving a degree of control over city elections even greater than that of the late nineteenth century. By that time city elections had been held off-cycle for twenty years, and voter turnout in city elections was extremely low. In 1925, only 28% of New York adults voted in the city election, far shy of the 61% who had voted in 1897. The machine, however, could still count on its supporters: city employees knew their jobs were at stake in each and every election, and the organization knew it could rely on them to vote and to mobilize their friends and relatives. Tammany's vote shares actually improved as overall turnout declined.[66] The great irony of the election timing reform the Progressives promoted in the 1890s is that in the long run, it appeared to work to the machine's advantage.

San Francisco

In San Francisco, the political context was quite different from that of New York, but the general explanation for the city's election timing changes of 1861 and 1866 was similar: the political parties competing in local elections tried to tamper with election timing when they thought it would help them win city elections.

When California was admitted to the union and the new state legislature granted San Francisco its first city charter, city elections were scheduled for the same day as state elections, which were held during the first week of September except in presidential years, when they were held in November.[67] That original decision to hold San Francisco elections concurrently with state elections in the early 1850s was almost certainly calculated. The man largely responsible for the choice was a powerful Democratic state senator who had moved to California from New York City, where he had been trained in Tammany tactics.[68] With local races held at the same time as state and national races, party competition at the local level in the 1850s closely mirrored state and national politics, with the Whigs competing against the Democrats and the Democrats generally commanding more support in the city.

In 1861, however, San Francisco's local elections were moved to the springtime. The primary promoter of the change was a purely local political party called the People's Party—a creation of the city's commercial and financial elite who had organized in response to the financial extravagance and political corruption of the city's fledgling Democratic machine. Most of the local party's support came from voters who supported Republicans in state and national politics (although also some upper-class Democrats).[69] As long as the new Republican Party agreed not to run candidates in the city's races, the People's Party fared well under the on-cycle city election timing regime of the 1850s.[70] However, by 1859, the party's informal collaboration with the Republicans had begun to crumble. With city elections held on the same day as state and national elections and the national issue of slavery heating up, parties resisted interparty cooperation, and San Francisco voters were less inclined to stray from national party lines. The People's Party's vote share in city races began to erode.[71] Thus in 1861 a member of the state assembly, who had previ-

TABLE 3.1 **Votes cast in San Francisco during on-cycle and off-cycle elections, 1856–69**

Year	May elections		September / November elections	
	Votes cast	Highest office	Votes cast	Highest office
1856			12,152	President
1857			10,372	Governor
1858			8,744	Congress
1859			10,889	Governor
1860			14,355	President
1861	11,544	Mayor	15,228	Governor
1862	11,383	Police Judge	9,122	State Senate
1863	10,147	Mayor	14,713	Governor
1864	10,847	Sheriff	21,024	President
1865	13,770	Mayor	13,267	State Senate
1866			13,371	City and County Attorney
1867			17,294	Governor
1868			25,055	President
1869			21,494	State Senate / Mayor

Notes: Number of votes cast in the 1865 autumn election is an estimate based on the total number of votes cast for all state senate candidates divided by the number of available seats. The highest office in years in which there was no executive race was whichever office was placed at the top of the ticket.

ously been a People's Party supervisor in San Francisco, proposed a bill that would move San Francisco elections to the first Wednesday of May in each year—a day separate from state and national elections. That year, the San Francisco delegation of the state legislature was made up of Republicans friendly to the local party,[72] and the bill was passed.[73]

One consequence of the change was that voter participation in the springtime city elections was far lower than voter participation in gubernatorial and presidential elections in the fall. Table 3.1 presents the number of votes cast in city and statewide elections from 1856 to 1869. Throughout that time period, voter turnout in autumn elections depended on which office was at the top of the ticket: presidential elections had the highest turnout, gubernatorial elections saw about 70 to 85% of the voters who participated in presidential years, and state legislative and congressional races drew the fewest voters. When city elections were moved to May, however, a much smaller number of voters cast ballots in the city races than in the autumn month elections for governor and president. Compared to gubernatorial elections held only four months later, the May mayoral elections of 1861 and 1863 saw about four thousand fewer voters, which amounted to turnout decreases of 24 and 31%, respectively. The turnout difference was even greater in presidential years, such as in 1864, when 21,024 voters cast ballots in the presidential election but only 13,770 voters participated in the mayoral election six months later.

The shift to off-cycle elections also affected interparty coordination. From 1856 to 1859, when city elections were held at the same time as state and national elections, party competition at the local level had mirrored party competition for state races.[74] Starting in 1861, however, party competition in city elections operated more independently of state and national politics, and in ways that did not entirely favor the People's Party. In fact, the People's Party discovered that off-cycle election timing actually made the major national parties more willing to combine their tickets in city elections in order to defeat the local party.[75] For example, in the first off-cycle city election, the Administration Union Party (the party of Lincoln) cut a deal with the Douglas Democrats and put up a fusion ticket to defeat the People's Party.[76] Similarly, in May 1862, pro-union Democrats and Republicans combined forces, calling themselves the Citizens' Party.[77] Even so, for the first few years of off-cycle city elections, the election schedule appeared to deliver a net gain to the People's Party. In the years leading up to the switch, the People's Party's vote share shrank from 61% in 1856 to 49% in 1859. In 1861, the first year of separate elections, it saw its vote share jump to 55%, 58% in 1863, and then a full 70% in May 1864 when it ran as the "People's Union" party.[78] In spite of the national parties' attempts to unseat them in city government, the People's Party won all municipal elections from 1861 to 1865.[79]

However, in 1866 the city's elections were once again rescheduled to coincide with state and national elections. This time, the Union Party promoted the election timing change. Internally, the Union Party was having trouble with factionalism. Externally, it was seeing its vote share in the city eroded by an increasingly popular Democratic Party. Eager to secure control of city government so that it could use the San Francisco spoils to bolster support for the party at the state level, the Unionists targeted the local People's Party.[80] Presidential Voters in San Francisco were decidedly in favor of the Union Party in 1865, and so the Unionists used their three-fourths majority in the state legislature to move city elections back to on-cycle.

Unfortunately for the Unionists, though, they never had the opportunity to reap the benefits of Presidential Voter turnout at a time when national tides were in their favor. In 1867 the Democratic Party had a resurgence in California, and the concurrence of city elections with the state election brought to victory the first Democratic mayor since the People's

Party came to power in 1856. The Democratic Party thus inherited a municipal election schedule that worked to its advantage, and throughout the 1870s, it kept it that way. The People's Party was no longer viable on its own, and when it attempted a brief comeback in 1871 under the name Taxpayers' Party, the state legislature responded by amending the act of 1866 so that city elections would *never* be held on a day without state offices accompanying them on the ballot.[81]

During the 1870s, competition between Republicans and Democrats was intense and relatively balanced. It was also a decade in which many third parties surfaced, occasionally winning sizeable percentages of the city vote.[82] The major parties rotated in and out of state government and often found that they had common interest in passing legislation that would help to corral the large and unpredictable San Francisco electorate into support of the major national parties. In the late 1870s, for example, when the Workingmen's Party became a powerful force in city and state politics, delegates to the California constitutional convention merged the date of the state election with the day of the national general election in November of even-numbered years. By consequence, as of 1882, San Francisco city elections were concurrent with state *and* national elections.[83]

The 1880s brought a wave of Democratic machine government to the city, but unlike the New York machine, whose strength was rooted in its reliable ward and precinct organizations, the San Francisco machine did not have a strong base of organizational support in the city's neighborhoods. Rather, "it was suspended like a marionette from above."[84] The Democratic Party was therefore never much stronger than its rivals in terms of its organizational capacity; Republicans and some third parties were also well equipped to turn out supportive voters on election day. The Democrats, however, had the advantage of on-cycle city elections at a time when national and state political tides were in their favor, and thus it was the participation of the Presidential Voters in city elections that sustained that decade of the Democratic machine.

A number of factors chipped away at the Democratic machine's dominance in San Francisco in the early 1890s, including the rise of organized labor, the Reform Ballot Act that mandated the use of the secret ballot in California elections, the indictment of the city's Democratic boss, the election of a Populist mayor in 1892, and the pro-Republican national tides of the mid-1890s. However, the final election timing change in San Francisco was not imposed at the state level; rather, it came from within the city itself. Specifically, city leaders took advantage of a provision of the California constitution of 1879 that allowed municipalities to draft their own city charters. Unlike the other election timing changes that took place in New York and San Francisco during the nineteenth century, all it took to switch San Francisco elections to off-cycle in 1898 was a city leader willing to push through the change.

Because the city initiated the change—not the state legislature or even a new state constitutional convention—which party controlled state government at the time is less relevant for the 1898 election timing switch in San Francisco. The traditional wings of both the Republican and Democratic Parties almost certainly favored retention of the long-standing on-cycle election schedule. However, the man who initiated the successful San Francisco charter effort was not a traditional Democrat or Republican. He identified with the reform wing of the Democratic Party, and he was also head of an organization of local businessmen that sought to redesign the electoral and administrative structure of the city. When he was elected mayor in 1896, he oversaw the drafting of a new city charter that incorporated many of the provisions that were, by then, being promoted by the national municipal reform movement, including a switch to city elections in November of odd-numbered years.[85] Thus when San Francisco voters approved his charter in November 1898,[86] the city's elections were shifted to off-cycle.

As in New York, San Francisco's switch to off-cycle elections in 1898 was permanent. However, unlike New York, San Francisco never supported a Democratic political machine after the 1890s, in part because its Democratic Party organization lacked the ward and precinct network of the New York City machine.[87] Therefore, when city elections were moved to off-cycle, the old San Francisco machine was not well equipped to overwhelm the small city electorate by mobilizing supporters.

Philadelphia

Like San Francisco, Philadelphia city elections were originally scheduled to coincide with state elections, which, in Pennsylvania during the Second American Party System, took place in October. In 1854, however, the state legislature shifted city elections to June. A mere seven years later, the state legislature again moved Philadelphia's elections, this time back to October, a schedule that stayed in place for a little over a decade before the state constitutional convention of 1873 moved all municipal elections in the state to February. Thus the timing of Philadelphia's elections changed frequently throughout the nineteenth century. The circumstances of each change were different, but the basic reason behind each one was the same: the political parties were manipulating city election concurrence to increase their chances of winning.

The first election timing change in 1854 was included as part of an effort to consolidate all of the townships, districts, and boroughs in the county of Philadelphia with the then-separate municipal government.[88] Election timing aside, that consolidation effort faced a major political obstacle: the Whigs were the majority party in the city, whereas the Democrats had a majority in the areas of the county outside of the city.[89] An early proposal for consolidation, which would not have made any changes to city election timing, was resisted by state Democrats,[90] and for good reason: a document circulated during the debate over the measure demonstrated that the Whig majority in the city was larger than the Democratic majority in the surrounding areas of the county, which meant that consolidating the two would "extinguish the hopes of Democracy for a long time to come."[91] That same document, however, noted that in Philadelphia, the decreased Whig majority in 1850 as compared to 1848 was due to a decreased aggregate vote, not to fewer votes for the Whigs, "thus demonstrating . . . that of the many who remained away from the polls in 1850, by far the larger proportion were Whigs and Natives."[92] Even if consolidation would create a Whig majority in the new city and county, it was believed that the low voter turnout of off-cycle elections would decrease the vote share of the Whigs. When state Democrats finally did pass the consolidation measure in 1854, they changed the timing of the city's elections to June, presumably to weaken the electoral strength of the Whigs.[93]

The Whigs held on to control of city government in the very short run, but following the disappearance of that party, the organizations of the Democrats and the Republicans were relatively well matched in the consolidated city of Philadelphia. The Democrats controlled the city in 1856 and 1857, followed by two years of Republican control in 1858 and 1859.[94] In the spring elections of 1860, however, the incumbent Republican Party had a close call—it won the city election by only a few hundred votes out of 72,000 cast—and it responded by convincing its copartisans in the state legislature to fight for yet another change in city election timing. Early in the 1861 session of the state House, Republicans introduced a bill to abolish the spring city election and combine all future city elections with the general state election in October. The debate that ensued in the legislature was intense, with Republicans arguing that their proposed city

election schedule would save Philadelphia citizens $20,000 to $40,000 in
election costs and Democrats calling the proposal a purely partisan ma-
neuver.[95] One Democrat from the Philadelphia delegation explained to
the other legislators:

> Let us be plain on this matter. A worthy friend of mine, on this floor, who is an
> active Republican member, said to me yesterday, that some of the friends of
> this bill, from the city, urged him to vote for it, because it was a foregone con-
> clusion that if the election takes place in May, the Democrats, or Locofocos,
> as he expressed it, will be successful.... I do not believe the members of this
> House are prepared for any such action.[96]

When that legislator pressed a Republican from Philadelphia on the
question of whether city Republicans wanted to change the election date
in order to increase their chances of staying in control of city government, the Republican simply replied, "Of course they want the bill passed.
They have beaten the Locofocos [Democrats] so often that they want six
months respite."[97]

Unfortunately for the Democrats, the state government was stacked
against them, and the new election schedule was put into effect that year.
Every single Democrat in the House voted in opposition to the bill. Every
single vote in favor of the measure was cast by a Republican legislator.
And the legislature had no trouble getting the bill past the Republican
governor.

Proponents of the spring city election were outraged. Reporters called
the act "a political move,"[98] "a political dodge,"[99] and "arbitrary parti-
zan legislation."[100] Newly organized reform groups were just as furious as
the Democrats.[101] From the events that followed, it seemed their frustra-
tion was warranted: In the first October election in 1861, the Republicans
elected a majority to the city council and won most citywide offices. As
the Civil War wore on, the on-cycle election schedule continued to come
to the aid of the Republican Party in local elections thanks to city voters'
increasing allegiance to the Republican national platform.[102] By the late
1860s, the Republican Party had a firm grip on Philadelphia government
and powerful electoral machinery for keeping it in power. Moreover, Republicans dominated the legislature for the next fifteen years, so there
was little motive at the state level to once again isolate city elections from
state and national elections.

As in New York and San Francisco, the nascent Republican machine in

Philadelphia provoked a reform movement, and, also similar to the other two cities, the Citizens' Municipal Reform Association and the Reform Club in Philadelphia had serious organizational problems. Most of the reformers called themselves Republicans in state and national political affairs, which made many of them unwilling to desert the Republican Party in municipal races—especially those conducted at the same time as state and national races—for fear that their desertion would assist in the election of Democrats who wanted to lower tariffs. The slates of candidates they fielded in the early 1870s were failures.[103]

When state-level corruption allegations resulted in a state constitutional convention in 1873, reformers seized the opportunity and arrived with a large set of proposals. One of the reformers' proposals that ignited the most debate was their plan to establish a uniform February election date for all Pennsylvania municipalities.[104] Just as in 1861, the debate on the scheduling of local elections split almost perfectly along party lines within the Philadelphia delegation, with Democratic delegates in favor of creating an off-cycle schedule and Republicans opposing both the requirement for a uniform local election date and the February schedule that had been proposed. One Republican delegate from Philadelphia felt that local governments should be allowed to choose whatever election date was convenient for them. His Republican colleague, also from Philadelphia, tried to insert a provision that would allow cities to change their election dates by a vote of the people at the next general election. Another Republican delegate from Philadelphia tried to pass an amendment that would ensure that the section on election timing would not apply to cities of over one hundred thousand inhabitants—meaning Philadelphia. Philadelphia Democrats objected to all of this, arguing that it was the practice of combined elections that had led to bad city government in the first place.[105]

After over a week of debate on the issue of local election timing— even before the convention had decided which offices would exist under the new constitution—the election timing proposal finally came to a vote. Delegates approved the uniform February local election date by a vote of eighty-four to twenty-four. Among the Philadelphia delegation to the constitutional convention, all but one Democrat voted in favor of the measure, and all but one Republican voted against it.[106] Thus, throughout the 1850s, 1860s, and 1870s, the timing of Philadelphia's elections was a hotly contested partisan issue, with Republicans and Whigs generally favoring on-cycle elections and Democrats and reformers favoring off-cycle timing.

For a few years after 1874, Republican candidates' vote shares in state races tended to be higher than Republican candidates' vote shares in city races, suggesting that off-cycle elections did undermine Republican electoral efforts in the short run. Moreover, the Republican Party was rife with factionalism during this time.[107] Reformers had some small wins in 1876, and in both 1877 and 1881 the Democrats and reformers claimed large city election victories against the Republicans. However, the short wave of anti-Republican victories in the 1870s did not mark the beginning of the end for the Republican machine. The early 1880s actually saw the rise of a new machine run by Matthew Quay and the state Republican Party organization. Therefore, even though the new state constitution mandated off-cycle elections for every city in the state of Pennsylvania, Philadelphia elections continued to be dominated by the Republican machine.

Summary

These accounts make it clear that by the time municipal reformers gathered in a national forum in 1894, New York, San Francisco, and Philadelphia already had long histories of election timing manipulation. Changing the dates of city elections was a partisan power play: it changed the number of voters who participated, altered the distribution of voters in support of each party, and caused the parties to shift their competitive strategies. In some cases, the partisan fight over election timing pitted one major national party against the other major national party, as in New York in 1849, Philadelphia in 1854, and Philadelphia in 1861. In other cases, a national party conspired against a local party organization, or vice versa, as in San Francisco in the 1860s. Many cases involved a bit of both, since weaker national parties often coordinated with local parties to defeat the dominant party, and in San Francisco, national parties coordinated to fight the local party. Regardless of the particulars, party leaders clearly recognized the importance of election timing for their electoral fortunes and sought to set the rules in their own favor.

For many cases, the theoretical framework I have developed yields the same predictions as other existing theories, but it can also account for cases those theories leave unexplained. Recall that Ethington and Negretto argue that the clash over election timing pits major national parties against smaller parties.[108] This was sometimes true, as in San Francisco in the 1860s and 1870s, where Democrats and Republicans worked together to try to weaken the People's Party and the Workingmen's Party, and in New York City during the 1880s, where reformers accused the Republicans of being complicit in the Democratic machine. However, there were also cases in which one major national party fought with the other over election timing. In Philadelphia, Republicans and Democrats regularly clashed over when city elections would be held. In New York in the 1840s, Whigs' and Democrats' election timing preferences were diametrically opposed. Thus not every national party in every electoral context benefited from on-cycle election scheduling during the nineteenth century.

Others, like Bridges and Trounstine, have argued that groups promote off-cycle elections in the interest of lowering participation among immigrants and the lower classes,[109] which was sometimes true in the nineteenth century but not always. Consistent with the disenfranchisement argument, in the second half of the nineteenth century, the Democrats benefited from on-cycle elections in New York City and San Francisco, where Democratic machines relied on immigrants and the poor for political support. Moreover, in all three of the cities, reform groups consistently favored off-cycle elections, which accords with Bridges's and Trounstine's arguments that reformers worked to limit the participation of the machines' lower-class constituents. However, there are also some counterexamples: The Whigs favored on-cycle elections in New York in 1849. Republicans favored on-cycle elections in Philadelphia in 1861 and at the Pennsylvania constitutional convention of 1873. At the same time that the Union Party in San Francisco enacted the Registry Act, which was intended to restrict the franchise of immigrants (who mainly voted for Democrats),[110] it also implemented *on-cycle* elections. Thus high voter turnout did not always improve the electoral presence of immigrants and the poor.

More generally, off-cycle election timing did not consistently favor one party in particular across the three cities, or even within cities over the course of the nineteenth century. As I have argued, because the parties competed with each other in a zero-sum fashion, a party's election timing preference depended on the distribution of party loyalties among Presidential Voters and Consistent Voters, its relative organizational capacity with respect to its main rival, and the degree to which election timing shaped the nature of party competition in a city. Ultimately, the parties were dependent on state legislatures to help them secure favorable legislation when they thought an election timing change would benefit them.

In each of the cities, I have presented preliminary evidence that the parties that engineered each of these election timing changes usually benefited from them in the short run. However, it is worth pointing out that oftentimes, exogenous changes to political conditions tilted the advantage of the changed election schedule in favor of their rivals in the longer run. In New York, for example, the Whigs moved city elections to on-cycle in 1850, but the party disintegrated shortly thereafter, and eventually, the Democrats came to benefit from the election schedule the Whigs implemented. Likewise, the Unionists changed San Francisco elections to on-cycle in 1866, but just a year or two afterward, the Democrats benefited from the participation of Presidential Voters. Thus while party leaders did their best to design institutions to increase their probability of winning, as time passed and political conditions changed, the institutions they chose sometimes worked against them.[111]

The National Municipal Reform Movement

I have focused here on three cities, but other US cities also experienced episodes of election timing manipulation during the nineteenth century. The Minnesota legislature, for example, changed the election timing of St. Paul three times in four years.[112] In New Jersey, Republicans changed Jersey City's and Newark's elections to on-cycle in order to expose them to a wave of pro-Republican national sentiment.[113] Moreover, machine politics was an issue in the majority of large American cities during the Third American Party System.[114] The St. Louis government was selling franchises and contracts for political gain, the A. A. Ames regime ran Minneapolis, and Cincinnati had Boss George B. Cox.[115] It is therefore likely that there were other cases of city election timing manipulation during the nineteenth century that remain to be explored.

Still, the conditions of American cities varied greatly, and the delegates to the National Municipal League in the late 1890s disagreed on a number of proposed remedies. They quickly came to consensus on one issue, however. In order to undermine the urban political machines, they had to separate city elections from state and national elections. Off-cycle local election timing then became a primary goal of the national organization of good government groups at a time when such groups were rapidly multiplying in number.[116]

Why did the reformers prioritize off-cycle elections, and why were the delegates to the National Municipal League unified in their advocacy of this particular reform? There are at least three possibilities. First, perhaps reformers actually did think that off-cycle election timing would help them to build large, better-informed electorates in the cities. That is, after all, what many Progressives said: For years, city government had been run by political parties whose main interests were in state and national policy, even though good city policy had nothing to do with the policies that dominated the parties' state and national policy platforms. The Progressives thought city government should be administered like a business, with an emphasis on honesty and efficiency. Yet with city elections held on the same day as national elections, voters got caught up in partisan competition and lost sight of the importance of electing "good men" to city office. Off-cycle elections, it was argued, would encourage city voters to consider their vote for city officials independently of their vote for president or governor, resulting in more responsive city government.

The second possibility is that the Progressives were simply set on weakening (or destroying) the political parties, and they viewed off-cycle election timing as a tool that would help them do so. There is no question that the eventual outcome of the Progressive Era was a significant decrease in the strength of American political parties, brought on by a combination of institutional reforms like nonpartisan elections, at-large elections, direct primaries, civil service laws, direct democracy, and the like. Perhaps the National Municipal League promoted off-cycle election timing as an institutional arrangement that was consistent with the broader Progressive movement's goal of loosening the grip of political parties on American government.

There is a third possibility, however, and one that I think is closest to the mark: the delegates to the National Municipal League wanted to help local reform organizations get their candidates elected to office, and they believed that off-cycle election timing would improve reform candidates' electoral prospects. The cases of New York, San Francisco, and Philadelphia make it clear that reform organizations did not have much success in on-cycle elections. Since the urban machines were run by local organizations of the national political parties, reformers likely figured their best chance of minimizing the influence of these rival organizations was by holding city elections on a separate day than national elections.

All three of these explanations are plausible, although there are reasons to doubt that the first two can tell the whole story. First of all, given the history of election timing manipulation in New York, San Francisco, and Philadelphia, the municipal reformers likely knew that separating local from state and national elections would lower voter turnout in local races. In the three cities I examined, there were also signs that reformers recognized that changing turnout levels would change the composition of the electorate. If so, that casts doubt on the claim that they were merely trying to ensure that voters considered the right sorts of things when they voted for local offices. Moreover, in 1894, only some of the delegates to the National Municipal League advocated the banishment of political parties from city government altogether. Some delegates thought that off-cycle election timing would reform the existing party system, whereas others anticipated that election separation would lead to the creation of a wholly municipal party system.[117] Thus it does not seem that the league's decision to promote off-cycle election timing stemmed from delegates' desire to destroy political parties. In fact, as I have mentioned, the league's decision to promote nonpartisan elections was not made until years later.

Besides, even if reformers did want to improve the quality of city government, they had to win local elections to do so. Furthermore, the goal of winning local elections and weakening the electoral dominance of the machines was, in a way, consistent with the broader Progressive goal of weakening the major political parties, since the machines *were* organizations of the major political parties. Admittedly, if the league was really just trying to help local reform groups win elections, it should have simply promoted whatever institutions would work best in a given local context—even if what would work best was *on-cycle* election timing.[118] However, across the three cities I examined, even as Democrats, Republicans, and Whigs went back and forth over which election schedule would help them win, there was never a case in which reformers anticipated that they would fare better in on-cycle elections. As long as reformers in other cities with delegates to the National Municipal League had had similar experiences, it would make sense for the league to advocate a uniform policy of off-cycle election timing.

Therefore, just as Bridges and Trounstine have argued that reformers throughout the twentieth century were electorally and institutionally strategic in promoting nonpartisan elections, commission government, and at-large elections, my argument is that the delegates to the National Municipal League were strategic in promoting off-cycle election timing in 1894. They anticipated that they would have an easier time winning local elections in the future if those elections were held separately from state and national elections. And in part, they were correct. Since the party of the machine in any given city tended to also be the party Presidential Voters favored, the incorporation of Presidential Voters into city elections worked to the machine's advantage. Moreover, on-cycle elections encouraged unity within the machine's party and discouraged fusion among the opposition parties. But the theoretical framework also suggests that off-cycle election timing would not necessarily deliver a fatal blow to the party of the machines. The machines in most cities were also dominant in organizational capacity: they were well resourced and well equipped to mobilize a massive army of supportive voters as needed, more so than any other city organization. Therefore, the low baseline turnout of off-cycle elections could actually work in the machine's favor. It is not clear whether the reformers did not consider the relationship between low turnout and party organizational strength, whether they thought they could overcome it in time, or whether they simply thought the advantages of off-cycle timing outweighed the disadvantages.

Importantly, though, it does not seem that the election timing changes during the 1890s in New York and San Francisco were isolated events—they were part of a much larger structural reform movement. In the same decade that New York and San Francisco made election timing changes, cities ranging from Baltimore to Indianapolis to Waterbury, Connecticut, got new charters that separated city elections from state and national elections.[119] This was the beginning of what became a full-fledged national reform movement in the early twentieth century. By the early 1900s, reformers had moved on to more sweeping measures, promoting a comprehensive remodeling of American city government, of which off-cycle election timing was an integral part.

Meeting in Providence in 1907, National Municipal League delegates noted their large-scale success in promoting off-cycle city election timing. Still, they lamented the continued presence of the machines in city politics, and some delegates argued that off-cycle election timing had not undermined the machines as anticipated. Others argued that off-cycle scheduling had never been intended as a cure-all—it had merely been a first step of many they expected to be necessary. At this time the league began to promote the elimination of party labels from ballots in municipal elections. Delegates also recognized the importance of ballot reform and reform of the nomination process should they ever expect success in dislodging the major parties from their positions of power in city government. Thus reformers set about designing new structures that would further weaken the machines.

From the Progressive Era to the Present: The Institutionalization of Local Election Timing

These studies of New York, San Francisco, and Philadelphia in the nineteenth century make it clear that the choice of city election timing is *not* an accident; rather, it has deep historical roots as a strategy for groups trying to gain the upper hand in elections. The local election timing maneuverings of political parties in New York, California, and Pennsylvania during this period support the predictions of the theoretical framework: political party leaders regularly considered how changes in election timing would affect voter turnout, the partisan alignments of the people who would and would not vote, and the parties' respective mobilization capacities.

As of right now, it is impossible to say just how many American cities experienced this kind of back-and-forth over the concurrence of local elections. Perhaps the partisan jockeying over election timing was limited to relatively large cities, a particular set of states, or certain regions of the country. Perhaps the practice of tampering with local election timing was widespread. To know how common the manipulation of local election timing really was during this period, and whether moments of change and phases of stability can be explained by the theory, more data need to be collected.

Furthermore, focusing on the nineteenth century only gets us so far toward answering the broader question I posed earlier: Why are local elections today held when they are? Even if the Progressive Era municipal reformers were responsible for the widespread implementation of off-cycle local elections, we can't assume there has been no impetus to change things since then. For starters, in order to be able to deal effectively with potential endogeneity issues in testing the *effects* of election timing, we have to know something about what happened in the years since the Progressive Era. Moreover, the theoretical framework should be able to account for the politics of election timing choice today—even though the overall political environment is quite different—as well as in the nineteenth century. And lastly, if we are interested in understanding why today's elections are held when they are, we cannot simply assume that schedules were set during the Progressive Era and were never again a source of political contention. In fact, the theory suggests that that would be unlikely.

Tracing the histories of election scheduling for all local governments throughout the twentieth century would be a monumental task, but two existing sources of data make it possible to draw some preliminary conclusions about what happened during the mid- to late twentieth century, after the Progressive Era had ended. The first data source is a 1986 survey of municipal governments carried out by the International City/ County Management Association (ICMA), which asked, among other things, when the municipalities held their regular elections. The second is a series of reference books also compiled by ICMA (then the International City Managers' Association). For a few years in the late 1930s and early 1940s, these reference books contained information on when municipal governments throughout the United States held elections. To the best of my knowledge, this is the oldest source (not to mention one of the only sources) of such information. By digitizing the governmental data from the 1940 *Municipal Year Book* and combining it with the 1986 ICMA data,[120] I created a dataset that allows me to compare the election schedules of 1,083 municipal governments in 1940 and 1986.[121]

Did city election timing continue to fluctuate a great deal after the Progressive Era ended, or did it remain relatively stable? To answer this question, I code elections held in November of even-numbered years as on-cycle elections and elections on all other dates as off-cycle elections.[122] I then group each of the 1,083 cities into four categories: cities that had off-cycle elections in 1940 and still had off-cycle elections in 1986, cities that had off-cycle elections in 1940 but switched to on-cycle elections sometime before 1986, cities that had on-cycle elections in both 1940 and 1986, and cities that switched from on-cycle elections to off-cycle elections sometime between 1940 and 1986. Table 3.2 presents the percentage of cities in each of the four categories, broken down by state. The fifth column presents the number of cities used to calculate the percentages, and the final two columns specify the percentage of the cities in each dataset (the 1940 dataset and the 1986 dataset, respectively) that are included in these calculations.

One pattern immediately stands out: the most common type of city by far is one in which elections were held off-cycle in 1940 and were *still* held off-cycle in the mid-1980s. In seventeen of the forty-seven states listed in the table,[123] 100% of the cities in the dataset held off-cycle elections in the early part of the twentieth century and continued to do so nearly fifty years later. In thirty-seven of the states, 70% or more of the cities in the dataset had off-cycle elections in both the earlier and later period. And in

TABLE 3.2 **Municipal election timing in 1940 and 1986, by state**

State	% Off-cycle to off-cycle	% Off-cycle to on-cycle	% On-cycle to on-cycle	% On-cycle to off-cycle	Number of cities	% of cities in 1940 data	% of cities in 1986 data
AL	100	0	0	0	14	58	22
AR	0	100	0	0	12	67	29
AZ	100	0	0	0	5	63	10
CA	71	26	0	3	77	82	23
CO	100	0	0	0	15	83	21
CT	85	0	0	15	13	45	16
FL	89	0	0	11	18	60	11
GA	89	0	6	6	18	58	19
IA	97	3	0	0	30	86	27
ID	100	0	0	0	6	100	24
IL	99	1	0	0	74	65	29
IN	0	0	14	86	29	47	40
KS	100	0	0	0	25	76	28
KY	84	11	0	5	19	66	26
LA	80	0	10	10	10	53	21
MA	98	0	0	2	65	59	33
MD	100	0	0	0	9	100	21
ME	58	33	0	8	12	67	10
MI	84	4	2	10	51	71	26
MN	43	48	9	0	23	72	15
MO	93	7	0	0	27	71	21
MS	67	8	0	25	12	71	29
MT	100	0	0	0	9	75	50
NC	100	0	0	0	30	79	25
ND	100	0	0	0	7	70	78
NE	8	85	0	8	13	76	31
NH	88	13	0	0	8	57	16
NJ	47	9	30	15	47	44	23
NM	100	0	0	0	4	57	17
NV	100	0	0	0	2	100	17
NY	96	4	0	0	51	47	34
OH	81	17	2	0	54	49	24
OK	100	0	0	0	21	55	29
OR	0	10	80	10	10	67	12
PA	70	18	0	11	71	37	25
RI	0	18	55	27	11	61	52
SC	92	8	0	0	13	59	25
SD	100	0	0	0	7	88	41
TN	92	8	0	0	12	55	15
TX	98	2	0	0	63	76	21
UT	100	0	0	0	3	43	6
VA	100	0	0	0	13	52	19
VT	100	0	0	0	4	40	15
WA	91	9	0	0	11	58	14
WI	100	0	0	0	37	79	30
WV	93	7	0	0	15	68	47
WY	0	67	33	0	3	60	17

a total of thirty-nine states, this was the pattern for a majority of the cities. If the Progressives were responsible for implementing off-cycle elections in cities across the United States, table 3.2 suggests their work has been quite resistant to change.

The few states that deviate from this dominant pattern are a mixed bunch. The only states in which most cities changed from off-cycle elections in 1940 to on-cycle elections by 1986 were Arkansas, Nebraska, and Wyoming. A few states, such as Minnesota, Maine, and California, had smaller percentages of their cities switch from off-cycle to on-cycle elections. An even smaller number of states started out with mostly on-cycle city elections in 1940—namely, Indiana, Oregon, and Rhode Island—and of those, Indiana was the only one to undergo a transition to off-cycle municipal elections over the course of those forty-six years. Thus when it comes to the concurrence of city elections, much of the scheduling that was in place in the late 1930s was still in use half a century later. While this analysis is merely suggestive—it cannot tell us what happened to these cities before the late 1930s or even between 1940 and 1986—table 3.2 gives the impression that in most states, off-cycle local election schedules have been relatively stable over the course of the twentieth century.

Given what this chapter has shown, this stability is somewhat surprising. There was a long period of US history during which the timing of local elections—at least in some cities—was *not* durable. Rather, it was frequently changed for the purpose of tipping the balance of political party power in elections. Election timing was a lever that political parties pulled to affect how many people voted, which parties fused, which factions ran separate slates of candidates, and what percentage of the vote went to each party competing for city office. And yet, after sixty years of frequent changes in city election timing from the rise of mass political parties to the early years of the Progressive Era, and in spite of the fact that the timing of elections has potential to affect election outcomes and policy, local election timing became relatively stable in the twentieth century. This raises several questions: First, how did off-cycle election timing become such a durable feature of the American political landscape? Second, does the stability of election timing in the modern period mean that the theory doesn't provide a valid account of today's politics of election scheduling? And third, does this mean that when using observational data to test the effects of election timing, we can simply assume that variation in election timing is exogenous to the political influence of today's organized groups?

My answers to the second two questions are *no* and *no*: Just because municipal election timing appears to have been relatively stable during the twentieth century does *not* mean the theory's predictions are inaccurate. Moreover, the absence of change in election timing does *not* mean we can assume that variation in election timing is exogenous to the influence of today's interest groups. To the contrary, the stability in the election schedule is likely a *product* of the influence of today's groups. As for why municipal election timing became relatively stable after decades of back-and-forth, I argue that the incentives surrounding election timing choice stayed the same, and that what changed was the context within which election schedules are decided. The latter, and *not* any decreasing relevance of the individual effect and group effect of election timing, explains why election timing became stable.

To see this, consider several trends of the late nineteenth and early twentieth centuries that were most likely important to the new stability of local election timing: The *way* in which the Progressive reformers enacted their proposals was different from the way election timing had been changed previously. Prior to the 1870s, localities were predominantly governed by special legislation, meaning legislation passed by the state legislature that applied to only a single city, such as legislation to pave a street, alter the structure of the police force in one city, or change the term length of the mayor in another. Legislatures dealt with hundreds of such local provisions each session. Notably, the election timing changes discussed in this chapter—with the exceptions of the final switches in each city—were the result of special legislation.

In the late nineteenth century, however, the landscape began to change. Reformers increasingly viewed special legislation as the cause of chaos and unpredictability in municipal governance as well as a vehicle for fiscal extravagance. Starting in the 1870s, constitutional conventions in many states created clauses that required state legislatures to enact general legislation that applied uniformly to all cities within their boundaries.[124] Thus the municipal reformers succeeded in convincing state politicians to enact off-cycle election schedules during a period in which it was generally becoming more difficult for state legislators to create laws tailored to individual cities. In some states, off-cycle city election timing was even locked in to new constitutions, as in Pennsylvania in the 1870s and New York in the 1890s. The push for off-cycle elections also coincided with the home rule movement, the very goal of which was to enhance the stability of city government. As Jon Teaford writes,

Nineteenth-century home rule was a product of those who opposed excessive
change, who sought stability, and who hoped to build a lasting foundation for
city government. They dreamed of legal monuments in an age of jerry-built law.
They were determined to block the traditional channels to structural change,
and . . . they largely destroyed the adaptive mechanism of special legislation.[125]

Ultimately, many of the largest US cities implemented off-cycle election
timing by crafting their own city charters, as in San Francisco. By the time
the National Municipal League promoted off-cycle election timing, many
state constitutions contained home rule provisions and required general
legislation. By consequence, it became more difficult for post-Progressive
state legislators to change the election timing rules of individual cities.

More generally, the Progressive movement made sweeping changes
to the American political environment, and as a consequence of those
changes, political parties played a less central role in local elections. For
one thing, the early twentieth century marked the end of the spoils system as the regular way of conducting politics in the United States. The
implementation and gradual strengthening of civil service laws undercut
political parties' ability to use government jobs to win votes and campaign contributions. Once city jobs had to be distributed according to
merit rather than party loyalty, the cities were no longer as appealing to
national political parties as sources of political power. Changes in ballot practices also affected the operation of politics. As states adopted the
Australian ballot, voters were presented with the names of all candidates
rather than only the nominees of their preferred party, and the result was
a rise in split ticket voting.[126] Therefore, even in places where city elections
remained on the same day as state and national elections, it became easier
for individuals to vote for a municipal candidate of a different party than
their preferred party in the state and national races. Other reforms such
as the direct primary and nomination by petition, direct democracy, the
nonpartisan ballot, and at-large elections weakened the parties' control
over elections at all levels of government. By 1917 the American political
scene looked quite different than it had in the 1880s.

The parties gradually relinquished their direct stake in local politics
in many places and declined to take an active role in the political fray in
newer cities, but the space they left did not stay empty for long. An important consequence of the party-weakening reforms of the early twentieth
century was the rise of political activity by nonparty groups like nonpartisan slating groups and special interest groups.[127] Chambers of commerce,

good government groups, labor organizations, businesses, and other interests became increasingly influential in political activities that the parties had previously carried out, such as financing campaigns, endorsing candidates, nominating candidates, and electioneering.[128] Therefore, after the Progressive Era, the local groups with the strongest organizational capacity in many cities were not political parties—they were interest groups. Unlike political parties, whose competition in city elections had been zero-sum, it was possible for city government to accommodate the demands of many different interest groups simultaneously, as long as the groups were not working at cross-purposes. Since off-cycle election timing increased the influence of interest groups in elections, many of those groups had a stake in protecting it from proposed changes.

Still, many of the large cities where political parties remained active experienced rule by party machines well into the twentieth century. The great irony of the Progressive reformers' push for off-cycle elections was that it probably actually *helped* the machines in the long run. In cities like New York and Philadelphia, the political machines continued to be the groups with the strongest organizational capacity, and the low turnout that accompanied off-cycle elections enhanced the effectiveness of machines' mobilization efforts. As Raymond Wolfinger notes, "These low-salience contests are particularly amenable to the resources typical of machine politics . . . since precinct work is effective in inverse relation to the salience of the election."[129]

With off-cycle election timing working in favor of many interest groups and old-fashioned machines, the deck was stacked against any state legislators and party leaders who might have found reason to try to alter local government election timing. Changing the election timing of a particular city would now mean, at a minimum, passing a law for all municipalities in the state. Cities with home rule charters and cities in states with election timing provisions embedded in the constitution were even more difficult to touch. These factors almost certainly have something to do with why, after decades of frequent changes to city election scheduling, the back-and-forth largely came to an end.

The politics of election timing choice today is set in a very different context from that of the nineteenth century. Fusion ballots are relatively rare.[130] In most places, political parties are not the most important groups active in local elections—nonparty groups like interest groups are. For the most part, states have to make rules by general legislation, not special legislation. Home rule has proliferated, and the number of local governments has increased dramatically. These changes in the American political arena have fundamentally changed the context within which decisions about election timing are made.

Even so, as I show in the next chapter, the basic dynamics of election timing are essentially the same today as they were in the nineteenth century. The organized groups that have a vested interest in election outcomes have preferences over when those elections are held, and we can predict those preferences by considering how the individual effect and the group effect alter the composition of the electorate. Ultimately, it is still the state governments that have final say as to when state and local elections are held. Therefore, by examining how organized groups get involved in state government decision making on election timing, and by considering how the activities of those organized groups matter to state legislators, we can get a clear picture of why state governments make the decisions about election timing that they do. Not only does this constitute another test of the theory in a very different political context, but it also illuminates why local election timing patterns established in the late nineteenth and early twentieth centuries have been so remarkably stable over the last hundred years.

CHAPTER FOUR

Interest Groups and Election Timing Choice in the Twenty-First Century

Around any [electoral] system there develops a set of strategies for the gaining of power. The strategists take account both of the "rules of the game" and each other's strategies, and there arises by mutual adjustment an equilibrium that becomes in time so familiar and taken for granted that the electoral system appears to be a purely technical, and therefore trivial, feature of the city's politics. But this is an illusion, for the electoral system profoundly affects the character of politics. It should not be surprising, then, that efforts to change fundamentally the distribution of power within a city are often directed toward changing the electoral system. And it should likewise not be surprising that the changes proposed are discussed by proponents and opponents as if they could be judged on purely technical grounds.—Edward C. Banfield and James Q. Wilson, *City Politics*

A century has gone by since the dawn of the Progressive Era, and yet nothing has undone the general tendency for state elections to be held concurrently with national elections and local elections to be scattered throughout the year at different times. There is little question that governments' election timing choices have an impact on voter turnout— and usually a big one. Off-cycle local elections are sometimes even referred to as "stealth elections," since a large percentage of eligible voters do not know that they are happening.[1] And yet few people stop to think about why elections for cities, school boards, counties, states, and special districts are held when they are. For most Americans, this is as obscure a topic as any.

As Edward Banfield and James Q. Wilson note, however, there is usually political tension behind the facade of unquestioning acceptance of existing electoral rules, for "the electoral system profoundly affects the character of politics."[2] The theory I developed in chapter 2 indicates that this should be true of election timing. The concurrence of elections—an important component of the broader electoral system—has potential to have a profound impact on the electoral process, election outcomes, and public policy. We should therefore expect there to be political tension surrounding the choice of election schedules—even if what we observe from a distance is that the election schedules of states, cities, and school districts have not changed much at all in the last hundred years.

In this chapter, I put the theory of election timing to the test in present-day American politics by examining the politics of election timing choice in state legislatures from 2001 to 2011. I begin by explaining how the theoretical framework can be used to make predictions about which organized groups benefit from a certain election schedule and therefore have reason to lobby election timing decision makers in support of it. However, just as in the previous chapter, in order to understand actual decisions on election timing, one has to understand the nature of the connection between those organized groups and the decision makers (which, in most cases, are state elected officials). Thus by evaluating the incentives of state officials with respect to the organized groups that pressure for certain election schedules, I can predict the stances of those officials on election timing matters and explain when and why election timing changes—or, as is more common, why it stays the same.

The empirical analysis proceeds in four stages. The first is an investigation of voters' preferences on local election timing using data from a nationally representative survey. This is a critical first step in evaluating the theory, since the theory posits that the preferences of organized groups—and not necessarily the preferences of average voters—play a central role in the politics of election timing choice. In the last chapter, it was easier to make this claim, because parties were so critical to every aspect of the political process in the nineteenth century. Today, however, political parties are much weaker. Moreover, most of the modern political science literature on representation stresses the importance of individual voters' preferences and focuses on the linkages between those voters and their legislators—not on linkages between legislators and interest groups. Before I test whether election timing today can be explained in terms of the preferences of organized groups, it is important to evaluate whether a simpler explanation is at work; that is, that legislators respond to the election timing preferences of voters.

The next stage is a descriptive analysis of a new dataset of election timing bills considered in US state legislatures from 2001 to 2011. This, too, is an important preliminary step toward testing the theory. Specifically, the theory suggests that there is likely to be considerable conflict over the scheduling of elections, and yet we know nothing about whether state legislatures even take up questions of election timing today. Therefore, provision of some basic information—such as how common it is for state legislators to propose changes to election timing, details on what those election timing proposals look like, and descriptions of what happens to them in the legislature—reveals a great deal about the politics of election timing choice and establishes a foundation for testing the theory.

In the third part of the empirical analysis, I focus on the politics behind the timing of a certain type of election: school board elections. First, I use the theoretical framework to generate predictions about what debates over school election timing should look like—specifically, which organized interest groups we should expect to be active and what positions we should expect state legislators to take. I then carry out two sets of empirical tests to see whether the data support those predictions. The first is a qualitative account of debates over election timing in three state legislatures— Michigan, South Dakota, and Montana—and the second analyzes data on partisan patterns in bill sponsorship and committee and floor votes. In both the case studies and the quantitative analysis, the patterns revealed closely align with the predictions I draw from the theoretical framework.

In the final step of the empirical analysis, I explore the contours of debates over election scheduling for state governments and other forms of local government. Because of the likely complexity of interest group competition in state elections and a general shortage of research on interest group activity in local elections like city elections, it is more difficult to move from the theory to clear predictions about which groups should benefit from off-cycle election timing in these contexts—and predictions about which legislators should support it. Even so, my empirical findings suggest that the theoretical framework is on the right track; the most plausible alternative explanation falls short of accounting for the observed patterns in the data.

Taken as a whole, this chapter makes it clear that it would be difficult to explain the politics of election timing choice today without an understanding of how election timing affects the composition of the electorate, altering the balance of power among organized groups.

Applying the Theory to the Politics of Election Timing Choice in the Twenty-First Century

Today's political environment is very different from that of the late nineteenth century. Political parties are weaker, and most local elections are formally nonpartisan. Even in state and national elections, in which most candidates are affiliated with a political party, party organizations play a less important role in election-related activities like nominations and mobilization than they did in the nineteenth century. Interest groups, on the other hand, have increased in importance and now actively participate in many of the activities that used to be the responsibility of political parties.

Despite the many changes that have taken place between the Progressive Era and today, however, I argue that the same two primary dimensions that shaped organized groups' preferences over election timing during the nineteenth century are still at work in the modern era. Specifically, I expect that organized groups benefit from off-cycle election timing if their members and supporters are more motivated to vote than the members and supporters of any directly competing groups, and if they are stronger in organizational capacity than their competitors. By contrast, if a group is organizationally weaker and has members that are less motivated than the competition, that group should fare better in on-cycle elections. As before, it is the anticipation of electoral benefit (or loss) from a change in election timing—stemming from the individual effect and the group effect—that shapes groups' preferences over election schedules.

In situations where elected officials are charged with making decisions about the timing of their *own* elections, moving from the theory's predictions about groups' election timing preferences to predictions about actual decisions is fairly straightforward. Consider, for example, state legislators deciding the timing of state legislative elections. Those legislators have a direct stake in that decision, and each legislator can roughly calculate whether she (or her party as a whole) would fare better in off-cycle or on-cycle elections. And if a sufficient proportion of legislators anticipate that they would benefit from a change in election timing, then presumably the assembly would pass a bill to enact that change.

In many cases, however, the decision makers are somewhat removed from the organized groups and elected officials who are directly affected. This, for example, was true for all but one of the election timing decisions I analyzed in the last chapter: For most of the nineteenth century, even if local party leaders wanted to change local election timing, they usually had to convince state elected officials to enact that change. For most local governments, this is still true today: state governments set the rules for when local governments hold elections. Of course, as I discussed earlier, state governments today usually have to pass general legislation rather than special legislation, which means that most of the time they cannot craft different election timing rules for individual local governments.[3] However, it remains true that a local organized group that wants to change local election timing is dependent on the state government for favorable legislation.

This raises an important question: Why would today's *state* legislators care about the timing of *local* elections? This was easy to answer for the context of nineteenth-century politics, because state and local candidates and officials were bound together by a system of strong political parties. It is no surprise, for example, that state Democrats in the nineteenth century took a deep interest in the political fates of Democrats running for local offices, because when Democrats won control of local government, the party gained patronage it could use to build and strengthen its organization. However, even today, in a political environment that is very much changed, I argue that state legislators *do* care about the balance of power among groups competing in local elections. To see why, one has to consider state legislators' electoral incentives and how those incentives link them to the groups directly affected by local election timing decisions. Once those electoral interests are taken into account, it becomes quite clear why interest groups' positions on local election scheduling would create predictable patterns in state legislators' positions.

As a starting point, I do *not* expect that the election timing preferences of average voters are especially important to state legislators. This is not to say that state representatives never care about the preferences of citizens—of course they do—but rather that when it comes to choosing election schedules, regular voters' preferences are not the main factor that state legislators consider. Election timing is an obscure political issue. In Banfield and Wilson's words, local election timing is "familiar and taken for granted" by most citizens.[4] It is highly unlikely that voters will judge the performance of their state representatives on the issue of election timing—and state representatives know that. Voter inattention therefore gives reelection-minded state legislators the flexibility to respond to their constituents who *are* paying attention: organized interest groups.[5]

The theory predicts that local interest groups are directly affected by changes to local election timing, and so I expect they pressure state legislators to enact (or protect) the election schedules they favor. That interest group pressure should interact with state legislators' electoral incentives in three distinct but interrelated ways. The first has to do with legislators' incentives to respond to the local interest groups that are active in their home districts.[6] All state legislators come from districts that contain local governments: county governments, municipal governments, school districts, park districts, and so on. If a change in local election timing will affect the balance of power among organized groups active in those local elections, those groups will likely voice their preferences to their legislator, backed (implicitly or explicitly) by the threat of retaliation or promise of support in the legislator's *own* reelection. If a particular local group is important to a legislator's reelection prospects, she will feel some pressure to respond to the group by adopting its preferred position on local election timing.

The second reason why state legislators may feel compelled to respond to interest groups' preferences on local election timing is that state legislators are members of political parties, and parties today depend heavily on interest groups for financial contributions, endorsements, recruitment, mobilization, and other electioneering activities. Some scholars, such as Kathleen Bawn and her colleagues, have even argued that political parties *exist* in order to further the goals of interest groups and activists.[7] Given the strong link between the fates of political parties and the fates of interest groups in American politics today, state legislators who care about the strength of their political parties (whether for electoral reasons or policy reasons) must also, by implication, care about the strength of the parties' interest group allies. A local election timing proposal that would alter the balance of interest group power should therefore cause state legislators and party leaders to take notice: if it would weaken an ally of one party, that party's members should tend to oppose it, while the competing party's members should tend to support it.

There is a third reason to expect that state legislators would take interest in local election timing: Local interest groups often have state-level organizations as well, and those state-level organizations can be active players in individual state legislative races—contributing money, phone-banking, coordinating mailings, and engaging in other activities on behalf of particular candidates. If local interest groups would be negatively affected by a proposed election timing change, and those local groups are part of a state-level group that, for example, contributed money to a legislator in the last election, that legislator would probably feel some pressure to oppose the change. This potential for direct alliance between individual legislators and state-level interest groups is yet another reason why state legislators might care about the timing of local elections.

The theory doesn't only lead to predictions about which groups should favor and oppose local election timing changes. Because of the linkages between the groups that would be directly affected by local election timing proposals and the state legislators who make election timing decisions, the theoretical framework can also be used to generate predictions about *state* legislators' positions on *local* election timing.

Are State Governments Merely Responding to Voters?

As a first step, how do we even know that state legislators' choices on election timing have anything to do with the preferences of organized groups? There could be a much simpler explanation for the variation in election timing we observe across the country; that is, American elected officials adopt election timing rules according to the preferences of the general public. Based on my descriptive analysis in chapter 1, that would imply that most American citizens actually prefer off-cycle local elections. If so, then I would not necessarily expect state legislators' positions to track the preferences of the organized groups directly affected by a proposed election timing change. This would not be evidence that the theory is wrong, of course; it would merely indicate that the effect of local election timing on interest group influence is not the main reason state legislators take the positions on election timing they do.

To the best of my knowledge, no study has ever asked American citizens whether they would prefer to vote on many offices on a single day or on different days. And so in the 2008 Stanford module of the Cooperative Congressional Election Study (CCES),[8] I did just that. Specifically, I asked each of the one thousand respondents in the module the following question:[9]

> In most states, elections for local government offices like mayor, city council member, and school board member are held on different days than elections for national government offices like US president and US senator. Some people favor having local elections on *different* days than national elections, because it allows voters to focus on a shorter list of candidates and issues during each election. Other people favor having local elections on the *same* day as national elections, because combining the elections boosts voter turnout for local elections. What do you think? Do you think local elections should be held on the same day as national elections or on different days than national elections?

TABLE 4.1 **Citizens' election timing preferences by party and ideology**

	Democrat	Republican	Independent
Different day	27%	39%	35%
	(73)	(90)	(81)
Same day	73%	61%	65%
	(200)	(143)	(150)
Total	100%	100%	100%
	(273)	(233)	(231)
	Liberal	Moderate	Conservative
Different day	27%	33%	34%
	(48)	(92)	(99)
Same day	73%	67%	66%
	(129)	(184)	(189)
Total	100%	100%	100%
	(177)	(276)	(288)

Notes: Numbers in parentheses are the number of respondents. Data are from the Stanford module of the 2008 CCES.

As it turns out, most American citizens do *not* prefer the prevailing norm of off-cycle local elections. Nearly 70% of respondents said they favored holding local elections at the same time as national elections.[10] Moreover, support for on-cycle election scheduling did not vary with respondent age, sex, education level, race, or ethnicity; these demographic predictors explain less than 1% of the variation in the responses.[11] Among various subgroups of American citizens, large majorities reported a preference for concurrent elections rather than elections held at different times throughout the year. It is thus very difficult to justify the fragmented American electoral calendar as being in accordance with what American voters want.

There are some notable differences between the responses of Republicans and Democrats in the sample, however. As table 4.1 shows, large majorities of Democrats, Republicans, and Independents favor holding local elections on the same day as national elections, but support for on-cycle elections is significantly stronger among Democrats than among Republicans and Independents: 73% of Democrats would prefer on-cycle elections, as compared to 61% of Republicans and 65% of Independents.[12] The same is true when I break down respondents into categories based on their ideology: 73% of self-identified liberals favor "Same day" local elections, as opposed to 67% of moderates and 66% of conservatives.[13]

This is notable because my descriptive analysis of state election timing rules in chapter 1 did not show that on-cycle local election timing is more common in liberal states than conservative states. The few states with uniform on-cycle municipal elections—Arkansas, Kentucky, Nebraska, Oregon, and Rhode Island—are a mixed bunch of "red" and "blue" states. If anything, the states with uniform on-cycle school board elections tend to be more conservative than the others. This, too, suggests that politicians aren't creating and maintaining election timing rules in response to the preferences of citizens. If liberal voters are more likely to prefer on-cycle local elections (as table 4.1 shows), then why would states with more conservative voters be more likely to have them?

My argument is that most voters don't monitor state legislators' positions on local election timing, and so state legislators can safely get away with responding to the preferences of organized interest groups. There is another possibility, however, which is that voters might be willing to answer a question about local election timing on a survey but do not actually care much about the issue. It is one matter if voters simply don't care about election timing and its implications for voter turnout; it is another matter if voters *do* care about election timing but don't (or can't) monitor what state legislators are doing about it.[14]

In an attempt to gauge respondents' level of concern about the election timing issue, I asked a second question as part of the CCES:

> In *presidential* elections, about 50 to 55% of eligible citizens typically turn out to vote. In most *local* elections for offices like mayor, city council member, and school board member, less than 25% of eligible citizens turn out to vote. Does the level of voter turnout for *local* government elections ... Bother you a lot? Bother you somewhat? Not bother you much? Not bother you at all?

The responses suggest that most Americans do care about the issue—at least when they are asked about it: A full 34% of respondents replied that the low turnout of off-cycle elections bothers them a lot. Thirty-eight percent said that it bothers them somewhat. Only 17% said that it does not bother them much, and a mere 11% said that it does not bother them at all. Liberals and Democrats indicated slightly greater concern over low turnout in local elections than moderates, conservatives, Republicans, and Independents, but in general, the differences were small.[15] Across the board a large majority of respondents expressed concern about the turnout gap between on-cycle and off-cycle elections.

Therefore, contradicting the hypothesis that elected officials have maintained the standard of off-cycle elections because American citizens like it that way, I find the vast majority of eligible voters would actually prefer to have local elections held on the same day as national elections. Moreover, Democratic citizens report slightly higher levels of support for on-cycle elections than Republicans, but it does not appear that *states* with more Democratic citizens are more likely to have on-cycle local elections. And voters do care when elections are held. When asked, most of them report that they are concerned about the low turnout typical of off-cycle local elections. On the whole, it does not appear that the fragmented American election schedule accords with public opinion.

State Legislatures' Activities on Election Timing

The discovery that state governments do not respond to voters' election timing preferences raises the question of what, exactly, state governments are doing on matters of election timing. How common is it for state legislatures to consider changes to the election schedule? What do the proposed changes look like? How successful are they? There is no existing research that provides answers to these questions, and yet I need some preliminary information before I can move forward with testing the theory. To this end, I have compiled a dataset of election timing bills proposed in state legislatures between 2001 and 2011.[16]

The starting point for that dataset is the National Conference of State Legislatures (NCSL) Database of Election Reform Legislation. NCSL researchers began work on this database in the wake of the 2000 US presidential election, a point at which leaders in many states attempted to reform their administration of elections. The NCSL began to track the various election administration bills introduced in the state legislatures, including bills affecting absentee voting, ballot access, candidate qualifications, registration, polling places, poll workers, and more. The result of their efforts was the Database of Election Reform Legislation, a rich source of data on election bills that have been introduced in state legislatures since 2001. For each bill, the database provides the bill number and year, its final status in the legislature, a brief summary of the measure (usually one sentence), and a bill category assigned by the NCSL staff. Importantly for my purposes, one of the categories within their database is Dates of Elections.

There are 479 bills categorized as attempts to change the dates of elections—a large number considering the obscurity of election timing as a topic of discussion and research. Moreover, while the coverage of the database is quite extensive,[17] it is not 100% comprehensive. Through my own outside research, I have discovered election timing bills that are not included in the Dates of Elections category of the NCSL database. Still, as a starting point, the fact that the NCSL tracks hundreds of state legislative proposals to change the dates of state and local elections suggests that state legislators are quite active in this area.

Digging a little deeper, it becomes clear that not every bill of the 479 in the NCSL database has to do with the combination or separation of different types of elections. For example, a bill proposing to move local elections to a Saturday rather than a Tuesday does not necessarily combine those local elections with (or separate them from) other elections. Likewise, a bill proposing to avoid scheduling elections on days of religious observance does not deal with making elections concurrent. Plus, some bills are listed twice in the database, either because they were considered in two different years, or because companion bills are listed separately. I therefore used the NCSL database of Dates of Elections bills as a starting point for the creation of my own original dataset of state legislative election timing bills.

First, since the NCSL database provides only the most basic information about the bills, I began by researching each individual bill using the bill tracking tools on state legislatures' websites. Using both the summaries provided by the NCSL as well as the information I gathered from the state legislatures, I pared down the original list of 479 bills to a subset of unique bills that satisfied one of the following criteria:[18]

- The bill proposed *combining* different types of elections in the state
- The bill proposed *separating* different types of elections in the state
- The bill proposed *restricting* the number of possible election dates in the state
- The bill proposed *expanding* the number of possible election dates in the state.

With that subset of bills, I then added in any bills that I had learned of in my background research on election timing that were not included in the NCSL database.

The product of this initial round of research was a dataset of 219 election timing bills introduced between 2001 and 2011. As I show in figure 4.1, the bills come from thirty-five of the fifty states, but a few states

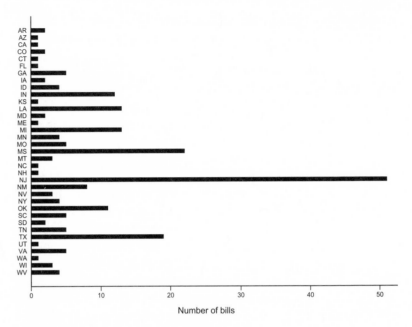

FIGURE 4.1. Election timing bills by state, 2001–11.

account for a large percentage of the bills. Nearly a quarter of the bills come from New Jersey (fifty-one bills). A few states in the South account for large numbers of bills as well: Mississippi had twenty-two, Texas had nineteen, and Louisiana had thirteen. In contrast, states like California, Maine, and North Carolina only had one bill each. Keeping in mind that the dataset may not be comprehensive, which means that I cannot draw firm conclusions about the frequency with which election timing bills are proposed, the sheer number of bills introduced as well as the large proportion of states that proposed changes to election timing suggest that efforts to alter election scheduling are quite common.

As a next step in the data collection process, I learned about the content of the 219 proposals by reading the information available on state legislatures' websites. The information available for each bill varied significantly. Many of the bills were never considered in committee, and so very little information was available. Even for the bills that made it to advanced stages of the legislative process, different state legislatures provided different amounts of information. For example, states like Texas provide an audio feed of committee hearings, lists of witnesses who testify in committee, detailed roll call information for all committee and floor votes, texts of the bills at various stages of the legislative process, bill summaries, fiscal notes, and more—all on their websites. Other states provide little more than bill histories and the text of bills.

At a bare minimum, I collected a few critical pieces of information on each of the 219 bills in the dataset. First, using the bill summaries, I coded the types of elections that would be affected if the bill were adopted. Second, I kept listings of which legislators authored, sponsored, or cosponsored each bill and coded the party affiliations of each of those legislators. Third, I tracked how far each bill advanced in the legislative process.

For many of the bills, there was a great deal more information available. When possible, I kept lists of the outside groups that testified for, against, or on the bills during committee hearings. When there was audio feed, video feed, or written minutes available from the bills' committee hearings or relevant floor debates, I took notes on those. Whenever there was a recorded vote on a bill, either in committee or on the chamber floor, I coded the party affiliation of each legislator voting along with information on whether he or she voted yes or no. While I only have these kinds of details for a subset of the 219 bills, the information helps to paint a fuller picture of what modern debates over election scheduling look like.

The first trend that jumps out from the data is the very clear *direction* of the proposals. Of the 219 bills, 203 of them—or 93%—proposed to either combine different types of elections on the same day or reduce the number of possible dates available for certain types of elections. Moreover, the vast majority of the 203 election consolidation bills proposed sweeping changes to election scheduling—for example, combining all municipal elections with national elections in November of even-numbered years. By contrast, the sixteen bills that proposed either an expansion of election dates or a shift from on-cycle to off-cycle elections involved what would be relatively minor changes. For example, one Wisconsin bill proposed to move county elections to the spring so that they would be held with other local elections rather than with national elections. A bill in West Virginia would have allowed municipal charter elections to be held at the time of primary elections in addition to the time of general statewide elections or general municipal elections. With few exceptions, today's election timing proposals are attempts to schedule more elections for the same day—not attempts to further fragment the electoral calendar.

Figure 4.2 provides a breakdown of the types of elections that would be affected if the consolidation bills were passed. Since a single bill can propose changes to multiple different types of elections, the numbers in

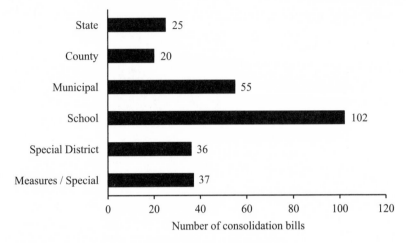

FIGURE 4.2. Types of elections affected by consolidation proposals.

figure 4.2 sum to more than 203. (For example, a bill proposing to move municipal *and* school board elections to November of even-numbered years would be counted as both a school board election timing bill and a municipal election timing bill.)[19] Clearly, regular school district elections are the most common target of state legislators' election consolidation efforts. In fact, half of the consolidation bills in the dataset proposed to combine school elections with some other type of election, whether national elections, state elections, municipal elections, or special district elections. After school elections, the next most common election consolidation target is municipal elections: fifty-five of the 203 bills would have pushed city, village, or town elections to the same day as other elections. In addition, thirty-seven of the bills proposed to limit governments' opportunities for holding ballot measure elections (including tax and bond elections) and other special elections. Moreover, thirty-six of the bills proposed to make nonschool special district elections concurrent with other elections.

Proposals to change county and state election timing were less common than attempts to change school and municipal election scheduling. This almost certainly has to do with the fact that most state and county elections are already held concurrently with national elections in November of even-numbered years. What is notable is that with so few states currently holding odd-year state and county elections, there were actually a sizeable number of bills that proposed to make state and county elections concurrent with national elections. The four states that hold elections for state legislature and governor in the odd-numbered years each had at least one proposal to move state elections to November of even-numbered years during this time period: Mississippi had fifteen, Louisiana had six, New Jersey had three, and Virginia had one.[20] Even at the state level there is a push to combine odd-year state elections with national elections.

However, a simple tracking of the legislative progress of the 203 election consolidation bills shows that almost all of them die early in the legislative process. A full 61% of them were introduced, referred to committee, and never even considered by committee. Five percent of the bills actually received committee hearings but were tabled by the committee before ever reaching consideration by the full chamber. Another 7% were voted down on the floor of the first chamber or were never debated on the floor. Thus, out of the 203 consolidation bills in the database, over 70% of the bills never cleared the hurdle of being passed by the first chamber. Twelve percent of the consolidation bills passed one chamber but were snuffed in the second one. Five bills were passed by both chambers of the legislature but were never reconciled by conference committee or were vetoed by the governor. And out of all the consolidation bills introduced in the state legislatures, a mere twenty-five became law—a 12% success rate.

Of course, this documentation of the legislative progress of consolidation bills does not account for the content of those bills, and the content varies dramatically. At the most extreme end, some of the bills would require all elections for a certain type of government throughout the state to be rescheduled for November of even-numbered years. Other bills were quite weak in their proposals. For example, contrary to the spirit of rules requiring general legislation, a few of the bills proposed to change the election schedule of a specific city. Others would merely combine school and municipal elections on a date in the spring or in the odd-numbered years, which clearly would not increase turnout as much as consolidation with national elections. Many of the bills would make the proposed changes to electoral timing discretionary; for example, a bill might simply *allow* cities to reschedule their elections for November of even-numbered years. Naturally, bills of the latter type might not be as controversial as bills that would require sweeping change to the context of elections. So when I say that 12% of the bills passed, what types of bills were they? Were they relatively weak or discretionary measures that would result in little actual consolidation of the election calendar, or were they mandatory, sweeping changes that would significantly reduce the frequency of elections?

To investigate what types of election consolidation bills advance in state legislatures, I created an ordinal, 0 to 5 measure of each bill's legislative progress: 0 indicates that the bill never received a committee hearing, 1 indicates that it died in committee in the first chamber, 2 indicates that it died before passing the first chamber, 3 indicates that it passed the first chamber but died in the second, 4 indicates that it passed both chambers but was either never reconciled in conference or was vetoed, and 5 indicates that the bill was signed into law. I then created three variables that describe certain characteristics of the bill. Since many of the bills' election timing provisions were amended along the way, usually to weaken the election consolidation provision, I coded each bill based on its status at the final stage it reached in the legislative process.[21] The first, Discretionary, equals 1 if the bill proposed to make election consolidation discretionary as opposed to mandatory. The second equals 1 if the proposed bill would have changed elections to November of even-numbered years and equals 0 if it proposed to consolidate elections on some other date. Last, I created a dummy to indicate whether the bill proposed a change for a specific government or a specific (and small) subset of governments rather than applying to elections in the state generally.

In table 4.2, I test whether certain types of bills are more likely to advance in the legislative process. The results in column (1) are from an ordinary least squares model with robust standard errors. The coefficient on Discretionary is about 1.9, significant at the 1% level, indicating that bills that propose discretionary election consolidation make it significantly further in the legislative process than bills that would require consolidation. I also find that the bills that propose moving elections to November of even-numbered years are significantly less likely to advance than those that propose consolidating elections in the spring or in the odd-numbered years. Bills that would affect specific governments also tend to be more successful. And all together, these variables explain about a quarter of the variation in the legislative progress variable, suggesting that these bill characteristics go a long way in accounting for which election timing bills advance and which bills do not.

When I use an ordinal logit model rather than ordinary least squares, as I do in column (3), the results suggest the same patterns. By making election consolidation permissive rather than mandatory, legislators are more likely to see their bills enacted. Asking governments to move their elections to November of even-numbered years as opposed to some other time lessens the likelihood a bill will advance. And, as before, bills that

TABLE 4.2 **Legislative progress of election consolidation bills**

	(1)	(2)	(3)	(4)
Discretionary	1.854***	1.439***	1.901***	1.885***
	(0.430)	(0.485)	(0.493)	(0.658)
November of even years	−1.022***	−0.72**	−1.254***	−1.146**
	(0.256)	(0.303)	(0.320)	(0.511)
Specific government	1.652***	1.261*	1.932***	1.472*
	(0.564)	(0.659)	(0.527)	(0.885)
Constant	1.592***	1.501**		
	(0.230)	(0.741)		
Observations	203	203	203	203
Model	OLS	OLS, State FE	Ordered Logit	Ordered Logit, State FE
R-squared	0.24	0.48		
Pseudo R-squared			0.09	0.26

Notes: Robust standard errors in parentheses. Dependent variable is the legislative progress of the election consolidation bill, 0–5, with 5 indicating that the bill was signed into law.
* significant at 10%; ** significant at 5%; *** significant at 1%

change the timing of specific governments' elections are more likely to be successful than those that propose more widespread changes.

Of course, legislative procedures vary quite a bit across states, and so it is important to account for the possibility that some states make it more difficult for bills to clear the necessary hurdles than others. Therefore, in columns (2) and (4), I include a full set of state dummy variables (not shown). Inclusion of the state fixed effects does dampen the estimated coefficients on the bill type indicators a bit, but across the board, I still find that each of the bill descriptors has a substantively strong and statistically significant effect in the same direction as in columns (1) and (3). Put simply, the bills that advance in the legislative process—and the bills that pass—tend to make election consolidation discretionary, tend to propose consolidation on days other than November of even-numbered years, and are more likely to propose changes to the election timing of specific governments than changes for all governments in a particular category.

This analysis reveals a great deal about the politics of election timing choice in the modern era. Although election timing appears to be quite stable over time, at least some state legislators are active in trying to change it—and not just for state offices but for school boards, municipal offices, and other local governments. However, bills that propose sweeping, mandatory changes to election timing are highly unlikely to pass; the bills that do tend to advance in the legislative process would not actually simplify the electoral calendar much at all.

School Board Election Timing Bills as a Test Case

The analysis of this chapter has been mostly descriptive up to this point. However, it has produced two important findings that establish a critical foundation for testing the theory. First, I discovered that most eligible voters would actually prefer an electoral calendar that combines many elections on a single day, which suggests that state legislatures are *not* responding to the preferences of voters in scheduling elections. Second, state legislatures regularly consider proposals to consolidate elections, but most such proposals—especially those that would make election consolidation mandatory for a large number of governments—fail in the legislative process. The findings so far are therefore consistent with my argument that organized groups lobby state legislators for election timing rules that benefit them and that state legislators cater to those groups in designing election schedules. My goal in this next section is to test that argument directly by focusing on bills that propose changes to the timing of school board elections.

School board election timing is an excellent test bed for the theory for several reasons. First, school board elections are the most common target of state legislative efforts to move elections from off-cycle to on-cycle, giving me a large sample of election timing bills to analyze. Moreover, the 14,500 public school systems in the United States elect between 15 and 20% of the five hundred thousand elected officials in the country, and as of 2010, annual state and local spending on elementary and secondary education amounted to $574 billion—34% of all local government spending in the United States.[22] Most importantly, though, the nature of interest group activity in school board elections is such that the theory makes clear predictions about which groups benefit from off-cycle election timing—and therefore which groups should be active in lobbying state legislators for favorable election schedules.

For starters, school board elections tend to feature a set of organized interest groups that is both more motivated and better organized than its opposition: public school employees and their unions. As Terry Moe explains, teachers and other employees of the public schools have strong incentives to be active in school board elections, since by getting involved, they help to select their own employers—the very people who set their salaries, benefits, and working conditions. That occupational self-interest is a powerful driver of turnout among public school employees. In a study of California school districts, Moe shows that not only do teachers vote in school board elections at disproportionately high rates, but they are also two to seven times more likely to vote when they live and work in the same district (and can therefore vote for their employers) than when they live and work in separate districts (and therefore cannot vote for their employers). A similar pattern holds for other public school employees, such as janitors, cafeteria workers, librarians, and bus drivers; there are typically large gaps between the turnout rates of employees who live in the district where they work and employees who live and work in different districts. And because overall turnout in many school district elections is so low, the high rates of public school employee turnout can be pivotal.[23]

Furthermore, as organized groups, teacher unions are highly active in local school board campaigns. In a survey of school board candidates in California, Moe shows that teacher unions employ a number of strategies to mobilize their members and other voters, including door-to-door canvassing, phone drives, and endorsements.[24] And of the various groups that are active in school board elections, teachers and their unions are the most consistent in their involvement. Using a nationwide survey of school board members, Frederick Hess and David Leal find that teacher unions top the list of groups cited as active in local school board elections.[25] Focusing on California, Moe finds that teacher unions are *the* most influential group in elections in at least half the districts in the state.[26] In districts where other groups are cited as influential, such as parent-teacher associations and other district employee unions, those groups are typically allies of teacher unions and are thus unlikely to compete with teachers over policy.[27] The main organized groups that potentially oppose public school employees—business groups—are less frequently active,[28] and besides, education is only one of the policy areas that they might focus on, whereas for teachers, it is *the* focus.[29]

Because public employee unions tend to be more motivated and stronger in organizational capacity than any direct competitors, the theory predicts that they should have greater electoral influence in off-cycle elections than in on-cycle elections. Therefore, in state legislatures, I expect that organizations of public school employees should be vocal opponents of proposals to consolidate school board elections with state and national elections.

In addition to public school employees, there is one other type of group I would expect to participate in debates over when school board elections are held: groups of school board members themselves. After all, proposals to change school board election timing affect their own elections, and school board members are usually organized into associations that promote their interests. How might associations of school board members approach state legislative attempts to change election scheduling? One possibility is that they would resist changes to whatever the existing rules are since they were successfully elected under those rules.[30] Another possibility is that school board members are favorably disposed toward the interest groups that are most important in school board elections—groups that, as I have just explained, tend to favor off-cycle election timing. Both of these explanations suggest that we should expect school board associations to generally oppose proposals to make school board elections concurrent with other elections.[31]

With public school employee unions and school board associations lobbying on behalf of off-cycle school board elections, group opposition to election consolidation should be strong. And I expect that far less group activity will be marshaled in support of on-cycle school board elections. Many of the policies education-related groups seek have concentrated benefits and dispersed costs, and so the proponents of those policies are likely to be better organized than their competition.[32] As I just discussed, the literature on group activity in school board elections suggests this is, in fact, the case.[33] Because of this, group opposition to school board election consolidation should be stronger than the support for it, and to the extent that there *are* local groups that actively pressure for on-cycle school board elections, they should be groups like antitax groups, businesses, and religious groups.

This suggests we should observe certain patterns of interest group lobbying in debates over school board election timing. But if state legislators respond to pressure from those groups—as I argue they should—then we should also observe state legislators responding to that pressure in predictable and revealing ways.

Consider the pressure state legislators likely face from organized groups operating in their home districts. All state legislators have public schools and school boards in their electoral districts. If interest group support for off-cycle school elections tends to be more vocal and better organized than interest group support for on-cycle school elections, then local pressure to maintain the status quo will be greater than local pressure to make school board elections concurrent. This should apply to legislators regardless of their party affiliation. I expect that legislators uniformly face some pressure from groups in their home districts to keep off-cycle school elections as they are. Thus, if legislators only responded to group pressure from their home districts, then I would expect to find a general, bipartisan tendency for legislators to vote *against* proposals to shift school board elections to on-cycle.

However, state legislators might also consider the interests of their political parties in taking stances on school board election timing, and if they do, we should observe some partisan division in their positions. The reason is that the organized interest groups that benefit from off-cycle school election scheduling are important constituents of the Democratic Party. Public employee unions in particular have been firmly aligned with the Democrats since the 1960s, and their involvement in elections—their mobilization efforts, campaign contributions, and the like—are critical to the success of Democratic candidates in elections at all levels of government.[34] And so if off-cycle election timing helps teacher unions and other school employee unions have increased influence in school board elections, then the Democratic Party should support it. In contrast, the Republican Party—in the interest of weakening this important constituency of the Democratic Party—should favor on-cycle school board election timing. In sum, to the extent that individual legislators adopt positions consistent with those of their party leaders, Democrats should favor off-cycle school elections and Republicans should favor on-cycle school elections.

The same partisan pattern would hold if state legislators respond to direct persuasion from state-level interest groups that are important to their individual reelections. After all, state-level organizations of public employees are highly active in state legislative races, and the vast majority of their support is dedicated to helping Democrats win. The upshot is that if state legislators cater to the preferences of the state-level groups that contribute (financially or otherwise) to their campaigns, then Democrats should tend to protect off-cycle school board elections. Republicans, on the other hand, should prefer on-cycle school board elections in the interest of weakening an interest group that helps their electoral opponents.

With these three sets of state legislators' incentives in mind, what should we observe in the data? To some extent, the predictions are complicated by the likely possibility that legislators face pressure from groups in their local districts, political party leaders, *and* state-level organizations of local groups. But even when all three sources of pressure are present, we should observe some basic empirical patterns. Most importantly, for Democratic state legislators, all three sources of pressure should push in the *same* direction: Democrats should oppose school board election consolidation because local interest groups in their home districts oppose it, because interest groups that support the Democratic Party oppose it, and because state-level interest groups that are important to their own reelections oppose it. Regardless of where, exactly, the electoral pressure is coming from, Democrats should oppose efforts to consolidate school board elections.

Republicans, however, are likely to be conflicted. On the one hand, just like Democrats, Republicans feel pressure from local groups in their electoral districts to *oppose* school board election consolidation. However, as members of the Republican Party, which would benefit from a weakening of the interest group constituents of the Democratic Party, Republicans might also feel pressure to *support* school board election consolidation. Republican legislators also might support school board election consolidation because most of them do not receive electoral support from public school employee unions—more likely, their opponents do. Thus the prediction for Republican legislators' stances on school board election timing is less clear. They could come out overwhelmingly in favor of school board election consolidation, they could be mostly opposed, or they could be split on the issue, and all of those patterns would be consistent with my argument. Importantly, though, if Republicans *do* tend to support on-cycle elections for school boards, that would unambiguously support the theory, since the most plausible explanation would be that off-cycle election timing in school districts works in favor of interest groups important to Democrats.

Empirical Analysis: School Board Election Timing Bills

With these predictions in hand, my examination of the politics of school board election timing proceeds in two steps. I first provide an up-close look at the debates over school election timing in three state legislatures: Michigan, South Dakota, and Montana. In presenting these case studies, I not only describe what happens to school election timing bills in state legislatures and give a sense of what arguments legislators use in favor of or in opposition to them, but I also look at who proposes the bills, which groups testify on their behalf, and how legislators vote on them.

Of course, the events of these three states are not necessarily representative of events elsewhere; I focus on them because their school election timing bills progressed beyond the committee referral stage (which means the bills were at least debated in committee) and because their legislatures make available records of committee hearings, floor debates, and roll call votes. As a second step, to supplement the findings from the case studies, I also carry out a quantitative analysis of the 102 state legislative bills that proposed to combine school board elections with other elections. Together, the two parts of the analysis provide strong support for the theory and also reveal patterns in the politics of election timing choice that would, absent the theoretical framework, be quite surprising.

Michigan

Legislators in Michigan have been working to move school board elections to November of even-numbered years for more than a decade. In 2002 the Michigan House Legislative Analysis Section summed up the state's problems as follows:

> The state has too many elections and not enough voters. For many years, legislators with an interest in election issues, along with state and local election officials, have been working on proposals to consolidate elections. . . . The problems being addressed have included the hodgepodge of election dates at various levels of government, the relatively permissive approach to the scheduling of special elections, and the existence of two parallel elections systems, one run by school districts for school elections and the other involving local, county, and state officials for all other elections. Critics of the current system say it contributes to the very low turnouts in some elections, including annual school elections, and that it creates a suspicion among some citizens that elections are being designed and scheduled so as to be "below the radar" and to produce a desired outcome rather than honestly inviting public participation. The consolidation effort has focused on reducing the number of election dates so as to provide more consistency and predictability for potential voters and bringing the administration of all elections under the clerks whose primary obligation is to the Michigan Election Law.[35]

Election consolidation efforts in Michigan have therefore targeted all local governments, but school elections have been viewed as particularly problematic. As of 2002 the vast majority of school board elections in Michigan were held annually in June, a time when no other offices were on the ballot. Most had very low voter turnout. In Washtenaw County, for example, turnout in the June 2003 school board races averaged 6.6% of registered voters, ranging from 0.2% in Saline, where only twenty-nine voters cast ballots, to 22% in Whitmore Lake.[36] Moreover, school districts administered and paid for their elections themselves, which many considered to be an unnecessary cost.

However, early attempts at school election consolidation in the state fizzled quickly. HB 4628, introduced in 2001 by nine Republicans, proposed to move all regular school board elections to November of even-numbered years, but the bill was never considered in committee. That same year, a package of bills sponsored by six Senate Republicans proposed creation of a uniform local election day in November of odd-numbered years, applicable to school districts, counties, cities, townships, villages, and community colleges. The election timing provision in the bill was gradually watered down in the Senate, first to allow school districts the option of holding odd-year May elections, then to carve out the same exception for cities and villages and to grant schools the option of holding annual elections. Ultimately, the bill passed the Senate on a near party-line vote, with nineteen Republicans and one Democrat voting in favor and eleven Democrats and three Republicans voting against.

According to the House Legislative Analysis Section, opponents then unleashed a whole host of arguments to weaken support for the bill, including the following:[37]

- "This package of bills represents an erosion of local control for school districts."
- "Perhaps not many voters turn up for school elections, but they are likely to be interested and informed voters. Combining elections might lead to more voters but many will have no connection to or knowledge about school district issues."
- "On a long, complex ballot, a local school district issue could get lost in the 'noise.'"
- "The combining of elections will be problematic because of the number of overlapping jurisdictions involved."

Shortly after passing the Senate, that bill was left to die in committee in the House.

State Republicans were more successful the following year. A group of thirty-three House Republicans sponsored a package of bills that would allow school board elections to be held according to one of four schedules: November of odd-numbered years, May of odd-numbered years, or annually in either May or November. City and village elections would be held in November of even-numbered years unless councils chose to hold elections in May instead. In order to win the degree of Democratic support necessary to pass the bill, Republicans eventually made some concessions: they added an amendment that would allow school districts to hold "floater" tax elections on days other than the state's four established election dates. This compromise silenced the opposition of the Michigan Education Association, the state's teacher union, which did not take a position on the final bill.[38] Even with these concessions, however, twenty-two of the thirty supporting votes in the Senate came from Republicans, and all eight opposing votes were cast by Democrats. In the House, where the bill also passed, some Democratic legislators defended their "no" votes in formal statements. Representative Andrew Meisner, for example, explained, "In my view this scheme would create an insurmountable barrier to informed voting. This bill package coming out of Lansing also flies in the face of local control."[39] But with the support of both legislative chambers and the governor, the bill was signed into law.

Between 2005 and 2010, efforts to further consolidate school elections with other elections continued, but all such efforts failed. As of March 2011, the vast majority of school districts in the state still held elections in May (352 out of the 550 whose election dates were tracked). However, the 2010 election dramatically enhanced Republicans' ability to advance their policy agenda; it ushered in a sixteen-seat Republican majority in the House, which was a big change from the twenty-three-seat Democratic majority of the previous session. At the start of the 2011 session, two Republicans introduced HB 4005, which proposed to schedule all school board elections at the time of statewide general elections in November of even-numbered years. That proposal met a flurry of opposition from outside groups, including the Michigan Education Association, the Michigan Association of School Boards, the Michigan Association of School Administrators, and the Michigan Association of Intermediate School Administrators, all of which testified against the bill in committee. The only outside support for the bill came from the Michigan Department of State and the state associations of municipal and county clerks. The House and Senate votes on the bill were highly partisan, with all but two of the thirty-six "no" votes in the House coming from Democrats, and only three of the twenty-four "yes" votes in the Senate coming from Democrats. This time, however, Republicans had enough votes to push the sweeping school election timing bill to success. In a press conference following its final passage, sponsor Kurt Heise praised the new law, saying, "Taxpayers, school students, and local government all benefit from this efficient reform that will save money and increase voter turnout."[40]

Clearly, though, most Democrats did not view the new law as a change for the better. Quite the contrary; they had lined up against it. This pattern of Democratic opposition and Republican support is difficult to reconcile with any explanation other than the one I have proposed. After all, the *Republican* Party has traditionally been the one to espouse the virtues of local control and decentralized government, and it is generally believed that Republicans benefit from low voter turnout. Yet in Michigan, when it came to school election timing, Republicans favored increased centralization, decreased local control, and an electoral rule that would dramatically *increase* turnout. Democrats, the party that traditionally favors more centralized control and decreased barriers to voting, mostly voted against school election consolidation, citing concerns about local control and the importance of having informed voters.

The most logical explanation is that interest groups like public school employee unions and school board associations have an advantage in off-cycle school board elections and lobby to keep those elections off-cycle— and those groups are important constituents of the Democratic Party and supporters of Democratic legislators. Indeed, those interest groups came out in force to oppose the measure in Michigan. The reason, as a former chairman of the Michigan School Board Leaders Association once said, is that, "Unfortunately, some people try to suppress voter turnout in order to allow school employees to more easily influence the election. In too many cases the elected school boards are heavily weighted with employee group representation, instead of a good cross representation of the electorate."[41] Democrats in the Michigan legislature responded to those groups and opposed the election consolidation measure, and Republicans, seizing an opportunity to weaken the interest group coalition supporting the Democrats, pushed it forward.

South Dakota

Similar divisions arose in South Dakota in 2001 when a seemingly minor election consolidation bill made it to the floor of the state's lower chamber. Under existing law, school districts in South Dakota have a great deal of discretion as to when they hold their regular elections. They can be held anytime between the second Tuesday in April and the third Tuesday in

June. While districts are allowed to combine their elections with municipal elections, typically held on the second Tuesday in April, or with statewide primary elections in June of even-numbered years, they are under
no obligation to do so. HB 1204, introduced by twelve Republicans, would
simply have required school districts and municipalities in the same area
to combine their elections sometime during the spring.

In the Committee on House State Affairs, the Associated School
Boards of South Dakota and the South Dakota Municipal League testified against the bill, but no groups testified in favor. And when the committee passed the bill to the floor, it was defeated in a vote in which
Democrats were nearly unified against it and Republicans were divided:
eighteen out of nineteen Democrats in the House voted against the bill,
and all but one of the twenty votes in favor of the bill came from Republicans. The Republicans had a large enough majority that they could have
passed the bill over Democratic opposition had they been unified, but
thirty-one Republicans joined the Democrats in voting against it.

During the half-hour-long debate over the bill on the House floor, the
arguments legislators made were similar to those made in Michigan. The
Republicans in favor of the measure spoke of the importance of increasing voter turnout and saving local governments money. As Republican
Representative Hal Wick explained,

> I believe that when we really have representative government, it's when we
> have the greatest possible turnout we can. The more people that turn out, the
> more you really have the people speaking on who they want to serve them. . . . I
> would very much encourage you to support this bill so that everybody will have
> a little better voice, or a little more of a voice, in the elections.[42]

Similarly, the bill's sponsor, Republican Bill Peterson, stated, "I simply
bring this bill forward as a way to help our local governments save money
and also, at the same time, and more importantly in my opinion, encourage greater voter turnout. I think we get a better representation of public
sentiment when we have higher voter turnouts."[43]

Opponents of the bill cited concern about the infringement on local
control and the problems that would arise in dealing with different school
district and municipal boundaries. Democratic Representative Thomas
Van Norman explained, "The problem for people is when the boundaries
are different or merged, it does lead to incredible voter confusion. . . . Instead of mandating [the election timing change], make it an option."[44] Re-

publican Larry Rhoden also objected, saying, "It's been said a thousand times and here we go again: local control. The people at the local level are already doing what's best for them.... There's no reason—*no reason*—to pass this bill."[45] And as Republican Representative Jim Holbeck said,

> If we're having a school board election, and those people don't choose to stand up to vote, and don't go because they don't care, I'm very sorry that that apathy exists. But to tell you the truth, I guess I will stand up here and say I *don't* want apathetic people showing up to make decisions. And if they're gonna be there for something that's dear to their heart, and then turn around and just cast a flippant vote for school board member, I would rather those school board members were elected by the people who wanted them to be elected.[46]

In response to these opponents, Republican William Napoli argued,

> We have our election in April. We've got about a 10–12% turnout. You know who goes out and votes? The people who support the candidate, and nobody else! So now we've got a rule by a minority. And I think what really bothers me most of all is 50 of you just passed a bill out of here that completely violated your principle of local control.... And now you very same people are standing up screaming local control on this bill. I find that ironic. And I also find it hypocritical.... It's an amazing contradiction that I've seen here today.... How in the world can we possibly get the best representation in this state, in this county, in this city, and the school systems, when you got 12% voter turnout? How can anyone on this floor stand up and defend that?[47]

But defend it they did. The bill was rejected twenty to forty-nine. Another Republican-sponsored bill, HB 1207, which would have required all school district and municipal elections to be held in November of even-numbered years, was tabled in committee. And that was the end of the consideration of school board election consolidation in South Dakota.

The debate in South Dakota was therefore similar to the one in Michigan, and it also featured Republicans extolling the virtues of higher voter turnout. In the case of South Dakota, *no* outside groups testified in favor of mandatory school and municipal election consolidation, whereas two interest groups testified against it. Unlike Michigan, however, Republican support for the bill in South Dakota was mixed, with about 40% of Republican legislators voting in favor and 60% voting against. However,

Democrats almost universally opposed the bill, which supports my argument that certain key interest groups benefit from off-cycle school elections and successfully pressure state legislators to uphold them.

Montana

Strikingly, events in Montana transpired in a similar fashion. There, regular school board elections are held annually in May at a time when no city, county, or state races are on the ballot. In 2001, Senator Alvin Ellis, a Republican, introduced SB 110, which proposed to move the statewide primary election and school board elections to the same day—the Tuesday before Memorial Day in May. Notably, even with this change, the two types of elections would only be concurrent in even-numbered years, since school board elections are held annually and state primary elections only take place in even-numbered years.

When the bill was considered in the Senate Education and Cultural Resources Committee in February of 2001, one person testified in favor of the bill, but he was not representing an organization. On the side of the opposition, however, several groups testified, including the Montana School Boards Association, a lobbyist for the Montana Education Association and the Montana Federation of Teachers, and the Montana Association of School Business Officials. In addition, a representative from the Montana Rural Education Committee objected that the measure would violate local control. A representative from the Montana Association of Clerks and Recorders complained that SB 110 would create technical problems because of the differences in boundaries used in state and school elections. Put simply, the opposition to SB 110 was organized and vocal, but there were no organizations to defend its merits.

Just as in South Dakota, the bill met with nearly unified Democratic opposition and splintered Republican support on the floor. Eighteen of the twenty votes in support of the bill came from Republicans, but that was not enough to overcome the twenty-nine votes against it, twelve of which were Republicans and seventeen of which were Democrats. That bill was postponed indefinitely.

Ten years later, Republican Representative Mike Miller introduced an almost identical bill, HB 242, which would have moved the statewide primary election date from June to the annual school election date so that in even-numbered years, the two would be held concurrently. In addition, the municipal primary in odd-numbered years would be moved back from

September to May, so that in odd-numbered years, school elections would also be concurrent with municipal primaries. In the House Committee on State Administration, there were a number of vocal supporters of the bill, almost all of whom were individuals from Helena who were unhappy with recent decisions made in their local school district. The only outside organizations present among the proponents were the Lewis and Clark Conservatives—a Tea Party Group—and the Montana Eagle Forum, a conservative, "profamily" group.

Proponents' arguments had a common theme: low turnout elections work to the advantage of special interests. One individual's submitted testimony read, "As things now stand elections are held off the radar for many ordinary citizens, and candidates who are favored by district employees, their relatives and friends enjoy a significant advantage."[48] Another's written testimony read, "It seems to me that the only people that vote in this election are people with vested interests."[49] A third explained that in the previous year, "the parents and grandparents of Helena learned firsthand how important it is to have a school board that represents their educational goals and interests instead of those of the special interest groups."[50] A teacher from the Helena district explained that under the existing election schedule, the deck is stacked in favor of mill levies passing.[51] And a political scientist from Winifred noted, "When you have millions of dollars in tax dollars being voted on, whatever subdivision of local government it is, these decisions shouldn't be made by an inside group of 20% or so voting."[52]

The opposition to HB 242 was just as vocal, however, and also highly organized. A representative from the Montana League of Cities and Towns asked that municipal governments be exempted from the bill. The Montana Clerks and Recorders as well as the Montana School Board Association protested that the issue of boundary confusion would be a major obstacle to implementation. The representative of the state's two teacher unions also opposed the bill:

> It's every citizen's responsibility to note when elections occur. . . . If it is that we the citizenry want to know about who our candidates are for the school board, are we going to know more about them if they are lost in a wash of primary candidates running for every office in the state? Legislators, statewide candidates, judicial candidates—even presidential candidates could be on the primary ballot. I mean, talk about being lost in the event. A race for school district trustees ought to be by itself singular, one that people really do concentrate on.[53]

After a long session of outside testimony, the House committee voted to table the bill. The floor then took a follow-up vote on whether to take HB 242 out of committee. That measure failed to garner sufficient support to bring the bill to floor consideration and was defeated thirty-five to sixty-one. However, all thirty-five of the votes in favor of considering the bill on the floor were cast by Republicans. All Democrats joined the remaining thirty Republicans in voting in support of killing the bill in committee. Just as in South Dakota, Democrats and a subset of Republicans defeated that attempt to consolidate school board elections.

Partisan Patterns in Bill Sponsorship and Voting

These case studies show that debates over whether to make school board elections concurrent with national, state, and other local elections are remarkably similar across states. In all three cases, proposals to consolidate school board elections were introduced by Republicans. The outside groups that opposed the proposals, which were predominantly organizations of public school employees and school board members, were more vocal and better organized than any groups that favored the proposals. And finally, Democrats in all three legislatures opposed the proposed changes to the status quo of off-cycle school elections, while Republicans were either supportive of the changes (Michigan) or split over the issue (South Dakota and Montana).

To examine whether there are similar patterns in other state legislatures, I turn to a subset of the data I described earlier: bills introduced in state legislatures between 2001 and 2011 that proposed to consolidate school board elections with state, national, or other local elections. There are 102 such bills, originating in the twenty-one states shaded light gray in figure 4.3.[54] Of those twenty-one states, some, such as New Jersey and Texas, considered more than ten bills apiece over the course of eleven years, whereas others, such as New York and Iowa, considered only a single proposal each. The remaining states did not see any school board election consolidation bills during this time period. However, some of those states (shaded dark gray) already *had* on-cycle school board elections as of 2001, and so there was no opportunity for their state legislatures to consolidate them further.[55] The states shaded white, however, had at least some off-cycle school board elections as of 2001 and yet did not see any state legislative attempts to consolidate those elections with other elections.

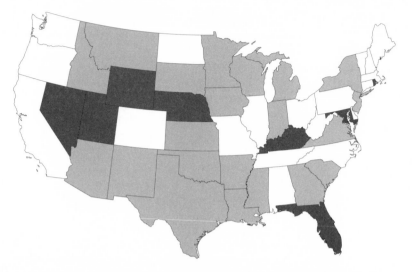

FIGURE 4.3. States with school board election consolidation bills, 2001–11.
Notes: States shaded light gray had at least one school board election consolidation bill introduced between 2001 and 2011. States shaded dark gray had no school election consolidation
bills but had on-cycle school board elections prior to 2001. States left white had at least some
off-cycle school board elections as of 2001 and did not see any school board election consolidation bills introduced between 2001 and 2011.

There is at least one notable difference between the states that appear
in the dataset and those that do not: aside from the states that already
had on-cycle school board elections as of 2001, the states where legislatures *did not* introduce any school election consolidation bills between
2001 and 2011 were, on average, more liberal than those shaded light
gray in figure 4.3. As one indicator of this, among the states with off-cycle
school board elections and no school election timing bills, the average
two-party vote for Al Gore in 2000 was 50%, whereas it was only 45% in
the twenty-one states that *did* see such bills.[56] In examining the set of 102
school election consolidation bills in the dataset, it is important to recognize from the outset that those bills come from a set of relatively conservative, Republican states.

I start by looking at the party affiliations of the legislators who author,
sponsor, and cosponsor each bill. Since some bills have multiple sponsors
and cosponsors and others have only one, I create a variable equal to the
percentage of sponsors and cosponsors of a given bill who are Republicans. Using those percentages, I divide the bills into five categories: bills
on which all sponsors were Democrats, bills on which more than half of

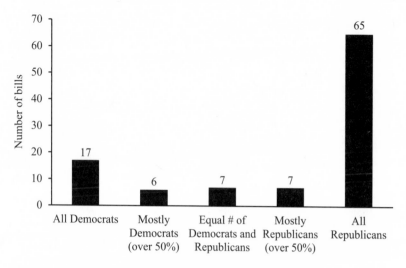

FIGURE 4.4. Sponsorship of bills proposing school board election consolidation.

the sponsors were Democrats, bills that had equal numbers of Democratic and Republican sponsors, bills that were sponsored by mostly Republicans, and bills for which all sponsors were Republicans.

Figure 4.4 breaks down the party affiliations of the sponsors, cosponsors, and authors of all the bills that proposed combining school board elections with other elections. The pattern in sponsorship indicates very clearly that the vast majority of the school bills in the dataset are introduced exclusively by Republicans: sixty-five out of the 102 bills are introduced by Republicans and Republicans alone, and only 17% of the bills are introduced solely by Democrats. The remaining bills are bipartisan in their sponsorship, with 6% introduced by mostly (but not exclusively) Democrats, 7% introduced by equal numbers of Democrats and Republicans, and 7% introduced by mostly (but not exclusively) Republicans. Moreover, the few school election consolidation bills that *are* introduced by Democrats tend to be weaker than those introduced by Republicans. For example, a quarter of the bills introduced exclusively by Democrats would have merely allowed school boards the option of consolidating their elections with other elections. In contrast, of the sixty-five bills proposed exclusively by Republicans, all but four of them would have made consolidation mandatory. In general, the partisan pattern of bill sponsorship in these twenty-one states looks a lot like what I found in Michigan, South Dakota, and Montana. Most of the time, in most places, efforts to make school elections concurrent are spearheaded by Republicans.

But looking at the party affiliations of legislators who sponsor bills only says so much about the patterns of support for those bills in state legislatures. After all, most of the bills were never even considered by committee, so clearly there is a strong current working against efforts to combine school elections with city, state, national, or other special district elections. To get a better sense of which legislators support and oppose these measures, I have identified all of the school election consolidation bills that received some form of vote in one or both of the states' legislative chambers. By looking at how Republicans and Democrats voted, I can evaluate whether state legislators' partisan divisions over school election scheduling follow a pattern that supports the predictions of the theory.[57]

Of the 102 school election consolidation bills, twenty-eight received some kind of vote.[58] Of that subset, twenty-one were voted on in a single chamber, and the remaining seven were voted on in both chambers. Since certain bills received multiple votes, whereas others only received a single vote, I selected one vote for each unique bill and chamber combination, which yielded thirty-five unique bill-chamber votes. Whenever a bill received a final passage vote in a chamber, which was the case for thirty-one of the bill-chamber votes, I use that vote in the analysis. For another three of the bill-chamber votes, the last vote on the bill took place in committee, and in those cases, I use the last committee vote on the bill for the analysis. The remaining bill was the one in Montana (discussed earlier) for which the final vote was a floor vote on whether to discharge the bill from committee. For all of the bill-chamber votes, a "yes" vote represented a vote in favor of making school board elections concurrent, and a "no" vote represented a vote in opposition. In total, the dataset contains 2,324 votes cast by individual legislators in twenty-one unique state legislative chambers and twelve unique states,[59] and the votes span all eleven years from 2001 to 2011. In total, Republicans cast 59% of the votes, and Democrats cast 41%.

Figure 4.5 depicts the probability of a "yes" vote in each of the twelve states, conditional on a legislator being a Republican or Democrat. Strikingly, in almost all of the states, Republican state legislators are more likely to vote in favor of school election consolidation than Democratic state legislators, and, in general, the differences across parties are large. In Georgia, Republican legislators vote in favor of consolidating school board elections at a rate of 99%, whereas Democrats vote "yes" at a rate

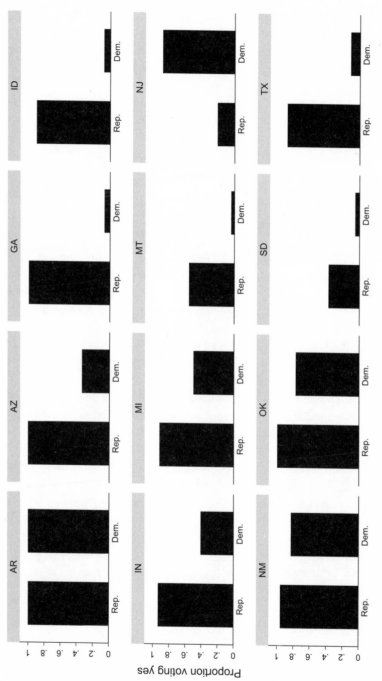

FIGURE 4.5. Proportion voting for on-cycle school board elections.

of less than 7%. In Idaho, Republicans voted for consolidation 90% of the time, and Democrats voted "yes" only 8% of the time. The large gaps in support between Republicans and Democrats hold for Arizona, Indiana, Michigan, Montana, and Texas, with support for the school election timing bills coming predominantly from Republicans, and "no" votes coming mostly from Democrats. Even in states like Oklahoma and New Mexico, where the probability of "yes" votes is high among both parties, and in a state like South Dakota, where support is fairly weak among both parties, there is a statistically significant difference in the degree to which the parties support school election consolidation.

The only two states that deviate from this pattern are Arkansas and New Jersey. However, the unanimous support in Arkansas can be explained by the fact that the bill was amended before it came to a vote in the full Senate; the bill was introduced as a mandatory requirement that school board elections be moved to November, but by the time the full Senate voted on it, the election timing provision gave school districts two options—either a September election date or a November election date. In New Jersey, the push to move school board elections to November of even-numbered years was combined with an effort to allow school boards to determine their budgets without a popular vote, and so it is not clear whether the partisan divide was over election timing or the process for deciding on school budgets.

These two anomalous cases highlight the fact that the particulars of the bills in the dataset vary quite a bit. Some would require school elections to be held in November of even-numbered years, whereas others call for changes that would make only small differences to voter turnout. Some would mandate concurrent school elections, whereas others would merely allow them. Many of the bills only proposed election consolidation, whereas some proposed other changes as well. To provide a clearer picture of the partisan divide over election timing, figure 4.6 excludes bills that propose to make election concurrence discretionary, bills that involve issues *other* than election timing, as well as one bill that made a very weak change to school board election timing.[60]

For the sixteen chamber and bill combinations represented in the bar graphs of figure 4.6, the gaps between Republican and Democratic support widen. In *all* of the states, Republicans are far more likely than Democrats to vote in favor of making school elections concurrent. In fact, state legislators' party affiliations explain 40% of the variation in their votes for or against these bills. In Oklahoma and Texas, party affiliation

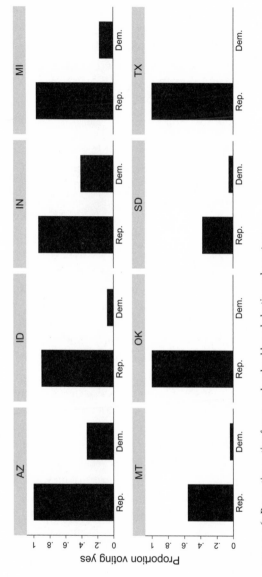

FIGURE 4.6. Proportion voting for on-cycle school board elections, clearest cases.

predicts legislators' votes perfectly: all Republicans vote in favor, and all Democrats vote against. For the cases where I know for sure that legislators were casting their votes in favor of or in opposition to mandatory election consolidation, I find clear evidence of Republican support and Democratic opposition. This finding strongly supports my argument that off-cycle election timing creates an advantage for certain interest groups—in the case of school board elections, interest groups that align with the Democratic Party.

Conclusion: The Politics of School Board Election Timing

In the absence of the theoretical framework, these findings would probably come as quite a surprise. Here we have seen a case in which Democrats—known as the party of the lower and middle classes—have taken a clear, consistent position in favor of a status quo electoral rule that dramatically suppresses voter turnout. It is a case in which members of the party that is generally amenable to policy solutions that centralize government control in order to alleviate society's ills have spoken out against infringements of local control and in favor of letting local governments do what they think is best. Meanwhile, in an equally strange turn of events, Republicans in state legislatures across the country have spearheaded efforts to enact election timing policies that would *increase* voter turnout and establish new mandates for local governments. For such an effort to stem from the party of decentralization and the party that is generally seen as benefiting from low turnout is quite remarkable.

Seen through the lens of the theoretical framework, however, these findings are not at all surprising. When it comes to school elections, there is good reason to expect that teacher unions, other school employees, and school board associations should oppose efforts to make school board elections concurrent with other elections. What is more, state legislators care about these groups for a number of reasons: they are active interest groups in legislators' home districts, they are key supporters of the Democratic Party, and their state-level organizations are important players in individual legislators' own elections. Thus Democratic state legislators have strong incentives to keep school board election scheduling off-cycle. While many Republicans can be persuaded to support the dominant interests in their districts and sustain off-cycle elections, other Republicans go the other way, supporting on-cycle elections in order to weaken a key constituency of the Democrats. This explains what would otherwise seem to be a baffling reversal in the major political parties' positions. In the case of school board elections, Republicans claim to be champions of increasing voter turnout, and Democrats have become the defenders of the status quo of off-cycle election timing.

Beyond School Board Election Timing Bills

Studying school board election timing bills is especially useful because the predictions of the theory diverge from what we otherwise might expect, but these findings should not be taken to imply that Democrats favor off-cycle election timing in *all* contexts. In fact, it is probably true that in other electoral contexts—such as environments where business groups or evangelical groups are the main beneficiaries of low voter turnout—Republican political elites fight to protect off-cycle election timing while Democrats support consolidation. My purpose in highlighting the school election timing case is not to make a general point about the parties' positions but rather to test the theory in a context where the theory's predictions are clear.

What should we expect of bills proposing to change the timing of other elections, such as city elections, state elections, or special district elections? It depends. First, it depends on the nature of organized group activity in those elections: Are the members of one group more motivated to turn out than their direct competition? Is one group much better organized to mobilize and persuade voters than directly competing groups? These questions are harder to answer for state elections, municipal elections, and county elections than for school board elections. State elections, for example, probably feature a large, diverse set of active interest groups, and many of them likely compete directly with one another. Political parties also have campaign organizations that raise funds, advertise, and get out the vote in state elections. This complexity of group activity in state-level elections makes it more difficult to evaluate how any given group will fare under different election timing regimes. Even if the theory leads to a clear prediction about a group or set of groups that should perform better under a particular election schedule, one then has to evaluate how election timing decision makers—usually state legislators—should be expected to respond.

Importantly, however, the difficulty of using the theory to generate precise predictions about the politics of election timing choice for state, municipal, or county elections doesn't mean that the theory doesn't apply to those electoral contexts. Actually, it should, and a few pieces of empirical evidence suggest that it does. When it comes to state-level elections, for example, recall that between 2001 and 2011, every state that holds odd-year elections for legislature and governor considered proposals to make state elections concurrent with national elections—and all of those proposals failed. State legislators therefore clearly don't view election timing as a mere technicality. Furthermore, the conventional wisdom about which party benefits from high turnout (Democrats) and which party benefits from low turnout (Republicans) does not go very far in explaining observed patterns in the sponsorship of state election timing bills. Mississippi, on the one hand, lines up with the conventional wisdom: Of its fifteen bills that proposed moving state elections to November of even-numbered years, the ones that proposed to schedule them during midterm congressional elections were introduced by Republicans, and the ones that proposed to schedule them during presidential elections were introduced by Democrats. In the three other states, however, state election consolidation does not appear to be a Democratic issue. New Jersey, for example, has seen three legislative proposals to make state elections concurrent with national elections, and a Republican sponsored all three. Virginia's one proposal was also sponsored by a Republican. Louisiana's six proposals have been introduced by a mix of Republican and Democratic legislators, and when those proposals have received votes, support (and opposition) has been bipartisan.[61] Thus, proposals to consolidate state elections with national elections do not pit supportive Democrats against obstructive Republicans—it is more nuanced than that.

Figure 4.7 reinforces this claim. There, I break down the party affiliations of state legislators who sponsor bills to consolidate or reduce the number of elections—excluding bills that propose changes to either regular state elections or school board elections. The figure makes it clear that Democrats are not always the initiators of election consolidation efforts. In fact, over half of the bills were introduced by Republicans and Republicans alone. Nearly 60% of the bills were introduced by mostly to all Republicans. Aside from the four bills that were equally bipartisan, only 35% of the bills were introduced by mostly to all Democrats.

Furthermore, Democrats often vote against election consolidation, and Republicans often vote for it. Take, for example, bills proposing to consolidate municipal elections.[62] Perhaps tellingly, there were only three municipal consolidation bills that received votes at a stage where the bills

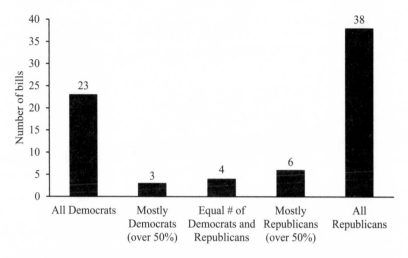

FIGURE 4.7. Sponsorship of consolidation bills, excluding state and school board bills.

were still mandatory (rather than permissive) in nature.[63] One of them, considered in Connecticut in 2008, featured strong Democratic support and Republican opposition, but that bill contained so many other changes unrelated to election timing that it is unclear whether the partisan nature of the support was due to the election timing provision or something else. For the other two bills, Democrats were almost universally opposed to municipal election consolidation, whereas most Republicans were in favor.[64] Democratic state legislators also tend to vote against bills that would limit the number of days available for special elections and ballot measure elections. A bill in Louisiana that would have limited bond, tax, and other proposition elections to either a single spring election date or the fall general election date was tabled in the lower chamber by a vote of fifty-nine Democrats and five Republicans, a move that was opposed by twelve Democrats and twenty-four Republicans.[65] In Utah, a 2004 bill that eliminated three of the five authorized dates for holding special elections was passed by the lower chamber with only two Democrats voting in favor and only six Republicans voting in opposition.[66] While this by no means constitutes a test of my argument that election timing tips the balance of power among organized groups, it does indicate that the conventional wisdom—that Democrats favor electoral rules that increase turnout—falls short of explaining the politics of election timing choice.

One final piece of evidence bolsters this point. In table 4.3, for all 101 consolidation bills in the dataset that would not affect school board elec-

TABLE 4.3 **State partisanship and the legislative progress of nonschool election consolidation bills**

	(1)	(2)
Discretionary	2.379***	2.857***
	(0.533)	(0.883)
November of even years	−1.326***	−1.695***
	(0.306)	(0.451)
Specific government	1.905***	2.693***
	(0.624)	(0.792)
% Democratic vote share	−5.578***	−8.723***
	(1.850)	(3.244)
Constant	4.388***	
	(0.939)	
Observations	101	101
	OLS	Ordered logit
R-squared	0.37	
Pseudo R-squared		0.15

Notes: Robust standard errors in parentheses. Dependent variable is the legislative progress of the election consolidation bill, 0–5.
* significant at 10%; ** significant at 5%; *** significant at 1%

tions, I regress the measure of legislative progress I introduced earlier on the same bill-type indicators used in table 4.2 but with one additional predictor: the Democratic percentage of the state's presidential vote in 2000. Using both ordinary least squares and ordered logit, I estimate a substantively large and statistically significant *negative* effect of Democratic vote share on the legislative progress of election consolidation bills. In light of the conventional wisdom that Democrats benefit from higher turnout, and in light of my earlier finding that Democratic voters are more likely to prefer on-cycle local elections, this result is quite striking. More Democratic states are significantly *less* likely to advance bills that would implement on-cycle elections. Thus, a conventional, individual-centric account cannot explain patterns of bill sponsorship, legislator voting, and legislative advancement. Something else is at work, and I argue that that something else is pressure from organized groups whose electoral fortunes change with changes to the election schedule.

Conclusion

Political actors use a variety of arguments to make the case for either consolidating elections or keeping them separate. The most common argument made in favor of on-cycle election timing is that it increases voter turnout; some point out that it also decreases the cost of administering elections. Proponents of off-cycle elections, on the other hand, usually argue that voters in off-cycle elections are more educated about the issues at stake than voters in on-cycle elections. They also argue that important issues get lost in the fray in on-cycle elections, that it would be technically difficult to combine elections, or that forcing governments to adopt on-cycle elections violates the principle of local control.

What the political players *say* is only so informative, however. The rhetoric political players use need not reflect their true underlying motivations. As Banfield and Wilson explain, advocates and opponents of electoral rules often couch their strategic political aims in language that makes it seem as though their preferred rules are desirable for normative or technical reasons. Higher voter turnout always sounds good. Saving money on election administration seems like a great idea. And few would disagree that having informed voters is more desirable than having ignorant ones. But all of these arguments over election timing are just a disguise for a very simple, strategic political calculus: Organized groups anticipate that changes to election timing would affect their political influence, and state legislators dependent on those groups try to be responsive to them in setting election schedules.

In the first part of this chapter, I made the case that state legislators are *not* tailoring election timing rules to the preferences of voters. Voters—Republicans and Democrats alike—quite clearly prefer on-cycle local elections, and yet off-cycle election timing for local elections remains the standard. Moreover, Democrats report being slightly more in favor of on-cycle local elections than Republicans, and yet it is not the case that states with more Democrats are more likely to have on-cycle local elections—if anything, they are less likely to have them. It therefore does not seem that state legislators craft election timing rules according to the preferences of their citizens.

Rather, I argue, election timing affects the influence of organized groups, and organized groups are tremendously important to state legislators. The case of school board election timing made this quite clear. School board elections in the United States tend to feature a type of interest group that is both more motivated to turn out than its competition and much better organized than any directly competing group: public school employee unions. The theory thus predicts that school-employee unions benefit from off-cycle election timing and should lobby state legislators to keep off-cycle school board elections in place. In addition, either because they favor the status quo rules or because they cater to the interest groups that are important in school board elections, organizations of school board members tend to prefer off-cycle elections as well. With the opposition to these groups so organizationally weak, state legislators who feel the need to please organized groups in their districts vote against proposals to consolidate school board elections with other elections. To the extent that any state legislators do support school board election consolidation, it should be Republicans, because the interest groups that benefit from off-cycle school board elections are important constituents of the Democratic Party and overwhelmingly support Democratic candidates in state legislative elections.

This is exactly what the empirical analysis showed. Most of the bills that proposed to move school board elections to the same day as other elections were introduced and sponsored by Republicans, not Democrats. When those bills were considered in committee or on the floor, interest group opposition was vocal and well organized—mainly composed of school employee unions and school board associations. In contrast, interest group support for the bills was weak. And in voting on school board election consolidation bills, Democrats were near unified in opposition, while Republicans were split on the issue with some voting in support and some voting in opposition. Together, these findings strongly support the theory.

Even beyond school board election timing bills, proposals to change election timing are quite common. State legislatures regularly consider bills that propose changes to the timing of municipal elections, county elections, state elections, special district elections, ballot measure elections, and special elections. In order to make predictions about interest groups' preferences over election scheduling in those contexts, one would need information about the organizations that are active in them. Moreover, one would have to verify that state legislators have a stake in when those elections are held before looking to activity of the state legislatures as a test of the theory. While examination of all these types of election timing bills is beyond the scope of this book, this chapter has at least provided a preliminary glance at what the politics of election timing looks like for those other types of electoral contexts. And the findings do not seem to fit the most plausible alternative explanation—that Democrats should favor on-cycle election timing because it means higher turnout. Instead, I find that there is mixed partisan support for (and opposition to) on-cycle election timing. If there is any general partisan pattern to speak of, it is that Republicans tend to favor on-cycle election timing more so than Democrats. The reason the conventional explanation does not fit the data well, I argue, is that that explanation is derived from a focus on individual voters and neglects the role of organized groups.

In the chapters that follow, I set out to estimate the causal effect of election timing on various measures of interest group success. In doing so, it is important to keep the lessons from this chapter in mind, since one of the main challenges to testing the causal effect of any institution is the likely possibility that the institutional variation we observe in the world is endogenous to the outcomes we are examining. To overcome that challenge, it would be tempting to assume that because election timing has changed very little over the last hundred years, election timing is exogenous to the influence of interest groups today. Given the findings of this chapter, however, that assumption would be incorrect. The *absence* of institutional change can be evidence of institutional endogeneity just as much as the presence of change. After all, groups often advance their interests by *blocking* change.[67]

As Banfield and Wilson explain, electoral rules might have the appearance of being "purely technical." But that appearance of stability and technicality "is an illusion, for the electoral system profoundly affects the character of politics."[68] If election timing does affect the character of politics, as I argue it does, then we should expect those who are affected to fight over election timing itself. And as I have shown in this chapter, they most definitely do.

CHAPTER FIVE

Estimating the Effect of Off-Cycle Election Timing

School Board Elections

The empirical analysis up to this point has treated election timing as the variable to be explained—an endogenous institution.[1] This approach has been productive, both in explaining why elections are held when they are and in testing the theoretical framework. It has also revealed striking similarities between the debates over city election timing in the nineteenth century and debates over school board election timing in the twenty-first. In both contexts, organized groups sought to implement (and protect) the election timing rules they expected to bring a more favorable electorate to the polls. In both time periods, the organized groups with a stake in election timing used normative arguments—and, actually, many of the same arguments—to make the case for their preferred schedule. And in political environments as different as present-day South Dakota and antebellum Philadelphia, those normative arguments masked a basic strategic calculus: organized groups supported whatever election timing rule they thought would give them an advantage. And because of the political linkages between organized groups and the state legislators charged with making election timing decisions, state legislators' stances on the issue are oftentimes quite predictable.

The study of election timing as an endogenous institution has also laid the foundation for the next two chapters, in which my goal is to test the *effects* of election timing on political and policy outcomes. In one sense, this is but another side of the same coin; rather than treating election timing as the phenomenon to be explained, in this chapter and the next, I use election timing as a predictor of organized groups' political success. In another sense, however, because of the methodological challenges to causal inference, the task of estimating the effect of election timing very much *depends* on an understanding of how election schedules are chosen.

The main methodological challenge involved in estimating the effect of election timing (or the effect of any political institution, for that matter) is the potential for bias. It is hard to imagine a scenario in which a policy maker would allow a researcher to randomly assign election schedules to governmental units (especially if election timing matters for outcomes), and so a study of election timing's effects has to rely on observational data. The problem with using observational data, of course, is that places that have on-cycle election timing are probably quite different from places that have off-cycle election timing—and in ways that may be correlated with the outcomes of interest. The potential for omitted variable bias is therefore considerable. In cross-sectional analysis, for example, it will be difficult to rule out the possibility that unobservable characteristics of the governmental units explain both the timing of their elections and the degree to which interest groups influence their political outcomes. Omitted variable bias can be substantially reduced by analyzing within-unit changes in election timing and political outcomes, but even a longitudinal study will still confront the problem of selection bias: if interest groups lobby for off-cycle election scheduling in the units where they expect it to help them most, then by comparing units with off-cycle elections to units with on-cycle elections, one risks overestimating the causal effect of election timing.

In order for an estimate of the election timing effect to be interpreted as causal, the estimation process has to deal with these concerns successfully. And by providing background on the politics of election timing choice, chapters 3 and 4 not only highlight the challenges inherent in estimating the causal effect of election timing but also hint at strategies for overcoming the likely sources of bias. In this chapter and the next, I use these strategies to develop quantitative empirical tests of the effect election timing has on the policy successes of organized interest groups.

The Effect of School Board Election Timing as a Test Case

The theoretical framework is relevant for a wide variety of electoral settings, including comparisons between on- and off-cycle local government elections, midterm and presidential-year congressional elections, and even- and odd-year state elections. However, designing an empirical test of election timing's effects is more difficult than concocting examples of where the framework should apply. In any given context, testing the theory requires some knowledge of the various groups active in elections as well as a measure of those groups' relative influence under different election timing conditions.

On these grounds, local school districts are an excellent starting place. As I described in the previous chapter, the literature shows that school board elections feature a set of organized interest groups that is both more motivated and better organized than its opposition: unions of public school employees.[2] Moreover, teacher unions in particular share many of the same basic policy goals. The most obvious example is teacher compensation: state and local chapters of the National Education Association (NEA) and the American Federation of Teachers (AFT) consistently press for higher professional pay at the school district level. Teacher compensation is largely determined by the school board members elected in school district elections, often in collective bargaining with teacher unions themselves. Therefore, we should expect school board members to be more responsive to teacher union demands for higher compensation when those teachers exert greater influence in their elections. As former AFT president Albert Shanker explained, "If teachers control both sides of the bargaining table in a substantial number of school districts, we should find many teachers with huge salaries, greatly reduced class sizes, longer holidays and vacations than ever before—you name it."[3] Therefore, if off-cycle school district elections confer greater electoral influence on teacher unions than on-cycle elections, then school board members in districts with off-cycle elections should be more responsive to teacher unions, and teacher compensation in those districts should be higher.

Beyond the usefulness of school districts for empirical testing purposes, district-level teacher compensation policies are important in their own right. American public schools employ 4.3 million full-time teachers, which is 40% of all full-time local government employees. In addition, over 40% of current expenditures in the average American school district are spent on instructional salaries and wages.[4] Changes to school districts' teacher compensation policies thus have a substantial impact on school district budgets and, consequently, government spending in the United States as a whole.

This chapter therefore presents the results of three studies of election timing in school board elections in the United States. My reason for conducting three separate studies is that each one has certain strengths. The first test, which I call the Eight-State Test, includes a particularly high quality dependent variable, which I will explain below. In the second test, the Minnesota Test, I actually have data on voter turnout in school board elections, which are not available for the other two tests. Lastly, the Texas Test, which is the third study, is the strongest in terms of its empirical design. Together, these studies paint a clear picture of how off-cycle election timing shapes the influence of teachers and teacher unions in school board elections across the United States.

The Eight-State Test

Because state governments make the rules for when school boards can hold elections, school board election timing is uniform within many states. In Florida, for example, all school board elections are held in November of even-numbered years. In Arkansas, they are all held annually in September. However, cross-state comparisons of the effect of election timing on teacher salary are likely to be problematic, because numerous state-level factors such as the school governance structure, education code, and financial equalization policies might be correlated with both district election timing and teacher salaries. The previous chapter highlighted two state characteristics in particular that are potentially problematic: First, more Democratic states are less likely to consider election consolidation bills, but school districts in more Democratic states may well spend more on teacher compensation—for reasons that have nothing to do with the timing of school board elections.[5] Second, and relatedly, states with strong teacher unions most likely have more generous teacher compensation policies than states with weak teacher unions, and since teacher unions actively lobby against proposals that would move school board elections to on-cycle, states with strong teacher unions are probably also more likely to have off-cycle school board elections. These are important relationships to account for in modeling the effect of off-cycle school board election timing on teacher salaries.

Fortunately, as I showed in chapter 1, there are a number of states that have internal variation in school district election timing, either because states assign school districts election schedules based on school district type, or because states give local school boards discretion as to when they hold elections. In the previous chapter, to the extent that I focused on such discretion, it was only to show that bills that allow discretion are significantly more likely to advance in the legislative process. Now that my focus is on testing the effects of election timing, the within-state variation discretion produces is quite useful; by limiting my analysis to a subset of the states that have within-state variation in district election timing, I can reduce the problem of omitted variable bias.

The next step is to develop a set of quantitative measures for the empirical analysis. To measure teacher compensation, I turn to the 2003–4 Schools and Staffing Survey (SASS), which is conducted by the National Center for Education Statistics (NCES) and contains a set of teacher compensation variables for a sample of 4,421 public school districts throughout the United States.[6] For each sampled district, it provides information on whether the district uses a salary schedule for teachers (97% do), the normal yearly base salary for teachers with bachelor's and master's degrees with zero and ten years of experience, and the highest step on the salary schedule. Unlike average teacher salary, which depends on the education and experience levels of teachers in the district, these variables allow comparisons in salaries across districts for teachers with similar levels of education, training, and experience. In addition, the SASS data include variables on district enrollment, student body composition, and district location. I combine the SASS data with variables from the NCES Common Core of Data (CCD) files from 2003–4, including school district finances and district-level demographics from the 2000 Census.

Since the data for the analysis come from the 2003–4 academic year and table 1.1 depicts election timing as of January 2012, I have to be careful about which states I include in the analysis and how I code the election timing of their school districts. New Jersey, for example, only recently passed a law that allows school districts to move their elections to November of even-numbered years; as of 2003, all of its school district elections were held off-cycle in April. As I discuss in detail below, it was not until 2007 that many Texas school districts had to shift their elections from off-cycle to on-cycle. Similarly, Oklahoma only recently passed a law requiring that annual school board elections in February be held concurrently with presidential primaries during presidential election years. For this study, therefore, I focus on eight states that had substantial within-state variation in school board election timing as of 2003–4: California, Minnesota, Georgia, North Carolina, South Carolina, Tennessee, Virginia, and Alabama.[7]

Within these eight states, I code the districts in the SASS sample according to whether they held off-cycle or on-cycle school board elections, using a variety of self-collected resources that are described in appendix C. I classify all school district elections held at the same time as a federal or statewide general election as on-cycle elections. In addition, I classify district elections held concurrently with statewide primary elections as on-cycle, mainly because voter turnout in presidential primary elections is, on average, 20 percentage points higher than turnout in local elections held at other times during the spring months or during the fall of odd-numbered years.[8] I exclude districts that are not either regular or component school districts as well as districts in which 50% or more of the schools are charter schools.[9] The remaining number of school districts with elected school boards in the eight-state sample is 672. There are 103 California districts with on-cycle elections and eighty with off-cycle elections. Respectively, there are eighty-one and thirty in Minnesota, thirty-nine and fourteen in South Carolina, sixty-nine and nine in Georgia, forty-nine and eight in Virginia, fifty-three and twelve in Alabama, sixty and five in Tennessee, and fifty-seven and three in North Carolina.

Empirical Analysis

To test the prediction that teacher unions exert greater influence when elections are held off-cycle, I compare teacher salaries in school districts that hold off-cycle elections to salaries in those that hold on-cycle elections. I focus on district salary for teachers with bachelor's degrees and no experience, master's degrees and ten years of experience, and the highest step on the salary schedule. I model district teacher salary linearly using ordinary least squares with state fixed effects:

$$\ln(salary_{ij}) = \alpha_i + \beta(Off\text{-}Cycle_{ij}) + X_{ij}\psi + \varepsilon_{ij}$$

Subscript i denotes the state, and j denotes the school district. The regression coefficients are β and ψ, $Off\text{-}Cycle_{ij}$ is a binary indicator variable equal to 1 if district j in state i has school board elections at a time other than federal or state elections in state i, X_{ij} is a matrix of district characteristics, α_i are state fixed effects, and ε_{ij} is an error term. The dependent variables are logged to reduce positive skew in the distribution of teacher salaries. Because the errors for districts within the same state are likely correlated, I cluster the standard errors by state.

The inclusion of state fixed effects, which partial out the effects of any school district characteristics that are constant within states, should substantially reduce omitted variable bias in the estimate of β, since, as I discussed above, certain characteristics make states more likely to have off-cycle school board election timing *and* more generous teacher compensation policies. The question then becomes whether there are certain *district*-level characteristics that could also bias the estimates of β. Since the previous chapter did not investigate the politics of election scheduling at the local level, it is important to consider various district characteristics that are plausibly correlated with election timing and teacher salaries and include them in the matrix X_{ij}.

One of the most important variables in the matrix X_{ij} is district size. As I showed in the last chapter, aside from increasing voter turnout, one of the main arguments used to advocate for on-cycle school board election timing is that on-cycle elections are less costly to administer than off-cycle elections. Large school districts are therefore more likely to have off-cycle elections than smaller districts simply because their heftier budgets allow them to cover the cost of holding stand-alone elections as opposed to relying on counties for support. They also pay their teachers more because they are typically found in large cities where the cost of living is higher and the day-to-day working environment is more challenging. For this reason, I include district size in all models, measured by the natural log of the number of enrolled students.

I also expect district affluence to influence both election timing and teacher salary. If administrators of affluent districts are equally likely as administrators of less affluent districts to prefer off-cycle election timing, but affluent districts have greater revenue with which to finance their own elections, then we would expect to see a positive relationship between district affluence and the presence of off-cycle election timing. For reasons unrelated to election timing, moreover, teacher salaries tend to be higher in areas of greater wealth. Therefore, in the models below, I include the natural log of median family income in the district as measured by the 2000 Census.

In addition, I include a variable equal to the percentage of the district's annual revenue that comes from state sources in order to account for the varying degree to which districts are dependent upon the state government for resources. I anticipate that districts that are more dependent on the state for resources are less likely to be able to fund increases in teacher salaries and also less likely to be able to fund and operate their own elections. Lastly, to control for districts' urbanicity, I incorporate in-

TABLE 5.1 **The Eight-State Test of the effect of election timing**

	Bachelor's, no experience (1)	Master's, 10 years (2)	Highest step (3)
Off-cycle	0.015***	0.037***	0.042***
	(0.005)	(0.005)	(0.011)
Ln(Enrollment)	0.007**	0.019**	0.037***
	(0.002)	(0.006)	(0.006)
Ln(Median income)	0.097***	0.121***	0.135***
	(0.017)	(0.030)	(0.022)
City	−0.007	0.009	0.007
	(0.006)	(0.013)	(0.013)
Fringe	−0.002	0.008	0.005
	(0.004)	(0.009)	(0.011)
% Hispanic	0.105***	0.145***	0.113***
	(0.010)	(0.037)	(0.013)
% Black	0.029	0.044	0.016
	(0.017)	(0.025)	(0.021)
% Asian	0.229***	0.149***	0.126***
	(0.011)	(0.016)	(0.025)
% Native American	0.139***	0.108**	0.047
	(0.023)	(0.041)	(0.036)
% Revenue from state	−0.026	−0.094	−0.136*
	(0.041)	(0.089)	(0.061)
Observations	665	658	665
R-squared	0.84	0.84	0.84

Notes: Robust standard errors clustered by state in parentheses. Dependent variables are district-level logged annual base salary for teachers of the three sets of qualifications. *Off-cycle* equals 0 if the district holds school board elections at the same time as the federal general election, a federal primary election, or a statewide general election; it equals 1 if school board elections are not held at those times. All models include state fixed effects. The test for *Off-cycle* is one-tailed; all other tests are two-tailed.
* significant at 10%; ** significant at 5%; *** significant at 1%

dicator variables for two of the three 2000 Census metro status code categories as well as variables describing the percentage of students in the district who are Hispanic, African American, Native American, and Asian or Pacific Islander. Teacher salaries tend to be higher in more urban districts, and the presence of municipal governments within urban districts' borders might allow them to more easily consolidate their elections with off-cycle city elections than districts that do not have large municipalities within their borders.

Table 5.1 presents the results from the specification described. The dependent variable in column (1) is the base salary in the district for teachers with bachelor's degrees and no experience. Column (2) presents the results from the same model using district-level salaries for teachers with master's degrees and ten years of experience. The dependent variable in column (3) is the highest step on the salary schedule, or the most a teacher can make in base salary in the district.

For teachers of all three levels of education and experience, I find that districts that hold off-cycle elections pay significantly higher teacher salaries than districts that hold on-cycle elections. Districts with off-cycle elections pay inexperienced teachers with bachelor's degrees an average of 1.5% more than districts that have school board elections concurrent with national or state elections. This coefficient is statistically significant at the 1% level. The salary gap between off-cycle and on-cycle election districts widens as teachers achieve higher levels of education and experience: a teacher with a master's degree and ten years of experience takes home 3.8% more in base salary in districts with nonconcurrent elections. A 3.8% increase from the average base salary for a teacher of these qualifications amounts to an extra $1,375 a year in Tennessee to $2,072 per year in California. The maximum base salary in a district—the highest step on the schedule—is approximately 4.2% higher in districts with off-cycle elections, amounting to $2,169 extra in Minnesota, $2,727 extra in Georgia, and $2,996 extra in California. The finding that the salary premium in districts with off-cycle elections increases with teacher experience is consistent with the literature, which shows that teacher unions are more responsive to senior teachers than to beginning teachers.[10]

The other predictors behave as expected. Enrollment is positively associated with salaries. Likewise, the coefficient on median income is positive and statistically significant in all specifications. The urbanicity indicator variables are insignificant, but I do find that districts with larger percentages of minority students tend to pay higher teacher salaries. This is most likely the case because the ethnic composition variables capture variation in district urbanicity and ideology. I find a negative relationship between teacher salary and the percentage of district funds that come from state sources, but the coefficient is only significantly different from zero at the highest salary level. Together, the control variables act to lower the coefficients on *Off-Cycle* relative to the coefficients estimated by a model that controls for state fixed effects alone: the state fixed effects model without control variables yields a coefficient of 0.023 (0.004) for beginning teachers with no experience, 0.056 (0.015) for teachers with master's degrees and ten years of experience, and 0.061 (0.029) for maximally qualified teachers.[11]

If I categorize school district elections held at the same time as statewide primary elections as off-cycle elections rather than on-cycle elections, the estimates of the coefficients on *Off-Cycle* for each of the salary categories are still substantively large and statistically significant at the 1% level. When I replace *Off-Cycle* with two binary indicator variables— one variable equal to 1 if the district's election is at the same time as a general election, the other variable equal to 1 if the district's election is at the same time as a primary election—an *F*-test of the regression coefficients shows that there is no statistically significant difference between teacher salaries in those two types of districts, although both pay lower teacher salaries than districts that hold elections independently of both primary and general elections.

One might suspect that if more Democratic states are more likely to have off-cycle school board elections than Republican-leaning states, then perhaps within a state, school districts in Democratic areas are more likely to have off-cycle elections than school districts in Republican areas. That would raise concerns if Democratic-leaning school districts also tend to pay higher teacher salaries than Republican-leaning school districts. However, since I control for certain district demographic characteristics in table 5.1, it is unlikely that district ideology—particularly constituents' preferences for greater spending on public education and teacher salaries—explains the positive coefficient on *Off-Cycle*.[12] As an additional test, however, I have matched each school district with the two-party presidential vote in its parent county in 2004.[13] In columns (1) and (2) of table 5.2, I estimate the effect of *Off-Cycle* on the salaries of beginning teachers and maximally qualified teachers controlling for the percentage of the 2004 vote for John Kerry in the district's parent county. The coefficients on *Off-Cycle* are essentially the same as those in table 5.1: beginning teachers earn an average of 1.4% more in base salary in districts with off-cycle elections, and maximally qualified teachers earn 4.2% more. Therefore, districts' ideological leanings do not account for the higher teacher salaries in districts with off-cycle elections.

Perhaps a bigger concern with the estimates in table 5.1 is that those models do not directly address the possibility that *within* a state, school board election timing is likely correlated with teacher union strength. The last chapter showed that teacher unions tend to oppose state legislative efforts to consolidate school board elections with other elections—and the theory predicts they should. That finding poses a challenge for causal inference here, however, because a reasonable hypothesis is that *districts* where teacher unions are strong are more likely to have off-cycle elections and pay higher salaries to teachers. If so, then even in this within-state analysis, I run the risk of attributing a positive relationship between off-cycle election timing and teacher salaries to the institution rather than to the combined effect of the institution and teacher union strength.

A good measure of teacher union strength in this context would capture both teachers' individual incentives to participate in school board elections as well as the organizational capacity of the union—how well it is equipped to mobilize voters. Unfortunately, I have no such measure, so I use data on the number of NEA members in each school district in 1999, a few years prior to the collection of the SASS data used in this analysis. The vast majority of unionized teachers in the United States are members of a state or local chapter of the NEA.[14] Therefore, in models (3) and (4) of table 5.2, I include the ratio of NEA members to full-time equivalent teachers as a control variable.[15] Admittedly, this is a crude measure of teacher union strength. However, it allows me to at least approximate how much of the effect of off-cycle elections persists once I include a measure of interest group strength.

As expected, the ratio of NEA members to teachers in the district is positively associated with higher teacher salaries for both beginning and senior teachers. The positive coefficient on the unionization rate variable is statistically significant for the highest step on the salary schedule and approaches significance for beginning teacher salaries ($p = 0.16$). Most importantly, the coefficient on *Off-Cycle* remains positive, substantively large, and statistically significant. On average, beginning teachers make 1.6% higher salaries in districts that hold off-cycle school board elections, controlling for the level of teacher union strength in the district. Column (4) shows that maximally qualified teachers earn 4.2% more in districts with off-cycle elections. The coefficients in both models are statistically significant. Granted, the overall weakness of the NEA ratio as a predictor of teacher salaries suggests that the endogeneity problem is not fully resolved by the inclusion of the unionization rate measure. However, these results do support the hypothesis that off-cycle election timing contributes to higher teacher salaries above and beyond the effect of teacher union strength.

In a final set of models for the Eight-State Test, I examine whether teacher unions' off-cycle election advantage is tempered by the strength of one possible source of competition: elderly voters. A large education finance literature hypothesizes that elderly voters are unlikely to support proposals to increase spending on public schools because they do not directly benefit from such spending. While the evidence for this hypothesis is mixed,[16] several studies do find a negative relationship between school spending and the share of elderly in the population.[17] Thus even if elderly voters aren't organized to mobilize voters, they might compete with teachers over public school compensation policies and also be highly motivated to turn out, and so I can test whether the effect of off-cycle election timing is smaller in school districts with high proportions of elderly voters.

In columns (5) and (6) of table 5.2, therefore, I interact the off-cycle indicator with the percentage of adults in a school district who are age sixty-five or over. The estimates do, in fact, suggest that the advantage teacher unions have in off-cycle elections decreases as the percentage of elderly residents grows. For example, when the elderly make up only 14% of the adult population in a district—which is the twenty-fifth percentile—off-cycle election timing has the effect of increasing beginning teachers' base salaries by 2.1%, significant at the 1% level. However, at the median level of percent elderly—17%—the effect is smaller: on average, off-cycle election timing increases beginning teachers' salaries by 1.5%. And at the seventy-fifth percentile value (20% elderly voters), the effect is only 0.9%. The same pattern holds for maximally qualified teachers: the effect of off-cycle election timing is 5.1% in school districts with 14% elderly, 4.5% in communities with 17% elderly, and 3.9% in districts where the elderly make up 20% of the adult population. Just as the theory predicts, the degree to which off-cycle election timing increases the influence of teachers depends on the strength of the competition they face.

The Minnesota Test

The results thus far are strongly supportive of my argument that off-cycle elections allow teachers to have greater influence in elections and policy making. Moreover, the finding that the gap between on-cycle and off-cycle districts widens with teacher experience and credentials is consistent with the fact that senior teachers tend to be more active in their unions and in politics than junior teachers.[18] Of course, my argument not only predicts that off-cycle election timing should have this effect but also that it should have this effect because *turnout* is lower in off-cycle elections. Unfortunately, I cannot test the effect of turnout directly with the Eight-State dataset, because most states do not have central, statewide repositories of local election data. Rather, in most states, one has to contact

TABLE 5.2 **The Eight-State Test and partisanship, union strength, and competition**

	Bachelor's (1)	Highest (2)	Bachelor's (3)	Highest (4)	Bachelor's (5)	Highest (6)
Off-cycle	0.014***	0.041***	0.016**	0.041***	0.046***	0.075***
	(0.004)	(0.009)	(0.007)	(0.011)	(0.014)	(0.022)
% Democrat	0.039	0.011				
	(0.024)	(0.095)				
NEA-to-teacher ratio			0.031	0.042**		
			(0.020)	(0.016)		
% Elderly					0.051	-0.216
					(0.036)	(0.163)
Off-cycle * % Elderly					-0.189**	-0.188**
					(0.072)	(0.097)
Ln(Enrollment)	0.007**	0.037***	0.008**	0.037***	0.007**	0.034***
	(0.002)	(0.006)	(0.002)	(0.006)	(0.002)	(0.006)
Ln(Median income)	0.095***	0.135***	0.093***	0.137***	0.095***	0.112***
	(0.017)	(0.019)	(0.015)	(0.023)	(0.016)	(0.021)
City	-0.006	0.007	-0.01	0.007	-0.007	0.002
	(0.006)	(0.013)	(0.006)	(0.014)	(0.006)	(0.013)
Fringe	-0.001	0.006	-0.003	0.006	-0.001	0.001
	(0.004)	(0.010)	(0.005)	(0.012)	(0.003)	(0.013)

% Hispanic	0.1***	0.112***	0.106***	0.113***	0.102***	0.09***
	(0.011)	(0.019)	(0.009)	(0.013)	(0.009)	(0.017)
% Black	0.015	0.012	0.023	0.007	0.029	0.008
	(0.025)	(0.029)	(0.020)	(0.022)	(0.017)	(0.023)
% Asian	0.216***	0.122***	0.218***	0.116***	0.233***	0.125***
	(0.008)	(0.026)	(0.009)	(0.020)	(0.011)	(0.028)
% Native American	0.134***	0.046	0.123***	0.032	0.144***	0.016
	(0.023)	(0.037)	(0.019)	(0.034)	(0.024)	(0.031)
% Revenue from state	-0.023	-0.135**	-0.043	-0.134*	-0.034	-0.168**
	(0.043)	(0.055)	(0.029)	(0.058)	(0.037)	(0.068)
Observations	665	665	643	643	665	665
R-squared	0.84	0.84	0.84	0.84	0.84	0.84

Notes: Robust standard errors clustered by state in parentheses. Dependent variables are district-level logged annual base salary. *Off-cycle* equals 0 if the district holds school board elections at the same time as the federal general election, a federal primary election, or a statewide general election; it equals 1 if school board elections are not held at those times. All models include state fixed effects. The tests for *Off-cycle* and *Off-cycle* * % *Elderly* are one-tailed; all other tests are two-tailed.
* significant at 10%; ** significant at 5%; *** significant at 1%

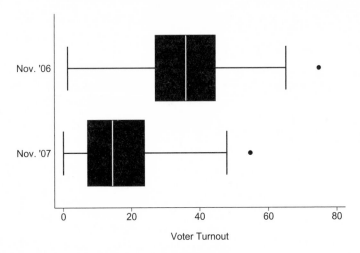

FIGURE 5.1. Voter turnout in Minnesota school board elections.

counties, cities, or school districts directly in order to collect information on voter turnout in local races. Fortunately, however, there is at least one state that gathers data on its school board elections: Minnesota.

Specifically, the Minnesota Office of the Secretary of State collects election data for the state's public school districts, which allows me to measure voter turnout in on- and off-cycle school district elections directly and examine its relationship to district teacher salary. Rather than rely on the sample of Minnesota districts in the SASS data, I use the full set of Minnesota school districts that reported to the secretary of state that they held elections in either November of 2006 (176 districts) or November of 2007 (62 districts). I combine these election data with a set of 2006–7 district-level data files from the Minnesota Department of Education as well as the variables from the NCES CCD database. The result is a cross-sectional dataset of 238 Minnesota school districts with variables describing district election timing, voter turnout, district finances, staff information, and student demographics.

As a starting point, I find that the relationship between election timing and voter turnout in Minnesota school board elections follows the pattern established in the literature.[19] To illustrate, the box plots in figure 5.1 show the distribution of voter turnout in Minnesota school board elections broken down by whether the elections were held in November of the even- or the odd-numbered year.[20] (Notably, the turnout figures only include people who voted in the local school board elections—not voters who turned out to vote for congressional candidates but abstained in the school board races.) The figure shows that in the vast majority of districts, turnout in the on-cycle elections exceeded turnout in the off-cycle elections, and the differences were quite large in most cases. Median voter turnout in November of 2007 was a mere 14% of registered voters, whereas turnout in November of 2006 was 36% of registered voters. In other words, off-cycle election timing decreased median voter turnout by a full 22 percentage points. Moreover, a third of the off-cycle elections had turnout rates below 10%, whereas only 2% of the on-cycle elections had turnout rates that low. As expected, turnout in Minnesota school board elections tends to be far lower when they are held separately from US congressional elections.

As for testing whether off-cycle timing (and low voter turnout) has the expected relationship with teacher compensation, the Minnesota Department of Education does not track teacher salary schedules, but it does provide figures for the average teacher salary in each of the state's districts. This measure is less than ideal since it depends on the education and experience levels of teachers in the district. However, the data also include variables on the average number of years of experience for teachers in the district as well as the percentage of teachers who are in their first year of teaching. I use these as control variables to account for any differences in average district salary due to differences in teacher experience.

First, in order to ensure that the results from the Minnesota data are comparable to the results presented in tables 5.1 and 5.2, I replicate that analysis. The results are presented in column (1) of table 5.3. The dependent variable is the natural log of average teacher salary, and the standard errors are clustered by county.[21] The results confirm that the salary advantage that accrues to teachers in districts with off-cycle elections is of a similar magnitude to the effects we observed in the previous tables: districts with off-cycle elections pay their teachers 2% more than districts with on-cycle elections. The results persist when I control for district-level presidential vote from 2000, as I do in column (2). I find that a 10-percentage-point increase in the district's vote share for the Democratic presidential candidate is associated with about a 1% increase in average teacher salary. The effect of off-cycle election timing remains unchanged. These results also persist when I include the NEA ratio as a predictor.[22]

Next, I estimate the effect of voter turnout directly rather than by the dichotomous off-cycle election variable. I include both turnout and its square because I expect the marginal effect of a decrease in turnout

TABLE 5.3 **The Minnesota Test of the effect of election timing and turnout**

	Average teacher salary			Superintendent salary	
	(1)	(2)	(3)	(4)	(5)
Off-cycle	0.02**	0.02**		–0.005	
	(0.009)	(0.009)		(0.025)	
% Democrat		0.096*			
		(0.051)			
Turnout			–0.167***		–0.048
			(0.066)		(0.148)
Turnout squared			0.184***		0.014
			(0.072)		(0.147)
Ln(Enrollment)	0.06***	0.059***	0.061***	0.122***	0.122***
	(0.006)	(0.006)	(0.006)	(0.019)	(0.019)
Ln(Median income)	0.055	0.068*	0.042	0.141**	0.096
	(0.035)	(0.034)	(0.040)	(0.068)	(0.080)
% Rev. from state	–0.289***	–0.257***	–0.301***	–0.486**	–0.566**
	(0.071)	(0.071)	(0.081)	(0.219)	(0.241)
City	0.002	0.003	0.007	–0.007	–0.025
	(0.015)	(0.016)	(0.018)	(0.035)	(0.034)
Rural	–0.007	–0.001	–0.012	–0.042	–0.059
	(0.023)	(0.023)	(0.025)	(0.040)	(0.042)
Town	0.005	0.007	0.001	–0.035	–0.043
	(0.021)	(0.021)	(0.022)	(0.035)	(0.040)
% Hispanic	–0.095	–0.091	–0.088	0.128	0.114
	(0.071)	(0.069)	(0.071)	(0.139)	(0.140)
% Black	0.218***	0.166*	0.177**	0.11	0.085
	(0.078)	(0.091)	(0.083)	(0.149)	(0.156)
% Asian	–0.184	–0.162	–0.193	0.15	0.022
	(0.132)	(0.117)	(0.139)	(0.268)	(0.240)
% Native American	0.027	0.013	0.007	0.023	–0.019
	(0.045)	(0.045)	(0.045)	(0.102)	(0.116)
Avg. teacher exper.	0.015***	0.015***	0.015***	–0.004	–0.004
	(0.002)	(0.002)	(0.002)	(0.005)	(0.005)
% New teachers	–0.354*	–0.36**	–0.363**	–0.067	–0.14
	(0.184)	(0.175)	(0.181)	(0.456)	(0.454)
Constant	9.707***	9.498***	9.883***	9.596***	10.163***
	(0.392)	(0.383)	(0.442)	(0.807)	(0.959)
Observations	235	235	228	226	219
R-squared	0.74	0.74	0.74	0.71	0.70

Notes: Robust standard errors clustered by county in parentheses. Dependent variables are logged. *Off-cycle* equals
1 if the district held its school board election in November 2007 and 0 if the district held its school board election in
November 2006. Turnout is the proportion of registered voters who cast a ballot in the school board election. The
tests on *Off-cycle, Turnout,* and *Turnout squared* are one-tailed. All other tests are two-tailed.
* significant at 10%; ** significant at 5%; *** significant at 1%

on teacher salary to diminish as overall turnout increases. For example,
a 5-percentage-point decrease in voter turnout should have a greater impact on interest groups' ability to influence elections when baseline turnout is 10% of registered voters as opposed to 40% of registered voters.

The results, presented in column (3) of table 5.3, are consistent with ex-

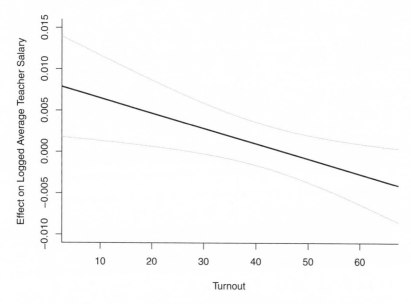

FIGURE 5.2. Marginal effect of a five-percentage-point decrease in turnout.

pectations. The coefficients on both turnout and its square are statistically significant at the 1% level, and the marginal effect of a decrease in turnout on average teacher salary is positive when overall turnout is relatively low. Figure 5.2 illustrates the marginal effect of a 5-percentage-point decrease in turnout on average salary. When turnout drops from 10% of registered voters to 5% of registered voters, the model predicts a 0.7% increase in district average teacher salary. When turnout drops from 30% to 25% of registered voters—still a 5-percentage-point drop, but at a higher level of overall turnout—the associated increase in average district teacher salary is 0.3%. Once overall turnout reaches 45% of registered voters, the estimated effect of a decrease in voter turnout on average teacher salary is zero, and the effect is not statistically significant above a turnout level of 28%. Clearly, if voter turnout is high enough, slight increases or decreases in turnout matter little for teacher union influence.

It is notable, moreover, that Minnesota leads the nation in voter turnout rates in national and state elections. If the same is true for off-cycle school board elections—if turnout in off-cycle Minnesota school board elections is higher than turnout in off-cycle school board elections in other states—I would expect the size of the off-cycle election effect to be even larger in other states than it is in column (1) of table 5.3. However, there is little evidence that turnout in Minnesota off-cycle local elections is higher than comparable elections in other states. Median turnout in the school district elections in 2007 in Minnesota was only 14% of registered voters, and that figure is an overestimate because it does not include same-day registrants in the denominator. Studies of off-cycle school district elections in other states have found even lower turnout figures—such as the 7.8% average in Michigan in 2000[23]—but based on figure 5.1, it does not look like participation levels in Minnesota elections are markedly higher. Most likely, the results from table 5.3 generalize to other states.

It is possible that something other than teacher union influence explains these results, although it is unlikely. Teachers are the most active interest group in school board elections and have strong pecuniary incentives to participate, and therefore it makes sense that they fare better when school board elections are off-cycle and turnout is low. One Michigan school board member explained the effect of election timing as follows: "The November election keeps unions from controlling the vote. If you have 3,000 people voting in June, teachers can get 1,600 people there; if you have 16,000 people voting, teachers are a minor factor."[24]

Still, a sizeable literature finds that minorities and individuals with low levels of income and education are underrepresented in the active electorate when turnout is low, such that policy tends to have an upper-class bias.[25] It is worth taking seriously the concern that the preferences of high-income voters are driving the results presented here. Perhaps those who turn out in off-cycle elections tend to be predominantly wealthy, well-educated individuals who also prefer greater spending on public education—including teacher salaries. How can we know that the higher teacher salaries in districts with off-cycle elections represent a private benefit for teachers as opposed to a broad policy of greater spending on public education?

Inspection of other expenditure variables in on- and off-cycle districts is of little help in answering this question, since teacher unions have many reasons to prefer greater spending on most district budget items, including facilities, support staff, and transportation. All such expenditures improve the quality of teachers' working conditions, and they also improve the employment terms of other school employees like bus drivers, janitors, and cafeteria workers.[26] However, there is at least one element of a school district's finances that the teacher unions typically have little interest in growing: the salary of the district superintendent. The superintendent is the district's chief school administrator. She is generally selected by the local school board and tends not to be affiliated with unions. If the effect of election timing on teacher salaries is truly the effect of teacher union influence in elections, then we should *not* expect to see higher superintendent salaries in districts with off-cycle elections.

Columns (4) and (5) of table 5.3 present the results of the same models as (1) and (3) but using the natural log of district superintendent salary as the dependent variable.[27] I find there is no difference in superintendent salaries between off-cycle and on-cycle districts, nor do superintendent salaries vary with voter turnout. As a robustness check, I have also estimated the model using the natural log of the average administrative salary in the district as the dependent variable (the district's general administrative salary expenditures in 2005–6 divided by the number of local education agency administrators and their support staff).[28] As in the model of superintendent salary, the coefficient on *Off-Cycle* is negative and statistically insignificant, and the effects on both *Turnout* and its square are not statistically distinguishable from zero.[29] The fact that there is no salary benefit for administrators in districts with off-cycle elections supports the argument that off-cycle elections help *teachers*, who are represented by a powerful interest group, not administrators.

The Texas Test

So far, my argument that school boards elected in low turnout, off-cycle elections should be more responsive to teachers in setting compensation policies is strongly supported by the data. However, one might still be worried that my estimates of the election timing effect could be biased. While my decision to conduct a within-state analysis—and the inclusion of a rich set of control variables—reduces that possibility substantially, neither the Eight-State Test nor the Minnesota Test addresses the problem fully. If characteristics of school districts that are difficult to measure—such as teacher union strength—make them more or less likely to adopt a certain election schedule *and* influence its teacher salary policies, then my estimates of the effect of election timing would be biased.

The situation would be improved if one could leverage within-district changes in election timing to estimate the effect, which is the general approach Christopher Berry and Jacob Gersen use.[30] If, for example, teacher union strength is constant over the time period being examined, then a longitudinal model with school district fixed effects would eliminate teacher union strength as a potential source of omitted variable bias. But even in such a district fixed effects model, the possibility of selection bias would remain. If teachers only lobby for off-cycle election timing in the districts where they think they will benefit from it, then by simply comparing districts where they secured off-cycle election timing to those where they did not make the effort, one would overestimate the average effect of off-cycle election timing. Since most within-district changes in election timing are the result of decisions made by elected officials within the district itself, it is possible that the officials who *choose* to alter election timing do so *because* they anticipate that it will have certain effects on the size and composition of the electorate. The problem this poses to causal inference is this: if officials in one district change elections to off-cycle while officials in another district opt for a continuation of on-cycle elections, we might not expect officials in those districts to make similar policy decisions, even in the absence of changes to election timing.

Therefore, the final tests of this chapter leverage a 2006 Texas state law that forced some school districts to move their elections to on-cycle while allowing others to retain their preexisting off-cycle election schedules. By examining changes within districts over time, I largely overcome the problem of omitted variable bias. Furthermore, since the rule the state used to assign school districts to on-cycle or off-cycle schedules was objective, teachers and administrators in districts forced to on-cycle elections were unable to alter the mandate. Thus the design reduces the incidence of selection bias as well.

A Quasi-Experiment: Texas House Bill 1

Prior to 2005, the Texas Election Code allowed for four election dates: the first Saturday in February, the first Saturday in May, the second Saturday in September, and the first Tuesday after the first Monday in November. All elections throughout the state had to be held on one of the established election dates.[31] When the Texas legislature decided in 2005 to eliminate the February and September uniform dates and move the May uniform date to the second Saturday in May, the move was relatively uncontroversial since 97% of governmental units in the state held elections either in May or November. Among school districts specifically, 99% held their regular trustee elections in May.[32]

In July 2006, state legislators passed HB 1, which for the first time required that all school districts throughout the state hold joint elections with either their parent county or with a municipality partially or wholly within the school district's borders. Since most municipalities in Texas hold elections in May, the majority of Texas school districts were able to retain their existing May election dates by combining their elections with overlapping municipalities. However, a sizeable number of school districts did not have incorporated cities within their borders, and those districts had no choice but to combine their trustee elections with county elections in November of even-numbered years. Another set of districts had incorporated municipalities within their borders but could not keep their May election dates since the overlapping municipalities held November elections. As long as those municipalities held elections in November of odd-numbered years, a school district could keep its elections separate from state and national elections. However, if the overlapping municipal elections were held in November of even-numbered years, those school districts had to combine elections with the counties. Therefore, with the passage of HB 1, several Texas school districts were forced to shift trustee elections to the same day as presidential elections and gubernatorial elections.[33]

I group school districts into four categories based on how their elections were affected by HB 1:[34]

TYPE 1 DISTRICTS: School districts that have an incorporated municipality within district boundaries, and that municipality holds elections in May. These school districts had the option of either having a joint election with the municipality in May (off-cycle) or having a joint election with the county in November of even-numbered years (on-cycle).

TYPE 2 DISTRICTS: School districts that have a municipality within district boundaries, and that municipality holds elections in November of odd-numbered years. These districts had the option of either holding a joint election with the municipality in November of odd-numbered years (off-cycle) or with the county in November of even-numbered years (on-cycle).

TYPE 3 DISTRICTS: School districts that have a municipality within district boundaries, and that municipality has elections in November of even-numbered years. These districts were forced to move their elections to November of even-numbered years (on-cycle).

TYPE 4 DISTRICTS: School districts that do not have an incorporated municipality within district boundaries. These districts were forced to combine elections with the counties in November of even-numbered years (on-cycle).

For the empirical analysis, I take advantage of the fact that a large number of Texas school districts had *no choice* but to hold on-cycle elections after 2006, whereas other districts maintained discretion over whether to conduct on-cycle or off-cycle elections. The former group, composed of type 3 and type 4 districts, makes up the treatment group, and the latter set of districts, including type 1 and type 2 districts, makes up the control group. My key design innovation is that the school trustees in type 3 and type 4 districts had no choice but to move to on-cycle elections, which meant that interest groups in those districts could not lobby for an advantageous school trustee election schedule. Moreover, the assignment of districts to treatment and control conditions was purely a function of whether or not the school district had a municipality within its borders and when that municipality held its elections. Importantly, assignment was not explicitly a function of interest group strength in the district.

That said, the assignment rule HB 1 established was created only after Texas Republicans tried for two years—unsuccessfully—to move *all* school trustee elections in Texas to November of even-numbered years. One such attempt was HB 855, which would have required all school trustee elections to be held at the same time as state and national general elections. Unsurprisingly in light of the findings of the previous chapter, the primary supporters of the bill were state Republicans and taxpayer organizations, who argued that it would increase voter participation in school elections as well as reduce the costs of holding elections for school boards across the state.[35] Also in line with what I found in chapter 4, state teacher unions, some school trustees, and the Texas Association of School Boards (TASB) opposed the proposal. The TASB representative who testified in committee argued that the higher November turnout would merely expose school trustee elections to uninformed voters. A representative from one of the state's three teacher unions explained that on-cycle trustee elections would strip districts of local control and make it more expensive for school board candidates to wage campaigns. A school trustee from one district defended his district's May elections by explaining:

> What we get in Spring Branch, and in most districts around the state, is an educated voter voting in our May election. . . . I think what you get is . . . the people who really care about the issues and who are passionate about their district.[36]

In response to the testimony of the opposition, Texas Representative Dan Gattis replied:

I think it's a little disingenuous at times to say, "We want to make sure that we have informed voters." No you don't. You want to make sure that you have *your* voters—your voters that are going to come and vote for your issue.... They mean the voters that they know they can turn out to vote for their deal.[37]

HB 855 was eventually dropped, and subsequent bills that proposed moving all trustee elections to November of even-numbered years were quietly snuffed in committee. The joint election provision that was later slipped into HB 1 in the summer of 2006 was a watered down election timing measure that only affected the elections of 20% of school districts in the state. State teacher unions and school board representatives testified against HB 1 in committee hearings, but the bill was first and foremost a bill that provided property tax relief and created new fiscal and academic accountability programs for school districts, so testimony did not focus on the election timing provision.[38] After HB 1 was passed in 2006, Republicans renewed their attempts to force larger numbers of districts to on-cycle elections, but all such attempts failed to gain traction in the legislature.

In sum, HB 1 created a rule for assigning districts to treatment and control conditions that applied uniformly to all 1,032 independent school districts throughout the state. Importantly, though, the creation of that rule in the legislature was likely the result of concessions made to the teacher unions and school trustees who opposed the move to on-cycle elections. Furthermore, even though the rule for assigning districts to treatment and control conditions was objective, it was not necessarily orthogonal to district attributes that were correlated with district teacher salaries. For example, since larger and more urban districts are more likely to have strong unions *and* to overlap with incorporated municipalities, the political clout of teachers might be greater in control districts than in the districts forced to on-cycle elections. To account for these differences between treatment and control districts, I use both matching techniques—which address selection on observable district characteristics—and fixed effects regression—which also addresses selection on time-invariant unobservable district characteristics—to estimate the effect of election timing on teacher salaries. I describe both strategies in the following sections.

Data

Since no state-level entity kept track of how the law affected each Texas school district, I employed a combination of strategies to classify the districts in the state as one of the four types described above. To create an exhaustive list of type 4 districts, I overlaid a shapefile of the boundaries of the 1,211 incorporated municipalities in Texas onto a shapefile of the boundaries of 1,023 Texas school districts.[39] I then used the intersect feature of ArcGIS to identify all areas of intersection between the independent school districts and incorporated municipalities, which enabled me to identify 150 independent school districts that do not overlap with any part of an incorporated municipality. These 150 districts form the comprehensive set of type 4 districts, which were all forced to switch to on-cycle elections following HB 1.

Type 3 districts also belong in the treatment group, but distinguishing type 3 districts from types 1 and 2 is challenging, because Texas does not have a central source of information on when municipal elections throughout the state are conducted. Therefore, I am unable to determine which municipalities hold regular elections in November of even-numbered years as opposed to May or November of odd-numbered years. As a next best alternative, I acquired a partial list of school districts that were forced to move their elections to November of even-numbered years from TASB. In its Election Advisory 2007-01, TASB asked all school districts to report whether they were forced to move their elections to November of even-numbered years as a result of HB 1. Ninety-seven school districts voluntarily reported to TASB that they had no choice but to hold on-cycle elections after the passage of HB 1, and of those, twenty-four were districts I did not identify as type 4 districts using the procedure described above. Adding those twenty-four type 3 districts to the 150 type 4 districts, I identify a total of 174 school districts in the treatment group.

Using this approach, it remains possible that I have failed to identify some type 3 districts, since not all districts responded to the TASB request. I therefore pursue one additional strategy to ensure that I do not erroneously classify treatment districts as control districts. Each year, TASB asks school districts whether they would prefer to receive the May election calendar or the November election calendar. In 2008, a total of 982 districts requested one of the two calendars. From this, I can be fairly sure that all districts that requested the May election calendar hold May elections and therefore are type 1 districts. Since I cannot be sure whether the districts that requested the November calendar are type 1, type 2, or type 3 districts, I limit the control group to the 743 districts that hold May elections.[40]

The dependent variable for the analysis is district teacher salary. In Texas, the state education code establishes a minimum teacher salary schedule, but independent school districts adopt their own teacher salary schedules each year as part of the annual budget process, and most of the state's districts pay teachers more than the state minimum.[41] While it would be desirable to have detailed annual salary schedule and benefits information for each district in Texas, unfortunately, no such data are available.[42] However, comprehensive data on average base teacher salary in each district and year are readily available through the Texas Education Agency (TEA). Average teacher salary has one major disadvantage in that it can change for reasons other than a change in the salary schedule. Still, since the data on average teacher salary are the best available, I use the TEA data files to compile annual average base teacher salary data for the panel of 1,023 independent school districts over seven years, from 2003–4 to 2009–10.[43] Salary figures and all other dollar values in the analysis are adjusted to 2009 dollars.

Since my argument is that election timing affects interest group influence by lowering voter turnout, an intermediate step for testing the theory is to establish that voter turnout in treatment districts increased following implementation of HB 1. As is true of most states, however, Texas does not have a statewide entity that compiles results from all school district elections held in the state. Rather, school trustee elections are administered by the counties, the municipalities, or the school districts themselves, which means that historical school trustee election results (including turnout statistics) in Texas are potentially kept by up to 2,497 different local governments, most of which do not report even recent election results on their websites. Therefore, collecting pre– and post–HB 1 turnout statistics for school trustee elections in Texas is a cumbersome task. For many districts, as I describe below, it is simply not possible.

However, there is little reason to expect that school elections in Texas would deviate from the empirical pattern established in the political science literature. Even so, to boost confidence that this link in the argument is sound, I called or e-mailed officials in a total of twenty-nine counties and 205 school districts in early June 2011 to request the returns of school board elections held between 2003 and 2011. Most of the officials I contacted either did not respond to the request or explained that they do not keep election returns more than twenty-two months old. However, with the returns I did receive, I was able to assemble a dataset of pre– and post–HB 1 turnout in thirty-one Texas school districts, thirteen of which switched to on-cycle elections.

Lastly, since the empirical analysis utilizes a pre-post design, I must also determine *when* the consequences of HB 1 would have taken effect. If the election timing effect works solely through the replacement of sitting trustees with new trustees who are less responsive to teachers, the first sign of a difference in teacher salary in treatment districts would appear in 2009–10, the academic year following the first on-cycle election. However, based on the testimony of various school board members during the committee hearings on election timing changes, it seems clear that even prior to HB 1, school board members in Texas were well aware of the consequences of switching to on-cycle elections. They knew that on-cycle elections would dramatically increase voter participation in their elections and that the composition of the electorate would be altered as a result. Therefore, I suspect that school trustees likely *anticipated* the effect of on-cycle election timing for the importance of teachers in elections— even before the first on-cycle election was held. If so, then any election timing effect would appear as soon as school board members became aware of the implications of HB 1,[44] which was in the spring of 2007.[45] I therefore treat the 2007–8 academic year as the first year of the treatment. However, in my empirical tests, I also explore the possibility that election timing did not have an effect until after the first on-cycle election in November 2008.

Empirical Analysis

Figure 5.3 presents a map of the geographic location of the treatment and control districts that are used for the empirical analysis. The 174 treatment districts—all type 4 districts and the type 3 districts I was able to identify—are colored dark gray. The 743 type 1 districts I identified as having May elections are colored light gray. The remaining districts—six common school districts, three districts that do not hold trustee elections, and all districts I was unable to classify as type 1, type 2, or type 3—are left white. Aside from the fact that there are relatively few treatment districts in the urban areas in and around Dallas and Fort Worth, Austin, Houston, and San Antonio, treatment districts are well dispersed throughout the state.

Moreover, as expected, voter turnout increased significantly in districts that shifted to on-cycle elections. Table 5.4 presents the results of two regressions of voter turnout on district and year fixed effects and an indicator for on-cycle election timing. The dependent variable in column (1) is voter turnout as a percentage of adults in the district.[46] The results show that the

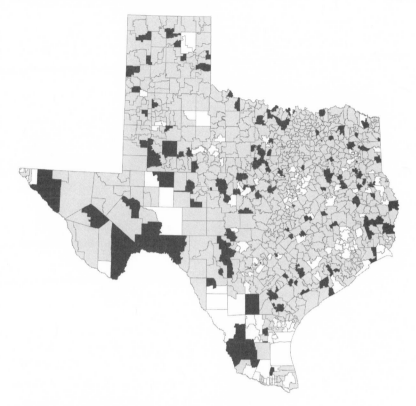

FIGURE 5.3. Treatment and control school districts, House Bill 1.

average effect of switching to on-cycle elections was a 16-percentage-point increase in voter turnout in the school board election. When I limit the analysis to the fourteen districts for which I can calculate voter turnout as a percentage of registered voters,[47] as I do in column (2), the estimated coefficient on the on-cycle indicator is even larger—about 18 percentage points. Based on this analysis of a subset of districts, it is safe to assume that voter turnout increased in treatment districts as a result of the change to on-cycle elections.

However, treatment districts differ from control districts on the basis of some attributes that tend to be associated with both teacher salaries and the political strength of teachers. For example, only 31% of the districts assigned to the treatment group are urban or urban fringe districts, whereas 49% of control districts are classified as urban or urban fringe. Since urban districts generally pay higher teacher salaries than rural dis-

TABLE 5.4 **The Texas Test of the effect of election timing on turnout**

	% of adults (1)	% of registered voters (2)
On-cycle	0.156***	0.182***
	(0.019)	(0.032)
Observations	110	65
Number of districts	28	14
R-squared	0.85	0.80

Notes: Robust standard errors clustered by district in parentheses. All models include district and year fixed effects. Dependent variable in column (1) is the percentage of adults who voted in the school board election. Dependent variable in column (2) is the percentage of registered voters who voted in the school board election.
* significant at 10%; ** significant at 5%; *** significant at 1%

tricts *and* tend to have stronger teacher unions, failure to account for these differences would result in biased estimates of the treatment effect.

In addition, treatment districts tend to be smaller in size and slightly less affluent than control districts, and they also paid lower average teacher salaries in the pretreatment period. I show these differences in figure 5.4. In the top two rows of the left-hand column, I plot the distributions of logged district enrollment in 2005 and logged median family income in 2000 for treatment districts (the solid lines) and control districts (the dashed lines).[48] The distribution of enrollment for treatment districts is clearly shifted to the left of the distribution for control districts. Moreover, due to the presence of a few control districts with extremely high values of median family income, income in treatment districts tends to be lower than in control districts. In addition, as the plot in the top right-hand corner shows, logged average teacher salaries in 2003 were slightly lower in treatment districts than in control districts. These differences between treatment and control districts pose a problem for the empirical analysis. Regardless of election timing, larger districts tend to have stronger teacher unions. Larger and more affluent districts also tend to pay higher teacher salaries than smaller, less affluent districts. And if treatment districts were starting out with slightly lower average teacher salaries even before the treatment, there might be something distinct about those districts that affected their salary growth after 2006.

Regarding other attributes that are likely correlated with teachers' political strength and average teacher salaries, the pretreatment values for treatment and control districts are similar. For example, teachers employed in more challenging work environments—for example, districts with more students for whom English is a second language—generally

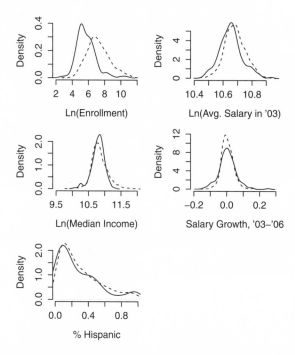

FIGURE 5.4. Pretreatment attributes of treatment and control districts.

earn higher salaries than teachers who work in less challenging environments.[49] Yet as we can see from the bottom left-hand panel of figure 5.4, treatment and control districts differ very little on the basis of the percentage of the student body that was Hispanic in 2005. Furthermore, if it were the case that teacher salaries were growing at significantly different rates in treatment and control districts *prior* to HB 1, it would be difficult to attribute any post-2006 salary difference to HB 1. However, the lower right-hand panel of figure 5.4 demonstrates that this was not the case; in spite of the differences in salary levels between treatment and control districts in 2003, there are only small differences between treatment and control districts in the distributions of average within-district teacher salary growth from 2003 to 2006.

The first method I use to handle the pretreatment covariate imbalance between treatment and control districts is matching. I match treatment districts to control districts on the basis of their metro status codes, their logged enrollment in 2005, and their logged median family income in 2000. I use exact matching for the metro status codes so that rural districts in the treatment group are only matched to rural districts in the control group, and likewise for urban and urban fringe districts. In order to achieve balance on district enrollment and income, I use a caliper equal to one-tenth of a standard deviation for both variables, discarding all treatment districts that fail to find acceptable matches based on this distance criterion.[50] The dependent variable is the percentage growth in district average teacher salary (in real terms) from 2006–7 to 2009–10, the period following the implementation of HB 1. All matching is one-to-one with replacement and is carried out using the Matching package in R.[51]

To provide a benchmark, the first panel of table 5.5 presents the results when I use all the treatment and control districts to calculate the average treatment effect on the treated.[52] Prior to carrying out any matching, I estimate a treatment effect of about –1 percentage point: districts that were forced to switch to on-cycle elections increased salaries by 1 percentage point less than districts that kept their May elections. This difference is statistically significant at the 5% level. However, the treatment and control groups are not balanced on enrollment, income, the percentage of students who are African American, or pretreatment salary level. Using a Kolmogorov-Smirnov (K-S) test, which tests for differences in the overall distributions of a variable in two groups, I also reject that the distributions of percent Hispanic and percent Native American are the same in the treatment group as in the control group. I do, however, find that there is *no* difference between the rates of average teacher salary growth in treatment and control districts prior to the implementation of HB 1. Therefore, whereas treatment and control districts had statistically indistinguishable teacher salary growth rates prior to HB 1, after the election timing change was implemented, treatment districts increased salaries 1 percentage point less than control districts.

The lower half of panel 2 of table 5.5 presents the same balance statistics after I carry out the matching procedure described above. I successfully match 106 treatment districts to 88 unique control districts and achieve balance on all of the critical covariates. Specifically, using the matched subset of districts, for enrollment, income, student demographics, and pretreatment salary, I fail to reject the null hypothesis that the average treatment group values are equal to the average control group values. In addition, a K-S test fails to reject the null hypothesis for enrollment, income, district demographics, and pretreatment salary, demonstrating that the distributions within matched treatment and control districts on those variables are exchangeable. As before the matching

TABLE 5.5 **The Texas Test of the effect of on-cycle elections, matching**

1. All districts

	Mean, treatment	Mean, control	Difference in means	t-test p-value
% Salary growth, 2006–9	–0.196	0.775	–0.971	0.032
Number of districts	174	742		

	Difference in means	t-test p-value	K-S Statistic	K-S Bootstrap p-value
Ln(Enrollment)	–1.489	0.000	0.500	0.000
Ln(Median income)	–0.050	0.005	0.125	0.018
% Hispanic	–2.538	0.245	0.110	0.053
% Black	–4.303	0.000	0.268	0.000
% Native American	0.191	0.275	0.274	0.000
Ln(Pretreatment salary)	–0.029	0.000	0.200	0.000
Pretreatment growth	0.063	0.882	0.084	0.242

2. Matched districts

	Mean, treatment	Mean, control	Difference in means	t-test p-value
% Salary growth, 2006–9	–0.593	0.155	–0.748	0.060
Number of districts	106	88		

	Difference in means	t-test p-value	K-S Statistic	K-S Bootstrap p-value
Ln(Enrollment)	0.001	0.927	0.038	1.000
Ln(Median income)	0.000	0.971	0.057	0.990
% Hispanic	0.248	0.922	0.142	0.217
% Black	–0.423	0.629	0.075	0.875
% Native American	0.041	0.889	0.104	0.501
Ln(Pretreatment salary)	0.012	0.225	0.123	0.372
Pretreatment growth	–0.117	0.856	0.113	0.475

3. Matched districts, excluding type 3

	Mean, treatment	Mean, control	Difference in means	t-test p-value
% Salary growth, 2006–9	–1.324	–0.697	–0.627	0.049
Number of districts	65	54		

	Difference in means	t-test p-value	K-S Statistic	K-S Bootstrap p-value
Ln(Enrollment)	0.006	0.583	0.046	1.000
Ln(Median income)	0.001	0.846	0.077	0.983
% Hispanic	–1.089	0.737	0.200	0.126

(*continued*)

TABLE 5.5 *continued*

	Difference in means	*t*-test *p*-value	K-S Statistic	K-S Bootstrap *p*-value
% Black	–1.419	0.208	0.123	0.679
% Native American	0.249	0.555	0.092	0.871
Ln(Pretreatment salary)	0.004	0.458	0.108	0.821
Pretreatment growth	–0.399	0.233	0.123	0.675

Notes: All *t*-test *p*-values for the ATT are from a one-sided test. For all the balance statistics, the *t*-tests are two-sided.

procedure, I find no significant differences between the means and distributions of average teacher salary growth in treatment and control districts prior to HB 1.

Using this comparable set of 194 districts, I estimate a treatment effect of –0.75 percentage points, statistically significant at the 10% level (p = 0.06). On average, therefore, districts that were forced to switch to on-cycle school trustee elections increased their teachers' salaries by 0.75 percentage points *less* following HB 1 than a set of districts of the same size, income, urbanicity, and pretreatment salary that were allowed to keep their off-cycle elections in May. This result supports the hypothesis that the dominant interest group in school district elections exerts less influence in on-cycle elections than in off-cycle elections.

To ensure that the result in panel 2 is not driven by the inclusion of the small number of type 3 districts in the treatment group, I present in panel 3 the results from the same analysis but excluding type 3 districts. Recall that type 3 districts are those that have incorporated municipalities within their borders but that were nonetheless forced to switch to on-cycle elections because those municipalities hold elections in November of even-numbered years. If there is some unobserved property of districts whose municipalities hold on-cycle elections that makes them different from control districts whose municipalities hold off-cycle elections, then the two types of districts would not be exchangeable. However, when I exclude the type 3 districts from the analysis,[53] the effect of the switch to on-cycle school trustee elections decreases by a mere tenth of a percentage point: I still estimate a –0.63 percentage point effect of on-cycle election timing on average district teacher salary, significant at the 5% level.

The results from the matching analysis are consistent with the hypothesis that teachers are less influential in on-cycle elections. However, the matching only accounts for potential confounders that are observable. One might be concerned that there are unobservable characteristics of treatment districts that not only differ from those of control districts but that also determine why their teacher salaries increased at lower rates after 2006. For example, the residents of type 3 and type 4 districts might place lower priority on education spending than residents of type 1 and type 2 districts such that they responded to the economic downturn by granting lower salary raises to teachers. The estimates in table 5.5 do not account for treatment and control group differences in residents' preferences over spending on teacher salaries—measures of which do not exist—and therefore cannot rule out this possibility. Furthermore, certain characteristics of districts that influence whether or not they contain an incorporated municipality, such as the political influence of private developers or population density,[54] might also influence the way districts set teacher salary policy after 2006.

In order to account for potential differences between treatment and control districts such as district preferences and propensity to incorporate, I model within-district changes in average teacher salary from 2003–4 to 2009–10 using district fixed effects regression. This approach allows me to estimate the effect of the forced switch to on-cycle elections while partialing out the effects of any time-invariant district characteristics. The model is as follows:

$$\ln(salary_{it}) = \alpha_i + \delta_t + \beta(On\text{-}Cycle_{it}) + X_{it}\psi + \varepsilon_{it}$$

Subscript i denotes the school district, and t denotes the year. $On\text{-}Cycle_{it}$ is the primary independent variable of interest. It equals 1 for all treatment districts from 2007–8 to 2009–10 and 0 otherwise. The α_i are district fixed effects, and X_{it} is a matrix of district characteristics that vary year to year. The δ_t are year dummy variables, which control for annual statewide trends in logged average teacher salaries (in real terms). The regression coefficients are β and ψ, and ε_{it} is an error term. Because the errors are likely correlated within districts over time, I cluster the standard errors by school district.

The inclusion of district fixed effects allows me to partial out the effects of any unobservable district characteristics that do not vary over time, but there are several time-variant district characteristics that likely affect yearly changes in district teacher salary policies. To this end, I have collected data on a number of school district characteristics that I expect to influence both teacher salaries and whether a district fell into the treatment group or control group with the passage of HB 1. I assembled annual data on district enrollment using the NCES CCD files from 2003–4 to 2007–8 as well as TEA enrollment records for 2008–9 and 2009–10, since teacher salaries generally grow as districts increase in size. Teacher salaries also increase with district income, but data on median family income are only available at the school district level for years in which the decennial census is conducted. As a substitute, I use the annual TEA data on total assessed property value in each district to control for increases in district income over time. Because the dependent variable is average teacher salary, and more experienced teachers are paid higher salaries than less experienced teachers, I use TEA data on the average number of years of teacher experience in each district and year to control for seniority.[55] Lastly, since teachers who work in districts with more minority students tend to earn higher salaries,[56] I use the same sources to compile measures of the percentage of enrolled students who are African American, Hispanic, Asian or Pacific Islander, and Native American.

The results of the fixed effects regression are presented in table 5.6.[57] The first column presents a simple model that includes only *On-Cycle*, the district fixed effects, and the year dummy variables on the right-hand side. The result is similar in magnitude to that of the results in table 5.5: relative to annual changes in average teacher salary throughout Texas, districts in the treatment group paid teachers 0.9% *less* in base salary once they were forced to conduct on-cycle elections. The estimate of the coefficient on *On-Cycle* is statistically significant at the 5% level, lending support to the hypothesis.

In column (2), I add the full set of control variables, including logged enrollment, logged assessed property value, average teacher experience in the district, and the ethnic composition of the district. The result is striking: once treatment districts were forced to consolidate their elections with national elections in November of even-numbered years, the school trustees in those districts granted teachers significantly smaller salary increases than they had given in earlier years. Specifically, relative to annual trends in average salary throughout the state, treatment districts paid teachers 1.3% less after implementation of HB 1. Of the average teacher salary in the average district in 2007, 1.3% amounted to $560, a nonnegligible amount of money for an individual who makes $43,000 per year in base salary. Moreover, the effect of on-cycle election timing is statistically significant at the 1% level. This result provides strong support for the prediction that the switch to on-cycle election timing decreased the influence of teachers in the elections.

TABLE 5.6 **The Texas Test, district fixed effects regression**

	(1)	(2)	(3)	(4)	(5)	(6)
	Average teacher salary					*Gen. admin.*
On-cycle	−0.009**	−0.013***		−0.013***	−0.017***	−0.001
	(0.004)	(0.003)		(0.003)	(0.006)	(0.016)
On-cycle				−0.013	−0.036*	
* Union				(0.011)	(0.022)	
Ln(Enroll.)		0.034***	0.034***	0.034***	0.028*	−0.753***
		(0.009)	(0.009)	(0.009)	(0.015)	(0.048)
Ln(Property		0.022***	0.023***	0.023***	0.023**	0.12***
value)		(0.006)	(0.006)	(0.006)	(0.011)	(0.027)
Avg. years		0.013***	0.013***	0.013***	0.01***	−0.004*
experience		(0.001)	(0.001)	(0.001)	(0.002)	(0.002)
% Native		0.029	0.032	0.023	0.063	−0.702*
American		(0.074)	(0.074)	(0.075)	(0.274)	(0.417)
% Asian		0.19	0.181	0.182	0.114	0.86
		(0.118)	(0.119)	(0.118)	(0.173)	(0.677)
% Black		0.15**	0.15**	0.151**	0.212**	0.234
		(0.061)	(0.061)	(0.061)	(0.095)	(0.243)
% Hispanic		0.088***	0.089***	0.087***	0.161***	−0.258*
		(0.027)	(0.027)	(0.027)	(0.057)	(0.144)
2004	−0.02***	−0.02***	−0.02***	−0.02***	−0.019***	−0.007*
	(0.001)	(0.001)	(0.001)	(0.001)	(0.002)	(0.004)
2005	−0.039***	−0.042***	−0.042***	−0.042***	−0.041***	−0.007
	(0.001)	(0.001)	(0.001)	(0.001)	(0.002)	(0.006)
2006	0.004***	−0.002	−0.002	−0.002	−0.004	0.009
	(0.001)	(0.001)	(0.001)	(0.001)	(0.003)	(0.008)
2007	−0.005***	−0.012***	−0.014***	−0.012***	−0.014***	−0.038***
	(0.002)	(0.002)	(0.002)	(0.002)	(0.004)	(0.010)
2008	−0.017***	−0.027***	−0.027***	−0.027***	−0.029***	−0.097***
	(0.002)	(0.002)	(0.002)	(0.002)	(0.005)	(0.012)
2009	0.01***	−0.007**	−0.006**	−0.006**	−0.01*	
	(0.002)	(0.003)	(0.003)	(0.003)	(0.006)	
Treatment			0.0004			
* 2004			(0.003)			
Treatment			0.004			
* 2005			(0.003)			
Treatment			−0.001			
* 2006			(0.003)			
Treatment			−0.007**			
* 2007			(0.004)			
Treatment			−0.014***			
* 2008			(0.005)			
Treatment			−0.015***			
* 2009			(0.005)			
Observations	6418	6407	6407	6393	2509	5491
R-squared	0.88	0.91	0.91	0.91	0.93	0.96

Notes: Standard errors clustered by district in parentheses. Models include district fixed effects.
* significant at 10%; ** significant at 5%; *** significant at 1%

The other independent variables behave as expected. Enrollment is positively correlated with average district teacher salary: a 1% increase in enrollment is associated with a 0.03% increase in average teacher salary. Likewise, rising property values are associated with increases in average district teacher salaries, as expected. As the average number of years of teacher experience in a district increases, teacher salaries rise as well, an effect that is statistically significant at the 1% level. While the proportion of students who are Native American or Asian does not appear to affect average teacher salaries, increasing proportions of African American and Hispanic students are associated with higher average teacher salaries.

In the model presented in column (3), I investigate the timing of the effect of on-cycle elections on average teacher salaries by including interactions between the treatment district indicator and all of the year dummy variables. Notably, there was no significant difference between the annual increases in average teacher salaries in treatment and control districts for 2003–4 to 2006–7, prior to HB 1: the coefficients on the interaction terms for all pretreatment years are statistically insignificant. In 2007–8, however, while teacher salaries were lowered from 2006 levels (in real terms) in both treatment and control districts, the dip was significantly more pronounced in treatment districts. That trend continued in 2008–9, when the gap between treatment and control districts widened further. In 2009–10, the difference in growth between treatment and control districts slowed, and both increased average teacher salary by approximately 2%. The finding that there was a negative effect in the years between the announcement of the election timing change and the first on-cycle election suggests that sitting school board members became less responsive to teachers as a result of the switch.

The results presented in columns (1) to (3) of table 5.6 are robust to a variety of alterations in the district sample and model specification. When I limit the analysis to the set of 194 matched districts, I estimate an effect of –0.7%, significant at the 10% level. The results are robust to the exclusion of type 3 districts, the exclusion of districts that pay the state minimum salary schedule, as well as to the inclusion (as control districts) of districts that I was not able to classify as treatment or control. When I use first differences rather than fixed effects regression, the effect is still negative and statistically significant. Finally, a battery of tests suggests that the results are not driven by fluctuation in teacher seniority over time, nor are they caused by differential effects of property tax reduction in treatment and control districts.

Moreover, it does not appear that the negative effect of on-cycle election timing is a product of within-district variation in teacher salaries. When I model specific steps of the salary schedule for a subset of districts and years—thus comparing salaries for teachers with equal levels of education and experience—the negative impact of on-cycle election timing persists.[58] One might also worry that the negative effect on salaries could have been offset by increases in other, unmeasured components of teacher compensation, such as health insurance. However, my analysis of NCES expenditures data shows that the switch to on-cycle elections had no effect on districts' expenditures on instructional employees' fringe benefits.

On the whole, these results demonstrate that there is a strong empirical link between election timing and teacher salaries in Texas school districts. However, can we be sure that the link is related to the decreased influence of teachers in on-cycle school board elections? One way of addressing concern about the mechanism would be to measure teacher electoral influence directly, perhaps using the percentage of voters mobilized by teacher organizations as a fraction of total active voters. Given that measures of teacher mobilization capacity are not available, one proxy for teacher mobilization strength is the percentage of teachers in a district who are members of unions. If unionization rates capture teacher organizational capacity, then the negative effect of *On-Cycle* should be greater in more heavily unionized districts.

Even unionization, however, is hard to measure; there are no current, publicly available data on teacher union membership in all Texas school districts. The best available resource on teacher unionization in all districts is the Census of Governments from 1987—the most recent year that the census conducted its labor-management relations survey. Admittedly, this twenty-year-old measure is a crude proxy for unionization rates today. Still, since it is the only available source of information on all of the districts, I use it to test whether the effect of the switch to on-cycle elections was larger (more negative) in more heavily unionized districts.[59] I interact the *On-Cycle* indicator with the unionization rate, centered on its mean, to test whether the shift to on-cycle elections had a greater impact in districts with better-organized teachers.

The results are presented in column (4) of table 5.6. For districts with the mean level of teacher unionization in Texas in 1987, I estimate a statistically significant effect of on-cycle election timing of –1.3%. As expected, the coefficient on the interaction term shows that the effect of the switch to on-cycle elections was more pronounced for districts in which a greater proportion of teachers were unionized. Granted, the coefficient estimate on the interaction term is imprecise ($p = 0.106$), and given the measurement error in the unionization variable, I do not put much weight on this result.[60] However, when I run the same regression on a subset of districts for which I have more current estimates of the teacher unionization rate, I find the same pattern. Specifically, using the information on Texas public school teachers available in the 1999, 2003, and 2007 SASS datasets, I create rough estimates of the percentage of teachers in each district who are members of unions, and then I interact that measure with the indicator for on-cycle elections. The results are set out in column (5).[61] I find that the districts where more teachers are in unions are those where the switch to on-cycle elections had the largest impact, and the negative coefficient on the interaction term is significant at the 10% level. Together, these results suggest that the districts with better-organized teachers were disproportionately affected by the switch to on-cycle elections.

As one last check on whether the negative effect is driven by the decreased influence of teachers, I use the original model to test whether the switch to on-cycle elections led to decreased school district spending on an item that teachers do *not* have a vested interest in expanding: general district administration. The dependent variable in column (6) of table 5.6 is logged per pupil district expenditures on general administration, as reported by TEA actual financial reports.[62] Since teachers have little stake in increasing expenditures on general administration, we would not expect the switch to on-cycle elections to have an effect if it is indeed decreased teacher union influence that is at work. The result in column (6) is consistent with this expectation: the switch to on-cycle elections did not affect per pupil spending on general administration. This evidence supports the claim that the switch to on-cycle elections affected one of the main items teachers seek—teacher salaries—but did not decrease spending on items that teachers should care little about.

Taken together, these results provide strong support for the prediction that off-cycle election timing enhances the influence of organized interest groups in elections. For decades, school districts in Texas had been accustomed to holding trustee elections in May, separately from state and national elections. As a school trustee explained during the hearings on a predecessor of HB 1, these elections were truly "their" elections; typical turnout was less than 10% of registered voters. In 2006, when the Texas state legislature handed down a mandate for districts to combine their trustee elections with either city or county elections, at least 174 districts had no choice but to move their elections to November of even-numbered years, the same time as presidential and gubernatorial elections. This was, no doubt, a massive change for those districts. Incumbent school trustees could expect more than twice as many voters to participate in future elections. I find that as soon as the joint election requirement was made clear to district officials, school trustees in the districts forced to on-cycle elections responded by granting smaller pay increases to teachers.

At first glance, 1.3% seems a small figure, definitely statistically significant but questionable in its substantive importance. Yet this is almost certainly an underestimate of the effect of on-cycle election timing on the relative influence of teachers in elections. As I described above, the election timing provision of HB 1—which affected 20% of Texas school districts—only passed after multiple failed attempts by Republican state legislators to move *all* Texas school trustee elections to November of even-numbered years. As is the case for the vast majority of such bills in state legislatures across the country, most of those proposals were never considered in committee. The ones that *were* considered in committee were vigorously opposed by Texas school boards and teacher unions. The repeated failure of those bills most likely persuaded Republican legislators to water down the election timing provision so as to only affect a small number of districts, which the teacher unions did not openly oppose. It is possible, if not likely, that the teacher unions let the election timing provision pass because they anticipated that it would only change election timing in districts where it was least likely to make a difference to their influence. If so, then the estimates presented in table 5.6 are lower bounds on the effect of on-cycle election timing on teacher union electoral influence. Had the change affected the remaining 80% of Texas districts, the estimated effect would likely be larger.

But it is important not to make too little of the −1.3% effect I do estimate. To an individual teacher who makes $43,000 per year, the loss of $560 is a noticeable decrease. Moreover, current spending by Texas public school systems amounts to $41.7 billion every year, and over 46% of that is used to pay instructional salaries and wages.[63] If all districts in the state cut average teacher salary by 1.3%, the $19.3 billion spent on instructional salaries in Texas would decrease by over $250 million. In the context of Texas school district budgets, therefore, the consequences of forcing districts to switch from off-cycle to on-cycle school trustee elections are highly substantively significant.

Conclusion

The empirical analysis of this chapter is strikingly clear on the question of how election timing affects the political influence of teachers. In the Eight-State Test, I found that teachers are paid more in base salary in districts with off-cycle elections and that the salary premium decreases as one potentially opposing group—the elderly—makes up a larger percentage of the eligible voter base. The Minnesota Test made clear that it is largely the low voter turnout of off-cycle election timing that is behind the higher teacher compensation levels in school districts with off-cycle elections: the lower the turnout, the greater the salary premium that accrues to teachers. And if there was lingering concern about whether these effects of off-cycle election timing are causal, the Texas Test should have put those concerns to rest. For even when I looked at the changes that occurred within individual school districts as a result of an election timing policy intervention made at the state level, I found that school districts that were forced to shift to on-cycle election timing responded by granting their teachers smaller salary increases than the districts that were allowed to retain their off-cycle election schedules. Together, these tests leave little room for doubt that teachers are more influential in low-turnout, off-cycle school board elections than in on-cycle school board elections.

In light of the theory I developed in chapter 2, these findings are exactly what we should expect. Teachers have powerful incentives to be active in school board elections, since those elections determine who will set their salaries, benefits, and working conditions. Thus we should expect that the lowering of turnout that comes with a shift from on-cycle to off-cycle elections would dampen teacher turnout far less than for other voters. Teacher unions are also the best-organized and most active groups in school board elections, and any organized competition they face tends to be weak in comparison. Therefore, it makes perfect sense that the increased effectiveness of teacher unions' mobilization efforts in off-cycle elections would make the electorate more favorable to teacher unions' policy preferences. For both of these reasons, we should expect teachers to be more successful in securing favorable policies in school districts that hold off-cycle elections. The empirical results of this chapter are unambiguous on the matter: the dominant interest group in school board elections has greater success when elections are off-cycle and turnout is low.

CHAPTER SIX

"What Election?"

Timing, Turnout, and Policy in California Cities

In April of 1988, the city of San Juan Capistrano, California, held its regular municipal election at a time when no other offices were on the ballot. Voter turnout was only 22% of registered voters. The next day, when a reporter from the *Orange County Register* interviewed a city resident named Jim about the election, Jim's reply was, "What election?"[1]

There are many people like Jim throughout the country—people who, when elections are held off-cycle, are either unaware that an election is taking place or simply decide not to vote because there isn't a presidential or gubernatorial race on the ballot. And because there are so many people like him, decisions about whether to combine local elections with other elections have large consequences for voter turnout rates.

Moreover, the last chapter showed that school board elections in the United States are very much affected by this little-discussed institution. Because most school board elections are held separately from state and national elections, voter turnout in those elections is low—oftentimes staggeringly low. For those who believe that increasing voter participation is a desirable end in itself, turnout rates of 20% or lower are a sign of a poorly functioning democracy. Others are merely skeptical that 20% of eligible voters can adequately represent the interests of all eligible voters. In defense of off-cycle election timing, supporters usually contend that the few people who do turn out in such elections are more knowledgeable about the issues at stake in the school district. Implied by such statements—even if not explicitly stated—is that a smaller, more knowledgeable electorate leads to better policies than a larger, less knowledgeable voter base. Regardless of one's personal views about whether off-cycle election timing leads to better or worse outcomes, the empirical pattern I demonstrated in the last chapter is that different school board election schedules lead to *different* policy outcomes.

At this point, however, one might wonder whether election timing *only* has an impact for school districts. After all, the interest group scenario in school board elections is somewhat unusual. The group that stands out as having the highest stake in school board elections—teacher unions—happens to be one of the largest and best-funded interest groups in the country.[2] This was a major consideration in my decision to test the theory in the context of school board elections; teachers and other public school employees are highly motivated to participate—far more so than the members of any potentially competing groups. It is also relatively safe to assume that in general, teacher unions are the best-organized groups in school board elections given their size, their high rates of political activity, and the fact that school board candidates often cite them as the most influential group in their elections.[3] So does off-cycle election timing have an impact on the success of *other* interest groups in different electoral contexts? That question has yet to be answered.

Moreover, school districts are special in another important way: they are single-purpose governments, and that may have implications for the number and diversity of groups that are active in their elections—and possibly the extent to which any single group faces direct organized competition over its policy goals. In his book on special districts, for example, Christopher Berry argues that the set of groups with a vested interest in single-purpose government elections tends to be limited, since those governments only make decisions in one policy area. In contrast, he writes, "a general-purpose government must balance the demands of many competing groups and make trade-offs when deciding policy priorities."[4] Because of this difference, he continues, special district officials are more likely than general-purpose government officials to grant interest groups the particularistic benefits they seek.

How does this distinction between special- and general-purpose government affect the theory's predictions? That depends. For one thing, if the turnout gap between on-cycle and off-cycle elections is smaller for general-purpose governments than for special-purpose governments—a plausible hypothesis given that general-purpose governments might attract greater political interest overall—then the off-cycle election timing effect should be smaller as well. However, the literature provides strong evidence that the turnout gap for general-purpose government elections is often quite large.[5] And as I showed in chapter 3, even in the nineteenth century, a time when overall participation rates were higher, there were often large turnout gaps between off-cycle and on-cycle city elections. While it may be true that off-cycle election timing has a larger dampening effect on voter turnout in special districts than in general-purpose governments, it still has a dampening effect in the latter, and so there is still great potential for election timing changes to shape group political influence.

That aside, there is another reason why the type of government (special- or general-purpose) might matter for the size of the effect of election timing on interest groups' policy success. To see this, recall that in developing the theoretical framework, I first explained that a shift to off-cycle election timing enhances the electoral presence of all organized groups. For groups like teacher unions, which have more motivated members and greater organizational capacity than any directly competing groups, the theory predicts that such a shift should increase their success in securing the policies they favor. But for a group that faces more direct competition in the electoral process, the effect of off-cycle election timing should be smaller. And actually, if a group is *weaker* in organizational capacity and has members who are *less* motivated to participate than a directly competing group, it should have greater success in *on-cycle* elections. This component of the theory may well be relevant in making comparisons between special districts and general-purpose governments. If the interest groups active in general-purpose government elections face greater direct competition than groups active in special-purpose government elections, then election timing should matter less to groups' policy successes in cities, counties, and states than in school districts and other special districts.

Importantly, though, it may not always be the case that the level of direct competition a group faces increases with the scope of government. After all, different groups have different sorts of goals. Political parties arguably have a broader set of goals than interest groups, and even interest groups seek different types of policies, benefits, and favors from elected officials. Some interest groups seek policies that demand a larger piece of the government budget.[6] Others seek environmental protections or zoning laws. Still others have values-based policy goals. Businesses might seek tax breaks, which certainly affect government revenue, but which may or may not directly compete with other groups' demands for public spending. Given the multidimensionality of group goals, simply increasing the number of active groups does not necessarily mean those groups directly compete with one another.

Moreover, it may not even be true that moving from special-purpose to general-purpose government always increases the number of participating groups. Eric Oliver, for one, argues that small to mid-sized municipal governments (those servicing fewer than one hundred thousand people) usually feature relatively *few* organized groups, because the politics of such places tends to be managerial rather than ideological in nature (land use and economic development being the dominant issues), and because aggregating preferences is easier in smaller polities. If Oliver is right, then there may not actually be a wide variety of groups active in the elections of most general-purpose governments—and that, in turn, could mean that any groups that *are* active encounter little more direct competition than teacher unions in school board elections.

My point is simply that the predictions of the theory hinge less on how *many* groups are active in an election than on whether any given group faces direct competition over its electoral or policy goals. Even in a general-purpose government election, if a group is more motivated and better organized than groups that compete with it, then I would still expect it to have a significant advantage in off-cycle elections. The more motivated and better organized the competition, however, the smaller a group's off-cycle election timing advantage should be—and it might even fare better in on-cycle elections.

The goal of this chapter is to evaluate whether election timing has an effect on interest group influence outside of school board elections, which, depending on the nature of group competition in a given context, the theory predicts that it should. I already provided some preliminary evidence of this in chapter 4 when I showed that political elites often clash over the timing of city, county, and state elections. Anecdotal evidence abounds as well. In June 2010, for example, the city of Torrance, California, considered a ballot measure that would move regular municipal elections from June of even-numbered years, the same time as the statewide primary election, to the last Tuesday in April of even-numbered years, a day when no other races would be on the ballot. Those who resisted the change to stand-alone city elections made the following argument:

> Just six years ago, Torrance residents voted overwhelmingly to abandon the March stand-alone election and combine with the State of California primary election in June.... Measure A creates an extra, stand-alone, low voter turnout election.... A Yes vote on Measure A gives "local control" to incumbents, city hall politicians, and special interest groups.[7]

In Torrance, as in other places around the country, politicians and activists seem to think that changing the dates of elections will change turnout levels, the degree of interest group influence in elections, and quite possibly election outcomes. The challenge for this chapter is to determine whether there is substance to these claims—and to my theory as a general framework for understanding changes to election timing.

California Cities: A Test Case

US city governments provide an excellent opportunity to further evaluate the empirical relationships among electoral timing, voter turnout, election outcomes, and public policy, first and foremost because there is a great deal of variation in city election timing across the United States.[8] As I showed in chapter 1, many states require that city elections be held on a day separate from state and national elections, such as Alabama, Idaho, Indiana, and Iowa, whereas a few other states, like Kentucky and Oregon, require municipal elections to be held in November of even-numbered years. Still other states give their municipalities discretion as to when to hold their elections. As in the previous chapter, this last feature of city government is particularly useful for testing purposes, since it means that there are some states in which municipal election timing varies within the state. Thus a comparison of city governments with different election schedules need not resort to a comparison of cities in one state to cities in another.

Municipal governments are also a critical component of American government as a whole. They are the most numerous of all general-purpose governments in the United States, at a count of 19,522 according to the 2012 Census of Governments.[9] They spend almost $478 billion each year, which makes up about 18% of overall state and local government expenditures,[10] and they employ over 2.4 million people on a full-time basis.[11] Moreover, they provide several essential public services like public safety, sanitation and sewerage, and parks. Municipal governments are therefore not only a great test bed for the theory but are also important in their own right.

In this chapter, I focus on municipal governments in the state of California, primarily for practical reasons. First, because of the concerns about the endogeneity of election timing that I laid out in the last chapter, I want to limit my comparisons to cities within a state so as to hold constant state-level factors correlated with both election timing and my outcome measures. This is possible in California, because its cities vary in their election timing. Charter cities—which are cities that have their own constitutions and therefore greater authority over municipal policy— have had discretion to choose their own election schedules since the late nineteenth century. California's general law cities were required to hold their regular elections in April throughout most of the twentieth century, but that changed in 1981, when the state legislature gave them the option of consolidating their elections with other elections in the state. Specifi-cally, after 1981, city councils could pass ordinances to combine their elec-tions with one of three other types of elections: the statewide direct pri-mary election, the statewide general election, or school board elections, most of which were held in November of odd-numbered years. The one caveat was that cities that petitioned to consolidate municipal elections with either state primary, state general, or local school board elections had to get the approval of their county boards of supervisors. Most county boards raised no objections to city officials' requests to consolidate elec-tions, but the Los Angeles County Board of Supervisors did not allow any cities within its borders to consolidate municipal elections with statewide elections, arguing that balloting for such combined elections would be too complex.[12] As a result, all but five cities in Los Angeles County still held elections off-cycle as of 2008.

The second main reason for my decision to focus on California is data availability. In general, city elections in the United States are either ad-ministered by the city governments themselves or by their parent coun-ties, and few states offer any centralized repository for city election re-sults. In order to get information on city elections, one usually has to collect the information from individual cities and counties. In California, however, thanks to a joint project between California State University and the California secretary of state, data from municipal elections are readily available in electronic format. The California Elections Data Ar-chive (CEDA) provides information on local elections held in California between 1995 and 2008, including the dates of the elections, basic infor-mation on the candidates, votes cast for each candidate, the number of seats up for election, and indicators for incumbents and winners.

The CEDA is an excellent resource in that it compiles the local elec-tion results from all counties in California, but it depends on the report-ing of the county clerks' offices for its information. One shortcoming of the CEDA database is that it is missing city election information for many cities in Los Angeles County prior to 2004.[13] Even with this omission, however, this data source is far more comprehensive and detailed than any other resource in other states that have within-state variation in city election timing, and it allows me to shed light on a number of questions relevant to this investigation of municipal government election timing.

The dataset I created using the CEDA indicates that as of 2008, California had 314 cities that held elections concurrently with state and national general elections in November of even-numbered years. Twenty-six cities combined their elections with statewide primary elections in the spring, and the remaining 137 cities held elections off-cycle, either concurrently with off-cycle school board elections or on their own separate day in the spring.

To give a sense of how these cities are distributed across the state, figure 6.1 depicts the number of cities in each county, with the bars for each county shaded by the timing of the cities' elections.[14] The black bars show the number of cities that had regular municipal elections in November of even-numbered years, the white bars show the number of cities that had elections concurrent with statewide primary elections in the spring of even-numbered years, and the gray bars depict the number of cities with off-cycle elections. The most noticeable feature of the graph is that Los Angeles County is home to a large percentage of the state's cities and also contains eighty-two of the state's 137 cities with off-cycle election schedules. Orange County, which is the county home to the second largest number of municipalities in California, is uniform in its city election timing, although it supplies only 10% of the on-cycle cities in the state.[15] Importantly, though, cities with off-cycle elections were present in many counties throughout the state in 2008, from Shasta County to Santa Clara County and down to Ventura County.

Election Timing and Voter Turnout in California Cities

An important first step in evaluating the suitability of the theory for the context of California city elections is to examine whether voter turnout in those elections is, in fact, lower when they are held off-cycle. As was the case for school board elections, there is little reason to doubt that this would be the case. Several studies, and one that specifically examines a sample of cities in California, find that voter turnout is much lower in off-cycle city elections than in city elections held concur-

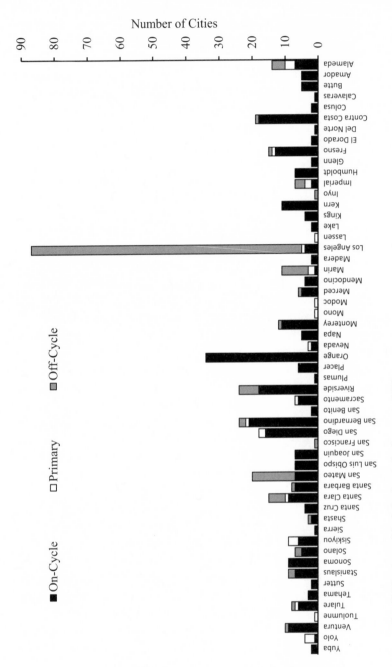

FIGURE 6.1. California municipal election timing by county, 2008.

rently with state and national elections.[16] Since most of these studies use cross-sectional data, it is possible that some unobservable trait of cities that choose off-cycle elections partially explains their low levels of turnout, but such factors are unlikely to explain away the turnout effect of off-cycle election timing. Moreover, many existing studies measure voter turnout only in terms of the voters who participate in local elections, and they still find large, significant effects.[17] That means the higher turnout of on-cycle elections is not eliminated by larger roll-off rates.

Even so, the CEDA database makes it easy to investigate how election concurrence affects voter turnout in the cities I will be using for the analysis. Therefore, using information from the CEDA, I have assembled a dataset of full-term city council elections held in California between 1999 and 2008.[18] I choose city council elections because every city has a city council, whereas only some cities have elected mayors. Because my interest is in explaining voter turnout, I include city primaries, runoffs, and special elections in addition to general elections.

Using the date of the election the CEDA provides, I create a series of binary indicator variables for concurrence with different types of elections. Specifically, I create indicators for concurrence with US presidential general elections, California gubernatorial elections, and presidential and gubernatorial primary elections in the spring of even-numbered years. In addition, I create an indicator for city council elections held concurrently with Governor Schwarzenegger's special statewide election in November 2005. Lastly, for 2008, since the statewide primary for US congressional and state legislative offices was not held at the same time as the presidential primary in February, I include an indicator for concurrence with the legislative primary in June 2008.[19]

While the CEDA reports the number of votes cast for each candidate in a city council race, it does not report either the total number of unique voters who cast ballots in the race or the total number of registered voters in that city. Moreover, in many city council races, multiple candidates are elected at large, which means that voters can vote for as many candidates as there are council seats up for election. I therefore estimate the number of unique individuals who participated in each local race in the following way: For cities with candidates both nominated and elected at large, I divide the total number of votes cast for all city council candidates in a given race by the total number of seats up for election. For cities that nominate candidates for particular seats or districts but elect them at large, I use the figure from the council race with the largest number of votes. I then merge in data on voter registration using files available through the California secretary of state's office to calculate turnout rates.[20] Because the registration files do not have the number of registered voters by district for cities that elect city councils by district, I focus my analysis on the cities that elect council members at large and then test whether the findings generalize to a subset of cities with districted elections.[21]

The dependent variable for the results presented in table 6.1 is therefore the estimated percentage of registered voters who cast ballots in city council elections between 1999 and 2008. In column (1), I use OLS to regress voter turnout in the city council race on the series of election concurrence variables, with off-cycle election timing as the omitted category. It does not appear that higher roll-off rates in elections concurrent with statewide primary or general elections erase any difference between participation in off-cycle and on-cycle city elections—in fact, the turnout gap in California city elections is quite large. While voter turnout in off-cycle elections averages 26% of registered voters, average turnout in city elections concurrent with primary elections ranges from 5 to 16 percentage points higher. Turnout in elections concurrent with gubernatorial and presidential elections averages 18 and 35 percentage points higher, respectively. The coefficients on all of the election concurrence indicators are highly statistically significant.

Most remarkable, however, is the R-squared from the regression in column (1). That statistic tells us that the concurrence of city council elections with state and national elections explains a full 67% of the variation in turnout in city council elections in California. Let me stress what this means. Here I have estimated a model of voter turnout that does not take into account the competitiveness of the elections, the characteristics of eligible voters in the cities, or any other features of the elections or the voters the literature suggests should be important predictors of turnout. It only includes indicators for election timing. And yet with those variables alone I can explain *two-thirds* of all the variation in city election turnout.

With that said, do the relationships between the election timing indicators and voter turnout hold up when I account for characteristics of the cities and races that are understood to affect voter participation rates? I investigate this in column (2). First, since voter turnout might increase when the city executive is up for election, I include an indicator for whether there is a mayoral race in the city on the same day as the council election. Also, voter turnout is often higher when elections are competitive, so I create a measure of the level of competition in a given city council race. I take the total number of candidates running for city council and divide it by the number of seats that are up for election. Since socioeconomic status is highly correlated with an individual's propensity to turn out, I use data from the 2000 Census to control for logged income per capita and the percentage of city residents who are African American, Hispanic, or Native American. In general, voter turnout is higher in smaller communities,[22] so I include logged city population as a predictor.[23] Lastly, I include an indicator for charter cities as well as a measure of the percentage of city residents who are sixty-five years old or over, with the expectation that they will be positively associated with turnout in city races.

The results in column (2) demonstrate that these variables have the expected relationship with voter turnout in city council elections. The presence of a mayoral candidate on the ballot increases turnout in city council races by about 1.7 percentage points, a small but statistically significant effect. More competitive council elections also attract higher turnout; a change from a totally uncompetitive race (with one candidate running per seat) to a race in which there are two candidates per seat corresponds to an increase in turnout of 2.9 percentage points. As expected, turnout is higher in cities with smaller populations, higher income per capita, smaller minority populations, and a larger percentage of elderly voters. There does not appear to be a difference in turnout between charter cities and general-law cities. But even with the inclusion of these variables, the coefficients on the election timing indicators are virtually unchanged. Moreover, the magnitude of the coefficients on the election timing variables dwarfs the size of the effect of having a mayor on the ballot, or even a competitive city council race.

In column (3), I add city fixed effects to the model to account for any unobserved city characteristics correlated with both election timing and voter turnout in city council races. Here, estimation of the coefficients on the election timing indicators is based on within-city changes in the concurrence of elections.[24] This dampens the coefficients on the indicators for concurrence with primary elections, which are positive but no longer statistically significant (most likely because only seven cities had both off-cycle elections and elections concurrent with primaries during this time period). Still, for council elections held concurrently with presidential elections, gubernatorial elections, and even Governor Schwarzenegger's special statewide election in 2005, the effects are strong and statistically significant. Within any given city, turnout in elections held at the same

TABLE 6.1 **Voter turnout and election timing in city council elections**

At-large elections	(1)	(2)	(3)	District elections	(4)	(5)
Presidential general	0.345***	0.353***	0.342***	General	0.35***	0.342***
	(0.008)	(0.007)	(0.023)		(0.024)	(0.024)
Presidential primary	0.158***	0.16***	0.05	Primary	0.168***	0.144***
	(0.025)	(0.020)	(0.043)		(0.023)	(0.029)
Gubernatorial general	0.179***	0.19***	0.182***			
	(0.008)	(0.007)	(0.023)			
Gubernatorial primary	0.086***	0.084***	0.001			
	(0.023)	(0.021)	(0.034)			
Other state primary	0.051**	0.057***	-0.029			
	(0.025)	(0.019)	(0.036)			
Special state	0.133***	0.143***	0.125***			
	(0.010)	(0.008)	(0.007)			
Mayoral race		0.017***	0.011			
		(0.007)	(0.010)			
Council competition		0.029***	0.032***			
		(0.003)	(0.003)			
Ln(Population)		-0.022***	-1.85***	Ln(Population)		-0.015**
		(0.003)	(0.053)			(0.007)

	(1)	(2)	(3)	(4)	(5)
Ln(Income)		0.049***			-0.067
		(0.008)			(0.041)
% Minority		-0.05***			-0.17**
		(0.019)			(0.080)
% 65 and over		0.168**			0.15
		(0.071)			(0.102)
Charter city		0.008			0.055***
		(0.007)			(0.017)
Constant	0.258***	-0.097		0.199***	1.081**
	(0.007)	(0.084)		(0.019)	(0.468)
Observations	1,916	1,904	1,904	34	34
R-squared	0.67	0.76	0.89	0.91	0.95

Notes: Robust standard errors clustered by city in parentheses. Dependent variable is the estimated percentage of registered voters who cast ballots in the city council election. Model in column (3) includes city fixed effects. Hypothesis tests on election concurrence variables are one-tailed. All other hypothesis tests are two-tailed.
* significant at 10%; ** significant at 5%; *** significant at 1%

time as a gubernatorial election averages 18 percentage points higher than in an off-cycle election. For presidential elections, the difference is a full 34 percentage points.

With the city fixed effects included, the effect of having a mayoral race on the ballot is no longer significant, but city council competitiveness still has a positive effect on turnout. Also, within cities, I find that as population increases, voter turnout rates tend to decrease. Again, however, these results pale in comparison to the effect of simply holding city elections at the same time as presidential or gubernatorial elections. The turnout effect of holding elections at the same time as presidential elections is *ten times* the size of the effect of increasing the competitiveness of a city council race from one candidate per seat to two candidates per seat.

Is the turnout gap between off-cycle and on-cycle elections different in cities where council members are elected by district? One reasonable hypothesis is that the turnout gap should be smaller, since districted cities tend to be large urban centers with perhaps more at stake politically— potentially inciting broader participation regardless of when elections are held. But larger cities and cities with higher proportions of minority residents also tend to have lower turnout rates, and so one could argue that their turnout gap between off-cycle and on-cycle elections should be bigger than for cities with at-large elections. The differences between at-large and districted cities are not the focus of this book, but because my argument hinges on the existence of an election-timing-induced turnout gap, and because I had to exclude cities with district elections from the models in columns (1) to (3), it is worth providing some confirmation that election timing also makes a difference to turnout in districted cities.

For districted cities, however, I cannot estimate turnout by simply adding up the votes cast in all of the council races in a given year and dividing that figure by the city's total registered voters, because council members' elections are staggered; only a fraction of the city's residents actually get to vote in a council race in a given election year. Therefore, for districted cities, I sum the total number of votes cast for council candidates in an election *cycle* (for example, November of 2002 and November of 2004) and then divide that figure by the average of the number of registered voters from those two years. Unfortunately, even this rough calculation was not possible for a large number of districted cities, because in many city cycles, the CEDA database lacks data on some of the city council district races. However, for a total of thirty-four two-year city cycles in twenty unique cities, the CEDA information was sufficient to estimate turnout in this way, and so I carry out the analysis using these thirty-four observations in columns (4) and (5) of table 6.1.

In column (4) I include just the timing indicators: a dummy for whether the city's elections in a given cycle were in November of even-numbered years (and thus concurrent with presidential and gubernatorial general elections) and a dummy for whether they were concurrent with state or national primary elections. (Again, off-cycle election timing is the excluded category.) The coefficient estimates are very similar to the coefficients in column (1): on average, compared to cities with off-cycle elections, turnout is 35 percentage points higher in cities with elections in November of even-numbered years and 17 percentage points higher in cities with elections during state and national primaries. Moreover, the two election timing variables alone explain over 90% of the variation in turnout across city cycles. The results change only slightly in column (5), where I include variables describing characteristics of the cities—including city population and percent minority. The results clearly demonstrate that the effect of election timing on turnout is just as large—if not larger—in cities with districted elections than in cities with at-large elections. In general, the effect of consolidating California city elections with state and national elections is a dramatic increase in voter turnout.

Election Timing and Interest Groups: Empirical Strategy

What difference does this make to election outcomes and policy? As I have argued from the outset, the predictions depend on which interest groups are active in a city, the types of policies they seek, and—if the groups compete with one another over policy—their relative levels of motivation and organizational capacity. And therein lies the main obstacle to testing the theory in the context of municipal elections: we simply do not know much about which interest groups participate in city elections, what policies they prioritize, whether they compete with one another, or which groups are organizationally strongest.

That is not to say there is no work on interest group politics in city government; there is, after all, a rich urban politics literature that argues, among other things, that business groups such as real estate developers and chambers of commerce, and sometimes neighborhood associations and citizen groups, play an important role in elections, coalition building, and policy making.[25] But that literature draws its conclusions almost exclusively from studies of the largest American cities, and as Eric Oliver notes, three-quarters of Americans live in governments that have fewer than one hundred thousand residents. When it comes to the role of interest groups in municipal elections, Oliver draws a very different conclusion from that of studies of large cities: he argues that in most small to mid-size municipal governments, there simply aren't many organizations active in politics.[26] Still, this is a theoretical argument and not one that has been empirically tested, and so the literature altogether leaves us with very little sense of which organized groups are active in city elections, what policy areas we might look at to evaluate how influential they are, whether they have direct organized competition, and how organizationally strong they are in comparison to any rival groups.

Of course, it is not as if this information is unknowable. One could imagine conducting a survey of city council candidates such as the one Terry Moe conducted in California school districts,[27] geared toward gathering candidates' knowledge of which interest groups are active in city council elections, what political activities they engage in during elections, what policies they prioritize, which candidates they favor, and who competes with whom. One could also gauge candidates' perspectives on the organizational strength of the various groups in city elections. With that basic information, I would be better equipped to make predictions about how city election timing affects the fortunes of various groups.

But those data don't yet exist. Out of necessity, then, the remaining empirical tests in this chapter are motivated by a theoretical argument, bolstered by related research, about how certain kinds of groups should be consistent and influential participants in city elections, and how the extent of their policy success should vary with election timing.

Specifically, I focus my analysis in this chapter on city employees—in many ways the obvious group to start with because, most simply, every city has them. In total, California local governments employ over 1.2 million people on a full-time basis.[28] Because they are employees of California local governments, they have a large stake in what local governments do, and by getting involved in elections, they are able to help influence the selection of their employers—the people who make many decisions that affect their daily lives.[29] Moreover, government employees in many places today are very well organized into public sector unions, which are some of the most politically active interest groups in the United States. In California specifically, two-thirds of all local government employees are members of unions, including 84% of firefighters, 83% of police officers, and 65% of nurses.[30]

As Terry Moe and I argue elsewhere, moreover, public sector unions are somewhat unusual in that they have two potential routes of influence over many of the policies they prioritize: they can push for higher wages, more generous benefits, and better working conditions through the collective bargaining process, *and* they can actively campaign to elect government officials who will be responsive to their demands.[31] It should therefore come as no surprise that public sector employees are more likely to vote than average citizens and that their unions are active in distributing literature, endorsing candidates, and mobilizing voters for elections that affect their members.[32] And there is strong evidence that their efforts have been quite successful over the years. The expansion of public sector unionism in the 1960s, 1970s, and 1980s led to significant increases in public sector wages and employment.[33] Moreover, cities with unionized employees today spend far more on workers' salaries and health benefits, and there is even evidence that public sector unionism is positively related to governments' pension obligations.[34]

What does this imply for how municipal employee unions are affected by changes in city election timing? For one thing, many of the policies municipal employees seek, such as better compensation, have concentrated benefits and distributed costs. Thus municipal employees should be far less likely to be affected by an overall decrease in voter turnout than voters who might oppose them on policy grounds. For this very reason, the organizational capacity of any opposition to municipal employees' interests is probably weaker than that of public sector unions.[35] It is therefore not much of a stretch to propose that in general, election outcomes and policy making should be more favorable to municipal employee unions when elections are held off-cycle. The literature even suggests some dependent variables that are worth investigating: unionized city employees' salaries and benefits should be more generous in cities that hold off-cycle elections, and city government expenditures on functions that depend on unionized workers should be higher as well.

I do not wish to imply that municipal employee unions are the *only* groups active in city elections, or that they are always the most important ones. Certainly, city elections might feature other organized groups, such as real estate developers and environmental groups. My claim is that in general, any direct competition to municipal employee unions in California city elections probably tends to be comparatively less motivated and less organized. To the extent that different groups of municipal employees in different places face different levels of direct competition, the theory predicts that the existence and magnitude of any election timing effect should vary accordingly.

This is yet another way in which municipal employee unions provide a useful context for testing the theory outside of school board elections; that is, certain groups of municipal employees probably face greater direct competition than others. This creates an opportunity to test whether the effect of city election timing varies with a group's relative organizational capacity, as the theory predicts it should. In the tests that follow, I take advantage of differences between municipal employee groups to examine whether the election timing effect is smaller for those that face greater opposition.

Salaries and Benefits: Firefighters and Police Officers

I begin by examining the effect of city election timing on the salaries and benefits of two groups of public employees found in the majority of municipal governments: fire protection employees and police protection employees. Both firefighters and police officers are highly unionized in California, and the literature suggests that both groups of public safety employees tend to be active in local politics.[36] Importantly, though, there are also differences between them, and those differences are useful for testing the theory.

Firefighter unions tend to be better organized and more politically active than unions of police officers, and they are widely viewed as more politically influential as well. As economist James L. Stern explains, "The International Association of Fire Fighters (IAFF) is a long-established, national union whose members are far more powerful politically at the local level than their numbers would warrant."[37] Firefighters also work long shifts together and have more down time between calls, a work setup that creates opportunities for coordinating political action. Police officers, by contrast, are not unified by a single, powerful, national organization,[38] and while they are "more numerous than firefighters, [they] do not seem to have proportionately more political influence."[39] This difference is shown in quantitative empirical work as well; multiple studies show that firefighters have been more successful than police in securing favorable policies through the political process and through collective bargaining.[40]

Police officers probably also face greater political competition than firefighters, purely because it is their job to enforce the law. Simply by carrying out their duties, police officers develop adversarial relationships with certain segments of the community. And this has been true for centuries. As Jon Teaford explains in his study of city government in the nineteenth century, the police regularly had to intervene in the important conflicts of that time. By enforcing the law (or not), they either upset labor or capital, teetotalers or saloonkeepers—and as a result, city police departments were constantly under attack by elected officials.[41] This probably has something to do with why police officers aren't as well organized as firefighters—firefighters were fairly insulated from politics early on[42]— but it also suggests that even today, police likely face greater competition in the political process than firefighters. It is entirely plausible that a community would have groups directly opposed to the interests of the police: neighborhood associations, church groups, and the like. But it is unlikely that most communities have groups that explicitly oppose firefighters. Because of this difference, I expect that firefighter unions face less direct electoral competition than police unions.

According to the theoretical framework, election timing should affect the political success of the two groups in different ways. For firefighters, my predictions are similar to those of teachers in school board elections; firefighter unions probably face little direct competition and also tend to be well organized, and so they should be more successful in cities with off-cycle elections than in cities with on-cycle elections. Police officers, on the other hand, are more likely than firefighters to face constituencies directly opposed to their policy interests, and they are also not as strong organizationally. Compared to firefighters, police officers' gains from off-cycle election timing (to the extent that there *are* gains) should be smaller.

To test these expectations, I turn to data on the compensation of firefighters and police officers in California cities: the Local Government Compensation Reports provided by the California State Controller's Office. For the first time in 2010, the state controller required all cities and counties to report compensation information for all of their employees in the 2009 calendar year. All but seven cities in the state filed compliant reports and are included in the database. For each city, the reports provide the department in which each employee works, his occupation classification, the minimum and maximum salary for employees within that classification, his total wages subject to Medicare in 2009,[43] the pension formula for the employee's classification, and the total amount the employer spent on his health, dental, and vision benefits.

Even within municipal fire departments and police departments in

California, there are many different types of employees, and I want to ensure that I compare employees of the same classification across different cities. First, I extracted from the database all fire department employees who had "fire fighter" or "firefighter" in their titles. From that list, I eliminated any individuals who were listed as trainees, on probation, apprentices, retired, part-time, or reserve. The remaining individuals were regular, full-time firefighters, although the classification names varied from city to city. I then took the median value of each of the compensation categories for each city. The resulting dataset summarizes median compensation levels for firefighters in a total of 177 California cities.[44]

In the analysis below, I focus on the minimum and maximum salaries for firefighters, the median firefighter Medicare wages, and the median amount the city employer spent on firefighter health, dental, and vision benefits. Average minimum salary for firefighters in these cities is $61,480, with a standard deviation of $13,843. The average maximum salary is $77,132, with a standard deviation of $17,168. Once overtime pay, payouts for unused paid time off, and bonuses are factored in, firefighter compensation looks quite a bit higher: the average across cities is $97,353. Of the 171 cities that reported health care expenditures for firefighters, the average amount across cities was $10,434, with a standard deviation of $4,471.

I performed a similar search for data on police officer compensation. For all police departments in the database, I extracted all rows that included "police officer" in the classification. I then eliminated any cases of individual police officers who were part-time workers, reserve officers, trainees, overfill, recruits, or temporary workers and took the median value for each compensation category in each city. This search gave me data on median police officer compensation in 273 California cities.[45] Across cities, the average minimum police officer salary was $60,747 and average maximum was $76,433. The average wages subject to Medicare were $88,603, and the average city expenditures on a police officer's health, dental, and vision benefits were $11,025.

My key independent variables are three election timing variables: *Off-Cycle*, *Primary*, and *On-Cycle*. The variable *Off-Cycle* is an indicator for whether the city's regularly held municipal elections are conducted at a time other than state and national primary and general elections as of 2008. *Primary* is a dummy variable that equals one if the city's regular municipal elections are held concurrently with state or national primary elections. *On-Cycle* indicates that the city's regular elections are held in

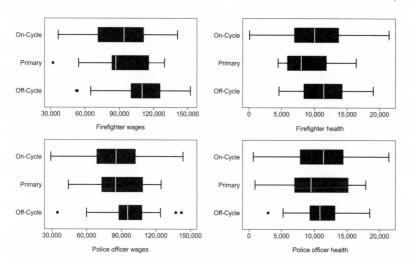

FIGURE 6.2. Firefighter and police officer compensation by city election timing.

November of even-numbered years, concurrent with state and national general elections.

As a starting point, some simple comparisons of compensation across cities with different election schedules provide preliminary evidence that firefighters and police officers tend to be better compensated in cities with off-cycle elections—but that the off-cycle premium is greater for firefighters. In figure 6.2, I present box plots of two of the compensation variables for both firefighters and police officers, broken down by cities' election schedules. The top left panel, which depicts firefighters' total wages subject to Medicare, shows that the interquartile range for cities with off-cycle elections is noticeably shifted to the right of the interquartile range for cities with elections concurrent with primaries. Moreover, for cities with elections concurrent with primaries, it is shifted to the right of the interquartile range for cities with on-cycle elections. The top right panel also shows that there is a slight difference in firefighters' health benefits between cities with off-cycle elections and the other cities (but not much of one between cities with on-cycle elections and cities with elections concurrent with primaries). For police, the general pattern in wages shown in the lower left panel is similar to that of firefighters, but it is more muted. And based on the bottom right panel, there is little difference in the distribution of police health expenditures across cities with different election schedules. Overall, figure 6.2 suggests that both police officers and firefighters benefit to some degree from off-cycle elections, but the advantage for firefighters appears to be greater.

This way of examining the data is revealing, but it is also simplistic. For one thing, compensation for firefighters and police officers is almost certainly correlated with the cost of living in a city, and more affluent cities might be more likely to hold off-cycle elections simply because they can afford the added expense. As a next step I use OLS to regress each of the dependent variables on two of the three election timing indicators— *Off-Cycle* and *Primary*—and logged income per capita in the city in 1999. (The omitted category is *On-Cycle.*) Since many of the cities that held on-cycle elections in 2008 had switched their election timing relatively recently, I also want to account for the possibility that a history of off-cycle or primary election timing affects employee compensation levels in the present period. Therefore, I include the variable *History of nonconcurrence*, which—for cities with on-cycle elections—equals the number of years since 1995 that a city held off-cycle or primary elections.[46]

I start with firefighter compensation, and table 6.2 presents the results. Controlling for income per capita and history of nonconcurrence, I find that firefighter compensation is, in fact, higher in California cities that hold off-cycle elections. In column (1), I estimate that on average, the minimum salary for a firefighter is approximately $5,731 higher in a city that holds elections on days other than state and national elections. The results in column (2) demonstrate that the maximum salary for firefighters averages $5,779 higher in cities that hold off-cycle elections than in cities that hold elections on the same day as presidential and gubernatorial elections. Moreover, once wages in addition to regular salary are included—overtime, bonuses, and time off paid out in cash—the premium in cities with off-cycle elections is over $13,000. The premium also carries over to cities' expenditures on firefighters' health care: the coefficient in column (4) is $1,051 and significant at the 10% level. Lastly, I find that for cities that hold on-cycle elections, a longer history of nonconcurrent election timing is significantly associated with greater total firefighter wages and greater expenditures on firefighter health care.

Unexpectedly, I find that there is no statistically significant difference between firefighter compensation in cities that hold elections concurrent with primaries and cities that hold on-cycle elections. As I showed in the previous section, voter turnout in city elections held concurrently with statewide primaries tends to be higher than turnout in fully off-cycle elections but lower than turnout in November of even-numbered years.

TABLE 6.2 **City election timing and firefighter compensation, basic model**

	Minimum salary (1)	Maximum salary (2)	Total wages (3)	Health benefits (4)
Off-cycle	5,731***	5,779***	13,295***	1,051*
	(2,009)	(2,429)	(3,894)	(700)
Primary	1,438	2,891	2,907	−709
	(3,408)	(5,415)	(5,983)	(1,088)
History of nonconcurrence	649	672	1,930***	480***
	(562)	(805)	(748)	(172)
Ln(Income per capita)	15,460***	18,926***	28,565***	1,847**
	(2,100)	(2,653)	(4,304)	(740)
Constant	−95,592***	−114,813***	−193,998***	−8,496
	(20,727)	(26,269)	(42,880)	(7,406)
Observations	177	177	177	171
R-squared	0.33	0.30	0.34	0.09

Notes: Robust standard errors in parentheses. Hypothesis tests on *Off-cycle*, *Primary*, and *History of nonconcurrence* are one-tailed; other tests are two-tailed.
* significant at 10%; ** significant at 5%; *** significant at 1%

Strictly speaking, I would expect responsiveness to interest groups in cities with elections concurrent with primaries to lie somewhere between that of off-cycle and on-cycle cities. One possible explanation for this null finding could be that like Minnesota school board elections, marginal decreases in turnout only matter for interest group influence when baseline turnout is low enough. Alternatively, there might be something different about the cities that choose the primary election date—something that is not captured in my model. It may be, however, that there are simply too few cases to estimate an effect. With only fourteen cities in this dataset that have elections concurrent with primaries, I don't place much weight on this result.

One might worry that there are other city characteristics correlated with both firefighter compensation and city election timing, and so in table 6.3, I add some other controls to the models. First, I add logged city population, because working as a firefighter might be more difficult in larger cities, and large cities are more likely to have the resources to sustain off-cycle election timing. In addition, perhaps cities with greater poverty tend to have greater incidence of fire as well as fewer resources with which to pay for off-cycle elections. This possibility might justify the inclusion of variables such as the percentage of people living in poverty, or the percentage of residents who are black or Hispanic. It is also possible that the work of a firefighter is more difficult in communities with large per-

TABLE 6.3 **City election timing and firefighter compensation, with controls**

	Minimum salary (1)	Maximum salary (2)	Total wages (3)	Health benefits (4)
Off-cycle	6,160***	5,225**	8,001**	1,926***
	(2,182)	(2,499)	(3,538)	(764)
Primary	–2,034	–3,304	–5,801	–494
	(3,600)	(4,760)	(5,809)	(1,232)
History of nonconcurrence	454	293	1,734***	379**
	(530)	(680)	(570)	(198)
Ln(Income per capita)	11,126***	14,496***	24,034***	–638
	(3,574)	(4,445)	(6,022)	(1,350)
Ln(Population)	2,247***	3,444***	6,811***	–156
	(703)	(870)	(1,352)	(274)
% in Poverty	–57,951***	–76,005***	–121,811***	–18,890***
	(18,579)	(23,283)	(34,975)	(6,689)
% African American	38,822***	69,839***	64,021***	7,690
	(12,821)	(23,494)	(21,553)	(5,922)
% Hispanic	–3,966	–1,398	3,969	–1,513
	(5,954)	(7,268)	(11,084)	(2,587)
% 65 and over	–54,340**	–42,313*	–111,997**	–608
	(21,951)	(25,425)	(45,243)	(7,720)
LA County	–2,789	–3,468	9,901**	–2,254***
	(2,255)	(2,907)	(4,348)	(851)
Charter city	1,588	3,729*	1,949	300
	(1,774)	(2,108)	(2,954)	(651)
Constant	–63,729	–96,610*	–198,419***	20,588
	(39,652)	(49,134)	(69,017)	(14,945)
Observations	177	177	177	171
R-squared	0.49	0.51	0.60	0.16

Notes: Robust standard errors in parentheses. Hypothesis tests on *Off-cycle*, *Primary*, and *History of nonconcurrence* are one-tailed; all other tests are two-tailed.
* significant at 10%; ** significant at 5%; *** significant at 1%

centages of elderly residents, which would be a reason to include the percentage of city residents over sixty-five. In case there is something special about firefighter compensation in Los Angeles County (which accounts for a large percentage of the off-cycle cases), I include a dummy equal to one for all cities in Los Angeles County. Finally, to account for the possibility that charter cities are able to use their greater flexibility to better compensate firefighters, I include an indicator for charter city status.[47]

As I show in table 6.3, the inclusion of these control variables changes the coefficients on the off-cycle election indicator only slightly. In column (1), I find that minimum firefighter salaries average $6,160 higher in cities that hold off-cycle elections than in cities that hold on-cycle elections. For maximum firefighter salary, shown in column (2), the effect is approximately $5,225. For total Medicare wages, presented in column (3), I find that firefighters earn an average of $8,000 more each year in cities that hold off-cycle elections. And in the final column, I estimate a positive and significant $1,926 effect of off-cycle election timing on firefighter health benefits expenditures. As before, I find no differences between the average firefighter salaries of cities that hold elections concurrent with primary rather than general statewide elections, but a longer history of nonconcurrent elections is associated with higher total wages and higher city contributions to firefighters' health benefits.

Many of the control variables behave as expected. In all but column (4), greater income per capita is associated with greater firefighter compensation. Firefighter salaries also tend to be higher in larger cities: a one standard deviation increase in city population is associated with approximately $2,800 more in minimum salary and $4,200 more in maximum salary. Cities that have higher percentages of African American residents tend to pay significantly higher firefighter salaries, but I find no significant relationship between firefighter compensation and the percentage of residents who are Hispanic.

However, some of the other variables have a relationship quite different from the expectations I set out above. For example, I find that a higher percentage of people living in poverty is associated with lower firefighter salaries, perhaps because it picks up a similar effect to that of income per capita. I also find a negative relationship between firefighter pay and the percentage of residents who are sixty-five or older, contrary to my expectation. I find that total firefighter wages tend to be higher, on average, in cities in Los Angeles County, but city spending on firefighter health insurance is significantly lower. And finally, the coefficients on the charter indicator are insignificant in three of the four models.

Most importantly, the results in table 6.3 make it clear that cities that hold their regular municipal elections at times other than state and national elections pay firefighters significantly higher salaries and spend more on their health, dental, and vision benefits than comparable cities that hold their elections on the same day as presidential and gubernatorial elections. However, my analysis in chapters 3 and 4 made it quite clear that if a group stands to benefit from a certain election schedule, it will fight to put that schedule in place—and fight to keep it that way. Could it be, then, that the estimates in table 6.3 capture both the effect of election timing *and* an effect of the strength of firefighter unions?

Actually, there is good reason to think that the risk of this is relatively low. Even if firefighter unions favor off-cycle elections, and even if they face little direct competition over their main policy priorities, there may well be other groups active in city elections, and some of those other groups might also care about when elections are held. Firefighters might prefer off-cycle city elections, but perhaps some other groups favor on-cycle elections, and how these varying group preferences should affect the actual choice of election timing is far from clear. It could be that the preferences of firefighters and other public employee groups are what matter most to city officials deciding on election scheduling, or—as for school board elections—that the groups that favor off-cycle election timing are more vocal and better organized than those that favor on-cycle elections. But it could also be that the preferences of groups that favor on-cycle elections matter just as much or more. And if firefighters' election timing preferences are *not* the dominant factor in city councils' decisions over election scheduling, then the strength of firefighter unions might not actually be highly correlated with the incidence of off-cycle election timing.

As a final robustness check, however, I carry out a test similar to the one I used in the Eight-State Test in the last chapter. That is, I control for the strength of firefighter unions using the percentage of fire protection employees in unions according to the 1987 Census of Governments. The inclusion of this variable forces me to drop twenty-six cases, but in results not shown, I still find strong, positive, significant effects of off-cycle election timing on firefighter compensation. For minimum salary, the effect is $5,563. For maximum salary, it is $4,372. As before, the effect is largest for firefighters' total salaries; firefighters earn an average of $6,072 more in cities that hold off-cycle elections than in cities that hold on-cycle elections. And finally, I find that spending on firefighters' health insurance is higher by an average of $1,883 in cities that hold off-cycle elections. Even controlling for a rough measure of firefighter union strength, therefore, I still find that firefighters are significantly better compensated—both in salary and health benefits—in cities that hold off-cycle elections.

This much is in line with the theory's predictions. But are the effects the same for police officers, or does off-cycle election timing confer a smaller advantage—or no advantage at all or even a disadvantage—on police officers? To test this, I model city police compensation using the full set of city characteristics I used in table 6.3. In addition, because police compensation likely depends on the level of risk involved in the job, I also introduce two new control variables: the log of the city's violent crime rate and the log of the city's property crime rate.[48]

TABLE 6.4 **City election timing and police officer compensation**

	Minimum salary (1)	Maximum salary (2)	Total wages (3)	Health benefits (4)
Off-cycle	2,221*	333	1,040	1,531**
	(1,554)	(2,048)	(2,716)	(659)
Primary	–1,831	–2,534	–3,715	–254
	(2,084)	(2,633)	(4,030)	(1,394)
History of nonconcurrence	467*	370	698	397***
	(313)	(414)	(549)	(104)
Ln(Population)	14,044***	19,067***	21,384***	630
	(2,245)	(2,962)	(4,040)	(1,232)
Ln(Income per capita)	3,492***	4,613***	6,016***	317
	(623)	(772)	(1,097)	(245)
% in Poverty	–56,296***	–56,187***	–88,209***	–4,246
	(13,459)	(16,386)	(21,871)	(5,280)
% African American	10,410	16,182	16,206	–2,738
	(9,830)	(13,706)	(15,663)	(2,998)
% Hispanic	13,385***	14,572***	16,121***	–2,284
	(4,044)	(4,745)	(6,064)	(1,824)
% 65 and over	–22,539*	–29,745*	–43,651*	–2,030
	(12,126)	(15,907)	(23,267)	(5,585)
LA County	–3,443*	–3,430	286	–2,119***
	(1,779)	(2,340)	(2,949)	(672)
Charter city	1,670	3,514**	5,029**	77
	(1,356)	(1,767)	(2,290)	(581)
Ln(Violent crime)	2,537**	1,871	2,938	1,411***
	(1,136)	(1,509)	(1,984)	(531)
Ln(Property crime)	3,176	5,264**	5,582*	–264
	(1,964)	(2,392)	(3,318)	(730)
Constant	–124,843***	–176,954***	–200,920***	1,833
	(26,598)	(33,420)	(47,939)	(13,403)
Observations	265	265	264	257
R-squared	0.56	0.57	0.57	0.14

Notes: Robust standard errors in parentheses. Hypothesis tests on *Off-cycle*, *Primary*, and *History of nonconcurrence* are one-tailed; all other tests are two-tailed.
* significant at 10%; ** significant at 5%; *** significant at 1%

The results of the police compensation models are presented in table 6.4. Overall, the evidence for a police union advantage in off-cycle city elections is weaker than the evidence for a firefighter union advantage. Column (1), on the one hand, shows that cities with off-cycle elections do pay higher minimum salaries to police officers than cities with on-cycle elections. However, the magnitude of the effect is a fraction of the size of the effect for firefighters in column (1) of table 6.3. Furthermore, in columns (2) and (3), in which I model maximum police officer salary and total police officer wages, I find that election timing makes no difference: the coefficients on both *Off-Cycle* and *Primary* are statistically indistinguishable from zero. In fact, the only compensation measure for which the off-cycle election timing effect is of approximately the same size for police officers and firefighters is health benefits, shown in column (4). On average, cities with off-cycle elections spent about $1,500 more per police officer on health benefits than cities with on-cycle elections.[49] As with firefighter compensation, I find no differences between cities with primary elections and cities with on-cycle elections.[50]

When I control for the percentage of police officers who were in unions as of 1987, my results are substantively the same.[51] I find that average minimum police salaries are $2,776 higher in cities with off-cycle elections than in cities with on-cycle elections, significant at the 5% level. I still find that election timing makes no difference to maximum police salary or total police wages. And in my model of police officer health benefits, I find that cities with off-cycle elections spent an average of $1,910 more per officer in 2008. Across the board, I still find no significant differences between primary cities and on-cycle cities.

Taken together, these findings provide strong evidence that election timing *can* and *does* have an effect in elections other than school board elections, and for groups other than teachers. Indeed, organizations of fire protection employees appear to reap significant advantage from the low turnout of off-cycle elections in cities, as the theory predicts they should. But my findings here also support the argument that the existence and magnitude of the election timing effect for a given group in a given context are conditional on the relative organizational capacity of any directly competing groups. Compared to firefighter unions, police unions are weaker organizationally and probably face greater political opposition. And in line with what we should expect on theoretical grounds, I find that the election timing advantage for police unions is more tenuous than the advantage for firefighters.

Election Timing and Spending in California Cities

In a final set of tests, I examine whether there is evidence that organizations of municipal employees, considered as a set of groups, tend to benefit from the lower turnout of elections held at times other than state and national general elections. The data for these tests come from the California Local Government Finance Almanac, a source of financial information on city governments sponsored by the League of California

Cities. I focus on a few key variables the Almanac provides, which are drawn from the California State Controller's Cities Annual Reports. First, as a way of linking this investigation of broader measures of city spending to the previous analysis, I use the reports on fire and police expenditures by city to obtain the amount of total spending on police and fire services in 2007–8. My expectation is that the election timing effects for these two outcome variables will mirror those of tables 6.3 and 6.4. Second, I then extend the scope of the analysis and examine cities' total expenditures on employee salaries and wages, retirement, and other employee benefits for *all* employees in 2007–8. If, as a set of groups, municipal employee unions generally tend to benefit from elections held separately from state and national elections, then I would expect overall spending on employee compensation to be higher in cities that have nonconcurrent elections. If so, then one might wonder whether the extra spending results in lower spending in other areas—or whether it results in bigger budgets overall. As a final step I look at the effects of election timing on total city operating expenditures, as well as the percentage of city operating expenditures dedicated to employee compensation.

In column (1) of table 6.5, I examine cities' expenditures on fire protection to test whether cities with off-cycle elections or elections concurrent with primaries dedicate more funds to the provision of fire protection services.[52] The dependent variable is the natural log of total fire protection service expenditures per capita in 2007, and I include the same control variables as in table 6.3 in an attempt to account for variation in demand for firefighting services across cities. I estimate that cities with off-cycle elections spend approximately 21% more on fire protection services per capita, an effect that is significant at the 5% level. This finding bolsters those from tables 6.2 and 6.3, suggesting that cities with off-cycle elections make policy that is more responsive to firefighter unions. Once again, however, there is no evidence that cities with elections concurrent with primaries are more responsive to firefighters than cities with on-cycle elections.

When I run the same regression using logged per capita expenditures on police protection in the city as the dependent variable, as I do in column (2), I find no significant differences between cities with off-cycle elections, on-cycle elections, and primary elections.[53] I do find that a longer history of election nonconcurrence is positively associated with greater spending on municipal police departments, but the coefficients on *Off-Cycle* and *Primary* are statistically insignificant. Therefore, while

TABLE 6.5 **Election timing and city finance**

	Exp. on fire protection (1)	Exp. on police protection (2)	Exp. on salaries (3)	Exp. on benefits (4)	Exp. on retirement (5)	Total operating exp. (6)	% Comp. (7)
Off-cycle	0.191**	0.047	0.282***	0.239**	0.334**	0.137**	0.047**
	(0.084)	(0.069)	(0.095)	(0.112)	(0.166)	(0.082)	(0.022)
Primary	-0.041	0.118	0.283***	0.303**	0.349**	0.145*	0.045*
	(0.158)	(0.105)	(0.103)	(0.143)	(0.190)	(0.088)	(0.027)
History of nonconc.	0.013	0.017*	-0.004	-0.007	-0.02	0.006	-0.002
	(0.013)	(0.012)	(0.017)	(0.023)	(0.026)	(0.014)	(0.005)
Ln(Income per cap.)	0.882***	0.124	0.251*	0.158	0.062	0.271***	-0.01
	(0.132)	(0.112)	(0.130)	(0.166)	(0.306)	(0.099)	(0.028)
% Poverty	0.819	-1.071	-0.089	0.088	-0.885	0.542	-0.206
	(0.810)	(0.859)	(0.759)	(0.915)	(1.283)	(0.604)	(0.159)
Ln(Pop.)	0.083*	-0.07*	-0.055	-0.091*	0.009	-0.124***	0.03***
	(0.049)	(0.040)	(0.039)	(0.045)	(0.055)	(0.032)	(0.007)
% Black	-0.048	0.422	0.1	0.135	0.812	0.594	-0.21*
	(0.637)	(0.622)	(0.517)	(0.610)	(0.740)	(0.418)	(0.117)
% Hispanic	-0.197	0.054	-0.144	-0.157	-0.418	-0.012	-0.07
	(0.261)	(0.238)	(0.225)	(0.303)	(0.365)	(0.196)	(0.050)
% 65 and over	1.017	-0.132	-0.025	0.278	0.656	0.334	-0.075
	(0.840)	(0.779)	(1.151)	(1.529)	(1.376)	(0.896)	(0.170)
LA County	0.128	-0.088	-0.282**	-0.251*	-0.213	-0.114	-0.068***
	(0.120)	(0.091)	(0.117)	(0.135)	(0.172)	(0.100)	(0.023)
Charter city	0.075	0.341***	0.536***	0.6***	0.607***	0.462***	0.024
	(0.116)	(0.082)	(0.089)	(0.106)	(0.124)	(0.075)	(0.019)
Constant	-5.065***	5.035***	3.696***	3.519**	4.33	5.247***	0.325
	(1.437)	(1.254)	(1.396)	(1.778)	(3.208)	(1.096)	(0.313)
Obs.	293	461	462	454	419	462	462
R-squared	0.37	0.12	0.18	0.12	0.14	0.21	0.11

Notes: Robust standard errors in parentheses. Hypothesis tests on *Off-cycle*, *Primary*, and *History of nonconcurrence* are one-tailed; all other tests are two-tailed.
*significant at 10%; ** significant at 5%; *** significant at 1%

cities with off-cycle elections do spend more on fire protection services overall, the same is not true of police protection services.

I next explore whether overall expenditures on employee compensation are greater in cities with off-cycle or primary elections. In column (3), I regress logged per capita expenditures on municipal employee salaries in 2007 on the same set of covariates as in columns (1) and (2). Consistent with the claim that municipal employee unions *in general* benefit from off-cycle election timing, I find that cities that hold off-cycle elections spent approximately 33% more on employee salaries that year, controlling for city income, size, demographics, and charter city status. Moreover, the coefficient on the indicator for primary elections is essentially equivalent, indicating that cities that consolidate elections with primaries spend over 30% more on employee salaries relative to cities with on-cycle elections. Both of these effects are statistically significant at the 1% level.

The same pattern holds for employee benefits. In column (4), I regress the city government's logged per capita expenditures on employee benefits on the same set of variables. On average, cities' expenditures on employee benefits are close to 30% higher in cities with off-cycle elections and elections concurrent with primaries, relative to the benefits expenditures in cities with on-cycle elections. Moreover, in column (5), I examine the amount that each city spent on employee retirement benefits over a period of three years, and I find a similar pattern. There, I regress logged per capita retirement expenditures on the election timing indicators and the control variables. I find that between 2005 and 2007, cities with elections at times other than state and national general elections spent over 40% more per capita on their employees' retirement benefits than cities that hold on-cycle elections. These tests demonstrate a consistent pattern of increased spending on employee compensation in cities with elections held at times other than state and national general elections, suggesting that as a set of groups, municipal employee unions tend to benefit from electoral contexts with low voter turnout.

Do these findings have implications for city spending in the aggregate? I investigate this in columns (6) and (7) of table 6.5. In column (6), the dependent variable is the city's logged total operating expenditures per capita in 2007–8. On average, cities with off-cycle and primary elections spend about 15% more per capita in total operating expenditures than cities that hold on-cycle elections. In column (7), I test whether cities with nonconcurrent elections spend a larger fraction of their budgets on employee compensation.[54] The dependent variable is the fraction of operat-

ing expenditures in 2007 that went to paying city employee salaries, benefits, and retirement costs. The coefficients on both the off-cycle election
indicator and the primary election indicator are positive and statistically
significant; on average, these cities spend about 5% more of their total operating budgets on employee compensation than cities with on-cycle elections. In sum, the greater spending on employee compensation in cities
with nonconcurrent elections results in larger budgets overall *and* a larger
percentage of spending dedicated to municipal employee compensation.

Conclusion

Stepping back, my analyses in this chapter have accomplished a number
of objectives and paint a clear picture of the difference election timing
can make to interest groups' success in California cities. The first analysis
demonstrated that whether or not there is a state or national race on the
ballot explains a full two-thirds of the variation in voter turnout in city
council elections. Moreover, the magnitude of the election timing effect
on turnout dwarfs the effects of other factors that are widely recognized
to be important predictors of turnout, such as election competitiveness
and demographic characteristics of the electorate. In showing this, I un-
derscore a pattern that several other scholars have already shown—but
one that remains underappreciated. As Zoltan Hajnal writes, "A healthy
portion of the differences in turnout among the nation's municipalities
can be explained by one simple factor—the timing of the local election."[55]

What is novel in this chapter is the finding that election timing matters
for things other than voter turnout—and not just in school board elections. Not only do *fewer* voters participate in off-cycle elections but also
different voters. It makes perfect sense: those who stand to benefit most
from an election will turn out regardless of when it is held. For interest
groups, off-cycle election timing provides two big advantages. Their members—who care deeply about the policies city government makes—will
be reliable voters in the city election and therefore make up a greater
proportion of voters when turnout is low, but in addition, their efforts to
mobilize supportive voters go further in a city election in which turnout is
20% rather than 60%.

The second half of the empirical analysis of this chapter tested the theory's predictions by looking at the effects of election timing on the influence of a type of interest group that is known to be active in city elections

and to have a vested interest in city election outcomes: municipal employee unions. I have found that cities with off-cycle elections spend more per capita on employee salaries, retirement costs, and health benefits. Not only are city operating expenditures greater overall in cities with non-concurrent elections, but also a greater percentage of those operating expenditures goes to employee compensation in cities with either off-cycle elections or elections concurrent with primaries. Thus it appears that municipal employee unions, examined as a set of groups, are more successful in elections held on days other than state and national elections.

But election timing should not have the same effect for all groups in all contexts; the effect of election timing on a given group's fortunes should depend on how strong that group is relative to its direct political competition. This, too, is a prediction I have put to the test in this chapter, and the evidence is supportive. Specifically, I have found that firefighters—an organizationally strong group with little to no direct competition—unambiguously fare better in off-cycle elections than in on-cycle elections. The advantage that accrues to police officers in off-cycle elections is weaker, which is precisely what we should expect given that police unions are less well organized and are more likely to face political opposition than firefighter unions. By comparing these two groups of employees, I not only show that municipal employee unions benefit from off-cycle elections, but also that the presence and size of the election timing effect varies in the way the theory predicts it should.

This chapter by no means answers all questions about how election timing affects general-purpose government; it doesn't even answer all questions about how election timing shapes interest group influence in California cities. To build on the findings of this chapter in the future, we will need a great deal more information on which groups are active in different elections, what they do in those elections, which groups compete with one another, and which groups are organizationally strongest and most influential overall. For now, though, I have shown that off-cycle election timing dramatically suppresses turnout in city elections, and that the lower turnout of off-cycle election timing creates distinct advantages for the organized groups that are best equipped to take advantage of it.

CHAPTER SEVEN

Implications for Democracy, Representation, and Institutional Stability

In the United States today, it is largely taken for granted that elections occur frequently, openly, and relatively free of corruption. And yet the international context regularly reminds us that a well-functioning electoral process is a critical part of a well-functioning democracy. Elections, after all, are the primary channel by which citizens exert control over their government. In the comparative politics literature, the voter turnout rate is sometimes even interpreted as a barometer of democratic health. As Seymour Martin Lipset once wrote, democracy is "a political system which supplies regular constitutional opportunities for changing the governing officials, and a social mechanism which permits *the largest possible part of the population* to influence major decisions by choosing among contenders for political office" (emphasis added).[1]

How, then, should we think about elections in which only 10 to 20% of the eligible population participates? How should we evaluate an electoral institution that drastically reduces the size of the electorate, oftentimes cutting the voter turnout rate to a half or a third of what it otherwise would be? Put simply, is off-cycle election timing bad for democracy?

For those who believe that more political participation by a larger number of eligible individuals is invariably better than less political participation, the answer is clearly yes. And among political scientists who have noted the negative impact of off-cycle election timing on voter turnout, the general sentiment seems to be that election consolidation would be a step in the right direction. Arend Lijphart, for example, explains that while there may be downsides to holding what he calls "second-order elections" concurrently with "first-order elections," doing so would no doubt increase voter turnout levels in the former, and he clearly sees that as desirable.[2] Likewise, Zoltan Hajnal stresses that off-cycle election timing is a major—indeed *the* major—contributor to low voter turnout in local elections in the United States and implies that combining more elections on a single day would be an improvement.[3]

But others suggest that having *informed* voters is just as important as having high voter turnout—perhaps more important. And it does seem to be true that smaller electorates are better informed about the issues at stake than larger electorates.[4] Thus one can reasonably argue that the separation of elections yields higher *quality* participation, even if that quality comes at the expense of the *quantity*. As Eric Oliver puts it:

> These voters [those who vote in local elections] tend to exemplify all that we expect in a classical notion of the ideal democratic citizen: they are politically engaged, knowledgeable, and have definitive preferences about local policies. If all citizens voted in local elections, it is unclear whether higher turnout would improve the communication of their wishes, because so many citizens are too ignorant about local affairs to have clear opinions on public matters.[5]

This is probably the most common argument made in support of off-cycle election timing: low turnout is a reasonable price to pay for a more informed electorate.

However, some political scientists don't think voters really need to be particularly well informed in order to make decisions at the polls that reflect their "true" policy preferences, because they can rely on heuristics.[6] Moreover, the level of information a typical eligible voter has about any given election might actually *depend* on when that election is held. Consider the incentives of an organized group with a vested interest in a local election. If that election is held during a presidential race, the group will probably anticipate high voter turnout and distribute information widely in the hope of persuading voters to support their candidates. If the election is held off-cycle, however, the group's incentives will likely be different: Why bother to inform voters who are going to stay away from the polls anyway? And so while it may be true that the average voter is more informed in an off-cycle election than in an on-cycle election, it is also possible that the overall informational environment is richer during on-cycle elections.

My goal is not to argue in favor of off-cycle or on-cycle election tim-ing—or on the merits of high voter turnout versus more informed elec-torates. I merely wish to point out that there is this participatory trade-off involved in setting election schedules. To be sure, some might object to my insistence that such a trade-off exists, wondering what ever happened to the avowed Progressive dream of increased opportunities to vote, greater openness of the electoral process, and voters who understand the per-tinent policy issues. In response, I would say that perhaps those goals are achievable—perhaps they *have* been achieved—but we should ex-pect them to come at the expense of voter turnout. Most Americans have little time for politics, simply because they are kept busy by the daily re-sponsibilities of work, friends, and family. It is unrealistic to expect large percentages of Americans to come to the polls multiple times each year knowing details about the candidates and issues at stake. Therefore, the trade-off for participatory democracy is this: One can either bundle many elections together on the same day and rely on top-of-the-ticket races to attract high voter turnout in other races, which means that many voters who cast ballots in those other races do not know very much about them, or one can separate different types of elections on different days such that only those people who have reason to turn out for the different races do so, with the consequence being lower voter turnout.

I don't take a position on which of these scenarios is preferable, but this book does make it clear that the low turnout of off-cycle election timing not only changes participation rates but also changes the compo-sition of the electorate and produces different outcomes than on-cycle election timing. Based on the theoretical framework I developed in chap-ter 2, this is as we should expect. Those who have a large stake in an elec-tion are more likely to weather an overall decrease in voter turnout than those who have less at stake, and because many "stakeholders" are mem-bers of organized groups, off-cycle election timing works to increase the presence of organized groups at the polls. Organized groups also actively mobilize voters to try to tip elections in their favor, and as voter turnout decreases, those mobilized voters have a greater impact on election out-comes. In both of these ways, off-cycle election timing enhances the elec-toral influence of organized groups. Depending on the nature of interest group competition in a given context, the greater influence of organized groups in off-cycle elections should result in predictable and observable differences in election outcomes and public policy.

The empirical evidence presented in this book strongly supports this argument. Chapter 3 revealed that even in the nineteenth century, voter turnout in city elections was lower when those elections were held off-cycle rather than concurrently with state and national elections. Moreover, the organized groups that competed for local office at that time—political parties—fought vigorously over the timing of city elections, crafting the schedule to their advantage (and to the disadvantage of their rivals) whenever they had requisite support in the state legislature. The same factors that explain the political parties' preferences over local election scheduling in the nineteenth century also explain why the Progressive Era municipal reformers promoted off-cycle local elections, which they ultimately locked in to new state constitutions, new city charters, and newly required general legislation.

The timing of local elections appears to have changed very little since then, but not because American citizens like things the way they are, and not for lack of effort by state legislators. As I showed in chapter 4, large majorities of American citizens are concerned about the low turnout of off-cycle elections and would prefer to have more elections held on the same day. Moreover, state legislatures regularly consider proposals to consolidate elections. But the vast majority of those proposals fail. The ones that do pass tend to be watered down bills that make election consolidation discretionary for governments, that consolidate elections on days other than national Election Day, or that affect the election dates of a small set of places. The reason, as I show using school board election timing bills, is that the interest groups that benefit from off-cycle election timing pressure state legislators to maintain it. And state legislators have good reason to respond to the preferences of groups—rather than the preferences of average voters—in taking positions on election timing. Interest groups are paying close attention; voters are not. The partisan patterns in state legislators' election timing positions I discovered in chapter 4 would be hard to explain any other way.

Chapters 5 and 6 then focused on estimating the causal effect of election timing on the policy success of organized interest groups in two different contexts: school board elections and city elections. In both chapters, the evidence showed that election timing has effects in line with the theory's predictions. In chapter 5, I found that the dominant group in school board elections—teacher unions—is significantly more successful in securing the policies it favors from school boards elected off-cycle than from school boards elected on-cycle. In chapter 6, I found that the same is true for firefighters in city elections—a group that, like teachers in

school board elections, is highly organized and faces little direct competition over its preferred policies. By contrast, police officer unions, which
tend to be less well organized and face greater competition than firefighters, reap a smaller advantage from the low-turnout environment of off-
cycle city elections. This last finding supports the theory as well, because
the extent of an interest group's advantage in off-cycle elections should
be a function of its organizational capacity relative to the organizational
capacity of competing groups.

Future Directions

All of this, however, is just the tip of the iceberg. Clearly, the bundling and
unbundling of different types of elections has important consequences for
voter turnout, the composition of the electorate, and election outcomes
and public policy. My finding that the timing of elections can have de-
tectable effects on outcomes that are of central concern in a democracy
should push students of politics to study election timing further.

For starters, in future work, researchers should investigate how the
timing of elections matters in contexts other than school board elections
and municipal elections. Does the composition of the electorate in state
legislative races and gubernatorial races depend on whether a president is
on the ballot at the same time? Do interest groups have greater influence
in midterm congressional elections than in presidential years, and do they
hold less sway in midterm House elections when there is a Senate race on
the ballot at the same time? Does it matter when special congressional
elections are held? How does the timing of ballot measure elections affect their outcomes? These are just a few possible contexts in which election timing may matter, with potentially profound consequences for politics and policy.

Future research should examine how election concurrence affects the
fortunes of organized groups other than the ones I have explored here,
both in the past and present. In this book, I have focused on how election
timing affected political parties vying for control of local government in
the nineteenth century as well as how the unions of teachers, police officers, and firefighters fare in off-cycle versus on-cycle elections today. Yet
even in school board elections and municipal elections, there are likely
other engaged and active groups, and it would be worth investigating
whether the theoretical framework presented in chapter 2 is helpful for

predicting how their success hinges on election concurrence. Do the fortunes of chambers of commerce, environmental groups, and developers depend on the timing of elections? If so, how?

That brings me to one important question this book leaves unanswered: Are the effects I estimated in chapters 5 and 6 driven by what I have referred to as the individual effect or the group effect? As I argued in the case of teacher unions and municipal employee unions generally, I suspect that *both* are at work in school board elections and municipal elections and that they tend to push policy in the same direction. However, in the future, researchers should devise tests that isolate these different effects. It need not be the case that these forces work in the same direction, and it would be interesting to see an evaluation of cases in which a group tends to lose electoral influence through one channel and gain influence through the other.

I should note, moreover, that while my focus in this book is on the United States, there is nothing US-specific about the arguments I have made. The United States is an interesting case because it has so many elections that are held at times other than regular national elections. However, other countries like Mexico and Switzerland have this feature as well, and scholars like Lijphart have noted that subnational election turnout in many countries falls below turnout in national elections.[7] This is another research avenue worth pursuing: How does election timing affect the composition of the electorate outside the United States? Does the theoretical framework I have presented here help to explain the effect of election timing elsewhere?

Even within the United States, this work could be extended in a number of potentially promising directions. For example, I have argued that the effect of election timing on election outcomes and public policy works primarily through its effects on voter turnout. This raises the question, however, of whether other electoral rules, events, or circumstances that lower voter turnout should be expected to have similar effects on the composition of the electorate and subsequent outcomes. In short, I believe the answer is yes, but election concurrence is somewhat special in that it reduces voter turnout by such a large amount. This sets it apart from motor-voter laws, voter ID laws, election day registration, and other rules that do affect voter turnout but only by a few percentage points.[8] If the effect of these electoral rules on turnout is small, the consequences for the composition of the electorate, election outcomes, and policy might be small as well, and perhaps more difficult to detect.

Another interesting question is whether the election timing effect is conditional on the presence of other electoral rules. Elections at different levels of government, in different parts of the country, and at different periods in time vary in how candidates are nominated, whether party labels appear on the ballot, and whether elections are at large or by district. The degree to which election timing aids interest groups in securing favorable policies might depend on some of these factors. For example, does off-cycle election timing have the same effect in partisan elections as it does in elections where no party labels appear on the ballot? One hypothesis is that political party activity might attenuate the interest group advantage in off-cycle elections. Turnout in partisan elections is higher than in nonpartisan elections,[9] in part because party labels provide informative cues to voters who might otherwise not feel sufficiently informed to vote.[10] If party labels mitigate the degree to which off-cycle election timing lowers turnout, the effect of off-cycle election timing should be smaller in partisan elections. But there is another interesting question, the answer to which is not obvious: If a different set of voters turns out in off-cycle elections than in on-cycle elections, are those voters more or less responsive to or dependent on the presence of the party cue? This, too, would make for an interesting project in the future.

Election Timing and Representation

At the bottom of all of this, of course, is a concern about representation. It is one thing to argue that off-cycle election timing and low voter turnout change the composition of the electorate and that interest groups have greater presence as a result. But does that mean that off-cycle electorates are less representative of the eligible voter population than on-cycle electorates?

I have used the word "representation" sparingly in this book, and for good reason: in order to say something about the representativeness of the electorate in school board and municipal elections, I would need to have information about voters' preferences in those elections. To the best of my knowledge, no such data exist for a large sample of school districts or cities. Not only do we not have much data on the policy preferences of citizens aggregated to the level of municipal government or school district, but also the issues that are relevant for elections and policy at those levels of government are typically not the ones that are asked about in surveys, most of which are designed to measure public opinion on *national* policy issues. What are voters' views on issues germane to county boards, city councils, school boards, and public library trustees? As of today, we don't have much information with which to answer those questions, and the lack of data makes it difficult to draw conclusions about how election timing affects the representativeness of the electorate.

The broader question, however—whether turnout rates matter for the representativeness of the electorate—is a well-studied one in the field of American politics. And to the extent that there is anything that resembles a consensus, it is that low turnout actually does *not* bias the electorate all that much. The reason, according to this literature, is that the distribution of political preferences among nonvoters is similar to that of voters, and so the outcomes of elections wouldn't be all that different even if everyone voted.[11] Yet as Zoltan Hajnal and Jessica Trounstine point out, almost all of the work that draws such conclusions focuses exclusively on national elections.[12] There are some studies that examine subnational elections and find that turnout levels *do* have consequences for political representation and policy.[13] But others draw a different conclusion. In his study of local government, Eric Oliver examines two groups of individuals with different propensities to vote in municipal elections—homeowners and renters—and concludes that low voter turnout usually does *not* distort the representation of the eligible electorate's policy preferences.[14]

No doubt some of the inconsistency in this literature is due to the different types of elections scholars study to learn about representation. At the local level in particular, the little work that *has* been done suffers from a lack of data on voters' preferences on the policies pertinent to local government. As I explained above, that is the main problem I face here, and the reason why I hesitate to draw firm conclusions about off-cycle election timing and representation. But while I cannot definitively say whether off-cycle election timing systematically produces outcomes that are less (or perhaps more) representative of the whole eligible electorate, I *can* conclude that off-cycle election timing systematically produces *different* policies than on-cycle election timing—and policies that are more favorable to certain organized groups. When it comes to the degree of electoral and policy success organized groups achieve, election timing does matter.

This brings me to another way in which this book contributes to the broader literature on representation: its focus on organized groups. The politics of election timing would simply be incomprehensible without an understanding of how election timing affects organized groups. If not for groups, why would Democrats in state legislatures want to protect low-turnout off-cycle school board elections? If not for groups, how could we explain why the standard of off-cycle election timing for local governments has persisted over the years, in spite of the fact that most American citizens would rather it be otherwise?

In today's American politics research on representation, however (and indeed, on other topics as well), organized groups are of secondary importance; most work puts the preferences of individual voters—and the preferences of the median voter in particular—at the center of the story. Recently, this individual-centric focus of the American politics literature has been the subject of criticism by a small group of scholars who argue that many aspects of politics and policy cannot be explained by theoretical accounts that downplay or ignore the role of organized interests. In a prime example of such a critique, Jacob Hacker and Paul Pierson explain that the overemphasis of the preferences of individual voters is one of the main reasons why scholars have been unable to provide a compelling explanation for the dramatic rise in inequality in the United States in recent decades, and they go on to argue that organized groups should be a serious focus of study.[15] My findings in this book lead to the same conclusion: much of the politics of election timing wouldn't make sense with an exclusively individual-centric view of American politics.

However, it is not as though organized groups have *never* been central to political scientists' understanding of representation. During the 1950s and 1960s, groups were the primary unit of analysis for the pluralists—scholars like David Truman, E. E. Schattschneider, and Robert Dahl. The pluralists envisioned the political arena as a place where interest groups compete with one another to influence policy, and they viewed policy as a direct product of group influence.[16] Like the pluralists of fifty years ago, I think organized groups deserve a central role in theories of American politics. But my findings also shed new light on some of their conclusions.

Both Dahl in *Who Governs?* and Schattschneider in *The Semisovereign People* conclude that while most interest groups have narrow, private interests, their ability to capture government is tempered by the electoral process. Dahl finds that members of the relatively small, well-informed, and actively engaged "political stratum" have greater direct influence over policy than those outside of it, but since leaders who run for public office have to cater to majorities of the population in elections, the electoral process prevents minority viewpoints from being enacted as public policy. Elections, therefore, are the mechanism by which citizens exert influence—even if indirect—over government.[17] Like Dahl, Schattschneider notes that most of the population participates very little in politics and that the pressure system is small, narrow, and unrepresentative of the larger populace. However, Schattschneider argues that pressure groups' effectiveness in securing favorable policies from government is tempered by electoral competition among political parties; majorities must form to make policy and to win elections, and political parties are critical to building those needed majorities. Schattschneider concludes that political party competition undermines the tendency toward interest group capture.[18]

What, then, of elections in which a small minority of the public votes? And what of electoral institutions, like off-cycle election timing, that ensure that the electorate is small? It seems likely that as the size of the active electorate gets closer and closer to the size of Dahl's "political stratum" or Schattschneider's "pressure group system," the *composition* of the electorate *also* gets closer and closer to that of the pressure group system. Political scientists concerned with low rates of political participation often focus on why the abstainers choose to stay home on Election Day. But a simple reframing of the question may get more to the point: When voter turnout gets as low as it does in many municipal elections and school board elections in the United States, the question to ask is not who is staying away from the polls but rather who actually has reason to show up. As Dahl writes in *Who Governs?*, "Instead of seeking to explain why citizens are not interested, concerned, and active, the task is to explain why a few citizens *are*" (emphasis added).[19] When it comes to election timing, there is good reason to think that the process by which eligible voters select into the active electorate during off-cycle elections is similar to the process by which people select into the pressure group system. And if so, then electorates in off-cycle elections probably look a lot like the pressure group system itself.

What is more, if the electoral process is supposed to be the force that protects government from the undue influence of interest groups, then we should expect interest group leaders to anticipate that and try to limit the tempering effect of elections. Just as interest groups don't sit around and hope their supporters turn out to vote—they actively mobilize their supporters—they also don't passively accept any electoral rule, regardless of its consequences. If interest groups are more likely to have their way when turnout is low, then they have good reason to try to secure and protect electoral rules that make the electorate smaller and more favorable to their goals. In doing this, they can minimize the threat from the latent force of majorities—and not just in one election but also for many elections in the future.[20] Off-cycle election timing is an institution that can do just that. From this perspective, off-cycle election timing is an electoral rule that substantially reduces the likelihood that elected politicians will have to answer to majorities. In a twist on the optimistic pluralist conclusion, the electoral process can become a vehicle for interest group capture rather than a force that prevents it.[21]

Furthermore, political parties are not always the solution. My analysis in chapter 4 showed that large majorities of both Democratic and Republican citizens would prefer on-cycle local elections to off-cycle elections, and yet state legislatures around the country—where the two major political parties are active and competitive—consistently ignore or vote down proposals to move local elections to November of even-numbered years. Thus, especially when it comes to issues not visible to the public, the positions political parties take can go against what majorities of citizens want if doing so pleases the interest groups that make up their coalitions.

American politics scholars today rarely speak of political parties in such ways. They conceptualize political parties as groups of like-minded politicians in government, as aides to legislators' reelection pursuits, or as providers of cues to voters. Fifty years ago, however, Schattschneider thought of political parties quite differently: as broad coalitions of interest groups formed out of the necessity of building majorities. Kathleen Bawn and coauthors have recently revived this perspective on political parties, arguing that they are dependent on interest groups and can hide a great deal of their activity from voters.[22] In fact, as this group of scholars argues, parties actually have incentives to grow the "'electoral blind spot,' within which voters are unable to reliably ascertain policy positions or evaluate party performance." The result, they explain, is that "Rather than pushing for policies that voters would like better, the majority party engages in bamboozlement. Groups get their desired policy outcome and voters can't figure out what is going on."[23]

The election timing debates I discussed in chapter 4 are consistent with this theory of political parties. The parties can afford to take unpopular stances on issues like election timing because it is an obscure issue, and when legislators do occasionally debate it, most voters never know those debates took place. More generally, when it comes to institutional politics, the issues are so hidden from the public eye that parties can cease to be voices for the majority—and cease to be a moderator of politicians' tendencies to cater to interest groups.

Election Timing and Institutional Stability

With a proper focus on organized groups and how they affect and are affected by election timing decisions, the otherwise puzzling stability of the American electoral calendar is not actually all that puzzling. It has little to do with what American voters want, nor do state legislators ignore election timing because they regard it as a mere technical detail. Instead, at least when it comes to local election scheduling, the persistence of off-cycle election timing has much to do with the fact that the groups that benefit from it are better organized and more vocal than any groups that might potentially oppose it.

This is actually a familiar theme in politics. Take, for example, what Terry Moe writes about the politics of designing administrative agencies:

> Most citizens do not get terribly excited about the arcane details of public administration. . . . People just do not know or care much about these sorts of things. . . . Organized interest groups are another matter. They are active, informed participants in their specialized issue areas, and they know that their policy goals are crucially dependent on precisely those fine details of administrative structure that cause voters' eyes to glaze over. Structure is valuable to them, and they have every incentive to mobilize their political resources to get what they want. As a result, they are normally the only source of political pressure when structural issues are at stake. Structural politics is interest group politics.[24]

This passage could just as well have been written about the choice of election schedules; the politics boils down to battles fought by interest groups. Interest groups with a focus on a given policy area know that election timing can affect who turns out to vote and how effective their mobilization efforts will be. And because they have a stake in policy, they take an active part in debates over when elections will be held. Regular voters, on the other hand, have little incentive to pay attention to debates on such an obscure topic. As with other choices about procedures, rules, and structure, the politics of election timing choice is the terrain of interest groups.

By itself, however, this does not explain why election schedules persist over time. For if interest groups are well organized and highly motivated on both sides of an issue, a group that stands to benefit from a change in the election schedule has reason to push for that change—and to implement it as soon as it has friends in control of government. Keith Krehbiel sums up this dynamic nicely, speaking of legislative organization: "If legislators cannot agree on stable policies, how can they be expected to agree on stable institutional forms (procedures) that are implicitly associated with those very policies on which they cannot agree?"[25] This is a sticking point in the study of political institutions more generally: If institutions affect political outcomes, how can we explain the persistence of so many political institutions over time?

There is no simple answer to this, although the case of election timing is informative for how we should understand institutional stability more generally. For starters, it would be tempting to observe the stability in the American election schedule and conclude that nothing is happening, that no one is attempting to change it. One might even go so far as to say that because most election schedules were fixed back in the Progressive Era and have changed little since, election timing is exogenous to interest group influence today. My findings indicate that such a claim would be erroneous. Beneath the institutional stability, a political tug-of-war is going on. In fact, not only is election timing *not* exogenous to interest groups—the structure of the interest group system today is one of the *reasons* that election timing has been so stable. In the case of school board election timing, the interests that benefit from the existing electoral calendar are well organized, whereas the interests that would benefit from a change are much less so. At least in part, then, the reason that off-cycle election timing has proven so resistant to change is that the interest groups that are active in election timing debates are predominantly in favor of keeping things as they are. And for state legislators, disrupting the status quo involves little reward and significant electoral cost.[26]

This dynamic might actually be quite common in American politics. James Q. Wilson explains that there are many policy issues for which one side of the policy spectrum is much better organized—and more politically active—than the other.[27] If the politics of institutional choice is interest group politics, as Moe argues, then these are precisely the policy domains where we should expect institutions to be stable over time—and in the direction favored by the organized. And there is another side to this as well, which is that once institutions are in place, interest groups that benefit from those institutions grow up around them, organizing to protect them from change.[28] With the creation of the institutions, those groups suddenly have something to lose. By contrast, the obstacles individuals on the other side face are formidable; not only do they have to overcome the collective action problem, but even if they do, they have to successfully navigate the numerous political hurdles that stand in the way of enacting a new institutional structure.

That brings me to another reason why the American electoral calendar has been so stable over time—and perhaps why many other political institutions are stable as well: Those who want to maintain the status quo have tremendous advantage over those who want to change it. Within a bicameral legislature, opponents of legislation have multiple points at which they can try to stifle it: They can work to kill it in committee. They can try to block it from being debated on the floor. They can work to get it defeated on the floor. If one chamber passes the bill, it still has to make its way through the other. Then it has to be approved by the executive, possibly reconciled by a conference committee, and so on. Any group or individual trying to get new legislation passed—such as a bill proposing to make elections concurrent—must successfully navigate every step of this obstacle course. Opponents, on the other hand, need only be successful at *one* veto point. Therefore, in a system of checks and balances, it is much easier to protect the status quo than it is to change it.[29]

The case of election timing also suggests that the *way* institutions are created can have important implications for how long those institutions last. Not all institutions are created equal; some are more difficult to change than others. A statute, for example, is usually easier to change than a constitution. And politicians who want to craft policies in the direction they prefer—not just in the current period but also well into the future— would like to embed their preferences in institutions that are as difficult to change as possible.[30]

As I explained in chapter 3, the Progressive reformers did not implement off-cycle election timing by the same means as the political parties did earlier in the nineteenth century. Rather, they pushed for general legislation rather than special legislation. They got involved in state constitutional conventions and the drafting of municipal charters. Presumably, embedding their preferred electoral rules in these structures made off-cycle election timing more difficult to change than it had been in the past—hence the greater stability of election timing starting in the twentieth century. That is not to say that constitutions and home rule charters are unchangeable, of course. But there are varying degrees of ease with which institutions can be changed, and that variation is probably quite important for understanding why some institutions persist and others do not.

In sum, by focusing on election timing, we not only learn a great deal about a political institution that has been studied very little—although that alone is an advance—we also gain insights into some of the broader ideas that can (and should) occupy the minds of anyone trying to understand politics, government, and policy. Studying election timing highlights the important role of interest groups in American politics. It underscores the explanatory power of a revised theory of political parties that recognizes parties' dependence on interest groups. And finally, by studying election timing, we gain a deeper understanding of why political institutions persist—and not just in the United States but also around the world.

Closing Thoughts

Since the nation's beginnings in the late eighteenth century, citizens' opportunities for voting in elections have expanded. Not only can more people vote today than two hundred years ago, but there are also many more elections. The United States now elects its senators directly. There are primary elections for national races, state races, and many local races. There are elections that invite American citizens to vote directly on public policy—elections on tax increases, on tax caps, and on whether marriage should be defined as a bond between a man and woman. Over the course of 200 years, the opportunities for citizens to have a say in what their government looks like and does have dramatically increased.

On its face, this seems like a transition that is good for democracy. The irony, however, is that over time, as the opportunities to vote have increased, the percentage of eligible American voters who take advantage of those opportunities has gone down. And since voter turnout is often taken to be a barometer of democratic health, the expansion of elections can also be viewed as a change for the worse.

Robert Dahl once wrote, "At the focus of most men's lives are primary activities involving food, sex, love, family, work, play, shelter, comfort, friendship, social esteem, and the like. Activities like these—not politics— are the primary concerns of most men and women."[31] Put simply, most Americans just do not have much time for politics. There could be elections every week throughout the year, and in some sense, that would be an expansion of democracy, but the fact of the matter is that most Americans would not have time or energy or motivation to vote in all of them. The question then becomes: In a democratic government, is it better to hold many different elections on the same day, or should elections for different types of offices and policy issues be held on different days?

My focus in this book has been on what *is* rather than what *should be*, but the theory and empirical findings herein provide new insights that can be used to inform debates about how election schedules should be structured. Needless to say, there is much more work to be done and much more ground to be covered. But my hope is that this book takes a significant step forward toward an understanding of how electoral timing affects political outcomes and why elections are scheduled when they are. What it shows is that the timing of elections matters for voter turnout, it matters for the composition of the electorate, and, in many cases, it makes a difference to election outcomes and public policy.

Appendixes

Appendix A: Additional Data Sources for Chapter 3

The listing below provides additional sources that I consulted for chapter 3.

CALIFORNIA ELECTION RETURNS
The JoinCalifornia site of the One Voter Project, compiled by Alex Vassar and Shane Meyers, has information on all state and national elections held in California since 1849. Prior to 1898, for state legislative offices, only the names and political parties of winning candidates are provided, but statewide election returns as well as full candidate and party information are available for all statewide offices. The JoinCalifornia information is available online at http://www.joincalifornia .com/.

SAN FRANCISCO ELECTION RETURNS
San Francisco Municipal Reports 1861, 1870, 1874, 1875, 1876, 1877, 1878, 1880, 1881, 1882, 1884, 1886, 1888, 1890, 1896–97.
Steamer Alta California, September 16, 1853.
Alta California, September 15, 1854; June 16, 1855.
Daily Evening Bulletin, November 7, 1856; September 4, 1857; September 4, 1858; September 11, 1858; September 12, 1859; November 9, 1860; May 20, 1861; May 23, 1861; September 3, 1861; September 7, 1861; September 14, 1861; May 19, 1862; May 27, 1862; September 4, 1862; May 6, 1863; May 20, 1863; May 26, 1863; September 5, 1863; May 25, 1864; November 9, 1864; May 18, 1865; September 7, 1865; September 6, 1866; September 7, 1867; September 5, 1867; November 4, 1868; September 3, 1869; September 9, 1870; September 19, 1871; November 6, 1872; September 8, 1873; September 8, 1875; October 1, 1884; November 7, 1884; November 5, 1886; November 23, 1886; November 8, 1888; November 24, 1888.
"The Legislature," *The Morning Call*, San Francisco, November 7, 1890, page 2.
"Vote of the City," *San Francisco Chronicle*, November 10, 1892, page 3.

"Budd's Plurality, 1156," *San Francisco Examiner*, November 10, 1894, no. 132, page 1.

"M'Kinley Carries California with Thousands to Spare," *San Francisco Chronicle*, November 5, 1896, page 9.

"Official Count Is Now Complete," *San Francisco Chronicle*, December 12, 1896, page 10.

"City Gave Gage a Majority of 3460," *San Francisco Call*, November 11, 1898, page 3.

"Republicans Make Many Gains," *San Francisco Chronicle*, November 10, 1898, page 9.

"Count of Votes in City," *San Francisco Chronicle*, November 11, 1898, page 7.

"In Assembly and Senate," *San Francisco Chronicle*, November 11, 1898, page 2.

"Official Count Now Complete," *San Francisco Chronicle*, November 19, 1898, page 7.

"Local Vote on State Offices," *San Francisco Chronicle*, December 3, 1898, page 5.

"The Count is Completed," *San Francisco Chronicle*, December 21, 1898, page 7.

"Official Returns on Late City Election," *San Francisco Chronicle*, November 26, 1899, page 23.

"Phelan Wins by More Than Six Thousand in a Quiet Election," *San Francisco Chronicle*, November 8, 1899, page 1.

"Seven Offices for the Republicans," *San Francisco Chronicle*, November 9, 1899, page 12.

"Seven Republicans Will Go to Congress," *San Francisco Chronicle*, November 8, 1900, page 7.

"How the Vote Was Cast and for Whom," *San Francisco Chronicle*, November 7, 1901, page 12.

"Returns from San Francisco," *San Francisco Evening Bulletin*, November 5, 1902, page 2.

"Official Vote Cast in the City," *San Francisco Chronicle*, November 25, 1902, page 8.

"Complete Figures on Election of Tuesday," *San Francisco Chronicle*, November 5, 1903, page 16.

MISCELLANEOUS SOURCES FOR CALIFORNIA AND SAN FRANCISCO

"The New Municipal Election Bill for San Francisco," *Daily Evening Bulletin*, February 18, 1860, issue 112, column E.

"Local and Political Elections," *Daily Evening Bulletin*, January 26, 1861, issue 93, column A.

"A Municipal Election Next May," *Daily Evening Bulletin*, April 18, 1861, issue 10, column A.

"Our Local Election—It Must Not Be Neglected," *Daily Evening Bulletin*, April 26, 1861, issue 17, column A.

"Republican Partizans and the Municipal Election," *Daily Evening Bulletin*, April 30, 1861, issue 20, column A.

"Letter from Sacramento: Political Legislation—Democrats 'Down' on San Francisco," *Daily Evening Bulletin*, May 4, 1861, issue 24, column E.

San Francisco Municipal Reports Fiscal Year 1863–1864. San Francisco: William P. Harrison, 1864.

"The Result of the Election in San Francisco," *Daily Evening Bulletin*, September 7, 1865.

San Francisco Municipal Reports 1866–67, 1869–70.

"General and Special Laws," *Daily Evening Bulletin*, April 11, 1872, issue 4, column C.

"The Legislature," *Daily Evening Bulletin*, April 16, 1880, issue 8, column B.

"County Government Bill Void," *Daily Evening Bulletin*, September 16, 1880, page 2, issue 138, column C.

"Municipal Election: Will There Be One in This City This Fall?" *Daily Evening Bulletin*, September 21, 1880, page 3, issue 142, column G.

"Supreme Court Decisions," *Evening Bulletin, San Francisco*, September 29, 1880.

"The Legislature," *Daily Evening Bulletin*, February 19, 1881.

"The Legislature," *Daily Evening Bulletin*, March 1, 1881.

"The Municipal Election," *Daily Evening Bulletin*, May 5, 1881, issue 22, column C.

"An Election to Be Held This Fall," *Daily Evening Bulletin*, June 3, 1881, page 2, issue 47, column C.

"A Survey of the Political Field," *Daily Evening Bulletin*, June 9, 1881, page 2, issue 52, column A.

"Supreme Court Opinions in the Election Case," *Daily Evening Bulletin*, June 15, 1881, page 3, issue 57, column F.

"The Ups and Downs of the Local Democracy," *Daily Evening Bulletin*, June 15, 1881, page 2, issue 57, column A.

"Local Politics at the New City Hall," *Daily Evening Bulletin*, June 16, 1881, page 2, issue 58, column D.

"Supreme Court Decisions," *Daily Evening Bulletin*, August 19, 1881, issue 112, column D.

"The War of Ballots," *Daily Evening Bulletin*, September 7, 1881, page 3, issue 128, column F.

"Municipal Election: One 'To Be or Not to Be' This Fall, 'That Is the Question,'" *Daily Evening Bulletin*, August 14, 1882, issue 109, column C.

"A New Deal: The Supreme Court Orders a Municipal Election," *Daily Evening Bulletin*, August 24, 1882, page 2, issue 118, column D.

"Freeholders Talk about Franchises," *San Francisco Chronicle*, January 29, 1898, page 7.

"The Question of Elections," *San Francisco Chronicle*, February 10, 1898, page 5.

"New Charter Is Finished," *San Francisco Chronicle*, March 26, 1898, page 7.

"Too Many Elections," *San Francisco Chronicle*, May 14, 1898, page 6.

"Seek to Beat the Charter," *San Francisco Chronicle*, January 8, 1899, page 14.

"Charter Ratified by the Assembly," *San Francisco Chronicle*, January 19, 1899, page 4.

"The New Election Laws," *San Francisco Chronicle*, March 24, 1899, page 6.

"Railroad Threatens New Charter; Solid Seven Has Lost One Member," *San Francisco Chronicle*, May 31, 1899, page 12.

"Non-Partisans Will Test the Primary Law," *San Francisco Chronicle*, June 21, 1899, page 12.

"Municipal and National Politics," *San Francisco Chronicle*, October 20, 1899, page 6.

"Phelan Wins by More Than Six Thousand in a Quiet Election," *San Francisco Chronicle*, November 8, 1899, page 1.

"The Result of the City Election," *San Francisco Chronicle*, November 8, 1899, page 6.

"Corporation Bosses Hurled from Power," *San Francisco Chronicle*, November 7, 1901, page 12.

Curry, C. F. *California Blue Book or State Roster*. Sacramento: State Printing Office, 1903, 402–4.

San Francisco Municipal Reports Fiscal Year 1909–1910, Ending June 30, 1910. San Francisco: Neal Publishing, 1911.

NEW YORK ELECTION RETURNS

"The Spring Election—Next Tuesday—Can the Whigs Win?" *Morning Herald*, April 11, 1840, column B.

The Politician's Register for 1841, 6th edition, enlarged. New York: H. Greeley, 1841, page 37.

New York Herald, April 19, 1841.

"The Election," *New York Herald*, November 4, 1841, column A.

Weekly Herald, April 16, 1842.

New York Herald, November 10, 1842.

The Whig Almanac and United States Register. New York: Greeley and McElrath, 1844, page 56.

The Whig Almanac and Politicians' Register for 1846. New York: Greeley and McElrath, 1846, page 57.

The Whig Almanac and United States Register. New York: Greeley and McElrath, 1847, page 60.

The Whig Almanac. New York: Greeley and McElrath, 1848, page 54.

"The Charter Election," *Weekly Herald*, April 14, 1849.

The Whig Almanac 1849. New York, 1849, page 54.

"The Charter Election," *New York Herald*, April 12, 1849.

"The Charter Election," *Weekly Herald*, April 14, 1849.

"The Election," *Weekly Herald*, November 10, 1849.

The Whig Almanac and United States Register for 1850. New York: Greeley and McElrath, 1850, page 57.

New York Herald, November 6, 1850.

The Whig Almanac and United States Register for 1851. New York: Greeley and McElrath, 1851, page 54.

New York Daily Times, November 4, 1851, page 1.

The Whig Almanac for 1852. New York: Greeley and McElrath, 1852, page 51.

The Whig Almanac for 1853. New York: Greeley and McElrath, 1853, page 50.

New York Herald, November 4, 1852.

"Presidential Election," *New York Daily Times,* November 2, 1852, page 5.

"The Election," *New York Daily Times,* November 7, 1853, front page.

The Whig Almanac for 1854. New York, 1854, page 54.

The Whig Almanac for 1855. New York, 1855, pages 54–55.

New York Herald, November 8, 1856.

"Elections To-Morrow," *New York Daily Times,* November 3, 1856, page 1.

"State Elections To-Day," *New York Times,* November 3, 1857, page 4.

"The Elections," *New York Times,* November 4, 1857, page 1.

New York Times, November 6, 1857, page 1.

"The City Election," *New York Times,* December 2, 1857, page 1.

Tribune Almanac and Political Register for 1861, pages 41–48.

The Tribune Almanac and Political Register for 1862. New York: Tribune Association, 1862, pages 57–58.

"The State Election," *New York Times,* November 6, 1862, page 8.

The Tribune Almanac and Political Register for 1863. New York: Tribune Association, 1863, page 52.

The Tribune Almanac and Political Register for 1864. New York: Tribune Association, 1864, pages 56–57.

The Tribune Almanac and Political Register for 1865. New York: Tribune Association, 1865, page 52.

New York Times, November 9, 1864.

The Tribune Almanac and Political Register for 1866. New York: Tribune Association, 1866, pages 62 and 63.

The Tribune Almanac and Political Register for 1867. New York: Tribune Association, 1867, page 55.

The Tribune Almanac and Political Register for 1868. New York: Tribune Association, 1868, pages 52–53.

The Tribune Almanac and Political Register for 1869. New York: Tribune Association, 1869, page 62.

New York Times, November 4, 1868.

"The Election To-Morrow," *New York Times,* November 1, 1869, page 5.

The Tribune Almanac and Political Register for 1870. New York: Tribune Association, 1870, pages 55 and 57.

"The Charter Election," *New York Times*, December 1, 1869, page 5.

"The Elections," *New York Times*, November 9, 1870, page 1.

The Tribune Almanac and Political Register for 1871. New York: Tribune Association, 1871, page 55.

"The City Vote," *New York Times*, November 7, 1872, page 8.

New York Times, November 7, 1872.

The Tribune Almanac and Political Register for 1875. New York: Tribune Association, 1875, pages 51–64.

The Tribune Almanac and Political Register for 1877. New York: Tribune Association, 1877, pages 96–109.

"The Result of the City Vote," *New York Times*, November 7, 1888, page 5.

MISCELLANEOUS SOURCES FOR NEW YORK

"Next Election—Next Mayor—A Popular Movement," *Morning Herald*, February 10, 1840, column A.

"The New York Legislature," *Weekly Herald*, March 31, 1849, page 102, issue 13, column A.

"The Approaching Election in the Fall—Interesting State of Things," *The Weekly Herald*, September 1, 1849, page 277, issue 35, column A.

"To-Day's Election," *New York Daily Times*, November 4, 1851, page 2.

"Municipal Reform," *New York Daily Times*, March 7, 1853, page 1.

"City Reform at Albany," *New York Daily Times*, March 19, 1853, pages 1, 4.

"Proposed Amendment of the New-York City Charter," *New York Daily Times*, March 31, 1853, page 3.

"City Reform," *New York Daily Times*, April 8, 1853, page 4.

"Two New City Charters," *New York Daily Times*, February 12, 1856, page 3.

"Another New City Charter," *New York Daily Times*, February 24, 1855, page 8.

"Important from Albany: The New-York City Bills Reported," *New York Daily Times*, March 3, 1857, page 1.

"City Reforms—Amended Charter, &c.," *New York Daily Times*, March 3, 1857, page 4.

"State Affairs," *New York Daily Times*, March 27, 1857, page 1.

"The Mayoralty," *New York Times*, December 1, 1857, page 1.

"The Party or the City," *New York Times*, December 1, 1857, page 4.

"The Election Yesterday," *New York Times*, December 2, 1857, page 4.

"The City Election," *New York Times*, November 28, 1863, page 6.

"The Charter Election," *New York Times*, November 30, 1868, page 4.

"The State Legislature. Senate. Assembly. The City Charter." *New York Times*, February 3, 1870, page 1.

"The New Charter and the Old," *New York Times*, February 4, 1870, page 4.

"Albany," *New York Times*, February 11, 1870, page 1.

"Honest Elections," *New York Times*, March 5, 1870, page 5.

"The Newest Charter," *New York Times*, March 11, 1870, page 2.

"Albany," *New York Times*, March 11, 1870, page 5.

"Albany," *New York Times*, March 31, 1870, page 1.

"Albany," *New York Times*, April 6, 1870, page 1.

"Our New City Government," *New York Times*, April 13, 1870, page 4.

"The Judicial Election," *New York Times*, May 9, 1870, page 4.

"The Republican Ticket," *New York Times*, May 14, 1870, page 1.

"Political," *New York Times*, May 15, 1870, page 8.

"To-Morrow's Contest," *New York Times*, May 16, 1870, page 8.

"The Election Today," *New York Times*, May 17, 1870, page 8.

"The Result of the Election," *New York Times*, May 18, 1870, page 4.

"Political," *New York Times*, August 24, 1870, page 5.

"Political," *New York Times*, October 4, 1870, page 5.

"Political," *New York Times*, November 2, 1870, page 5.

"How the Democrats Love Honest Elections," *New York Times*, January 9, 1871, page 4.

"Albany," *New York Times*, March 25, 1871, page 1.

"Repeal the Ring Charter," *New York Times*, September 5, 1871, page 4.

"Hints about the Charter," *New York Times*, November 13, 1871, page 4.

"The Charter," *New York Times*, December 24, 1871, page 1.

"The Completed Charter," *New York Times,* January 20, 1872, page 1.

"Work of the Legislature," *New York Times*, February 3, 1872, page 3.

"The Progress of the Charter," *New York Times*, February 28, 1872, page 4.

"Party Spirit in Local Politics," *New York Times*, February 29, 1872, page 4.

"What the Charter Election Ought to Give Us," *New York Times*, March 10, 1872, page 4.

"The Charter," *New York Times*, April 19, 1872, page 5.

"The New Election Law," *New York Times*, April 21, 1872, page 4.

"Albany Affairs," *New York Times*, April 21, 1872, page 1.

"The New Election Law," *New York Times*, April 21, 1872, page 4.

"Albany," *New York Times*, April 24, 1872, page 1.

"Albany," *New York Times*, May 1, 1872, page 5.

"Veto of the Charter," *New York Times*, May 17, 1872, page 1.

"Municipal Reform," *New York Times*, August 31, 1872, page 8.

"The Charter," *New York Times*, January 8, 1873, page 5.

"The Charter," *New York Times*, February 17, 1873, page 9.

"The Charter," *New York Times*, February 20, 1873, page 8.

"Anti-Charter Meeting," *New York Times*, February 26, 1873, page 4.

"The State Legislature," *New York Times*, February 28, 1873, page 4.

"Meeting of the Reform Association," *New York Times*, May 25, 1873, page 8.

"The Seventy," *New York Times*, July 8, 1873, page 8.

"The Charter in the Senate," *New York Times*, March 10, 1873, page 4.

"Albany," *New York Times*, April 17, 1873, page 5.

"Two Objectionable Bills," *New York Times*, January 23, 1874, page 4.

"Albany," *New York Times*, March 6, 1875, page 5.

"The Legislature and the City," *New York Times*, December 14, 1875, page 4.

"The Lecture," *New York Times*, February 8, 1876, page 2.

"Albany," *New York Times*, March 30, 1877, page 1.

"Albany," *New York Times*, April 13, 1877, page 4.

"City Reform and the Late Election," *New York Times*, November 11, 1877, page 6.

"A New 'Omnibus' Bill," *New York Times*, December 28, 1877, page 1.

"Our Local Government," *New York Times*, February 3, 1880, page 1.

"Independence in Municipal Elections," *New York Times*, February 17, 1881, page 4.

"Changing the City Charter," *New York Times*, March 3, 1881, page 1.

"City Reform Measures," *New York Times*, March 23, 1884, page 14.

"A Spring Election for Mayor," *New York Times*, March 29, 1884, page 4.

"The Local Problem," *New York Times*, September 27, 1884, page 4.

"The Machine Ticket," *New York Times*, October 23, 1884, page 4.

"Reasons for Spring Elections," *New York Times*, November 7, 1884, page 4.

"City Elections in April," *New York Times*, February 12, 1885, page 4.

"In Favor of Spring Elections," *New York Times*, January 20, 1885, page 3.

"Local and General Elections," *New York Times,* February 21, 1885, page 4.

"The Spring Election Bill," *New York Times*, March 18, 1885, page 4.

"Defeated in the Senate," *New York Times*, March 25, 1885, page 1.

"The Elections Amendment," *New York Times*, April 18, 1885, page 4.

"A Real Measure of Reform," *New York Times*, May 20, 1886, page 4.

"The Long Expected Veto," *New York Times*, June 16, 1886, page 3.

"Gov. Hill and Municipal Reform," *New York Times*, January 6, 1887, page 4.

"Separate Municipal Elections," *New York Times*, November 3, 1888, page 4.

"Reform in Elections," *New York Times*, December 4, 1888, page 2.

"The Citizens' Movement," *New York Times*, June 17, 1890, page 4.

"Partisanship and City Government," *New York Times*, June 28, 1890, page 4.

"The Way to Defeat Tammany," *New York Times*, September 26, 1890, page 4.

"The Anti-Tammany Ticket," *New York Times*, October 10, 1890, page 4.

"Want a Straight Ticket," *New York Times*, October 3, 1890, page 1.

"The Opportunity for Reform," *New York Times*, October 11, 1890, page 4.

"Separate City Elections," *New York Times*, December 17, 1890, page 4.

"Municipal Reform Movements," *New York Times*, June 30, 1891, page 4.

"The Republicans and Tammany," *New York Times*, October 24, 1891, page 4.

"New York City Reforms," *New York Times*, February 2, 1893, page 5.

"Separate the Elections," *New York Times*, November 9, 1893, page 2.

"Non-Partisan Organization," *New York Times*, December 8, 1893, page 4.

"Not Ready to Commit Itself," *New York Times*, December 15, 1893, page 1.

"Essential to Permanent Reform," *New York Times*, January 18, 1894, page 4.

"To Destroy Platt's Power," *New York Times*, January 25, 1894, page 9.

"The National Association," *New York Times*, January 26, 1894, page 3.

"The Platt Fight 'Up the State,'" *New York Times*, March 3, 1894, page 4.

"For Better Rule in Cities," *New York Times*, May 18, 1894, page 8.

"Self-Government in Cities," *New York Times*, May 25, 1894, page 5.

"Self-Government in Cities," *New York Times*, May 29, 1894, page 5.

"Platform of Municipal League," *New York Times*, May 30, 1894, page 4.

"Self-Government in Cities," *New York Times*, May 31, 1894, page 5.

"Hearing on Municipal Reforms," *New York Times*, June 1, 1894, page 2.

"Self-Government in Cities," *New York Times*, June 1, 1894, page 5.

"For Separate Elections," *New York Times*, June 8, 1894, page 4.

"The Benefit to the State," *New York Times*, June 13, 1894, page 4.

"Tickets and Ballots," *New York Times*, June 21, 1894, page 4.

"The 'Good Government' Movement," *New York Times*, July 1, 1894, page 4.

"Bitter Talk against Platt," *New York Times*, July 27, 1894, page 1.

"The One Thing Essential," *New York Times*, August 11, 1894, page 4.

"Simplify the Matter," *New York Times*, August 14, 1894, page 4.

"Home Rule for Cities," *New York Times*, August 23, 1894, page 8.

"Dragged Deep in Politics," *New York Times*, August 28, 1894, page 3.

"For Separate Elections," *New York Times*, September 1, 1894, page 4.

"For Good Rule in Cities," *New York Times*, May 30, 1895, page 2.

"For a Municipal Party," *New York Times*, February 24, 1897, page 12.

"A Grand Opportunity," *New York Times*, February 25, 1897, page 6.

"Republicans for Low," *New York Times*, October 22, 1897, page 1.

"The Municipal Principle," *New York Times*, November 24, 1897, page 5.

"Independents to Persist," *New York Times*, October 1, 1898, page 2.

"The Independent Ticket," *New York Times*, October 11, 1898, page 3.

Washington Gladden, "Reform in City Government," *New York Times*, November 26, 1899, page 23.

PENNSYLVANIA ELECTION RETURNS

The county-level results of all presidential and gubernatorial elections in Pennsylvania from 1790 onward are made available by Wilkes University, *Pennsylvania Election Statistics: 1682–2006*. This resource also makes available a legislative directory for Pennsylvania, 1682–2006. Available online at http://staffweb.wilkes.edu/harold.cox/index.html.

PHILADELPHIA ELECTION RETURNS

Inquirer and Daily Courier, October 19, 1838.

Pennsylvania Inquirer and Daily Courier, October 9, 1839, issue 86, column C.

North American and Daily Advertiser, October 31, 1840, issue 500, column B.

Philadelphia Inquirer and Daily Courier, October 14, 1841, issue 90, column B.

North American and Daily Advertiser, October 12, 1842, issue 1104, column A.

Pennsylvania Inquirer and National Gazette, October 12, 1843, issue 88, column C.

North American and Daily Advertiser, October 11, 1844, issue 1724, column C.

North American and Daily Advertiser, October 16, 1845, issue 2039, column B.

North American, October 17, 1846, issue 2351, column C.

North American and United States Gazette, October 14, 1847, issue 16,139, column G;
  October 10, 1849, issue 16,747, column B; October 9, 1850, issue 17,056, column
  B; October 16, 1851; October 13, 1852; October 15, 1853; June 7, 1854; June 8,
  1854; October 11, 1854, issue 19,220, column B; May 2, 1855; October 10, 1855,
  issue 19,527, column C; May 7, 1856, page 2; October 17, 1856; May 6, 1857, page
  2; October 14, 1857, issue 20,146, column F; May 5, 1858, page 2; October 16, 1858,
  issue 23,956, column H; May 4, 1859, issue 24,126, column B; October 15, 1859,
  issue 25,266, column I; May 3, 1860; October 10, 1860, issue 25,572, column B; November 7, 1860, issue 25,596, column B; October 9, 1861, page 2; October 12, 1864,
  issue 26,318, column B; October 11, 1865, issue 26,622, column A.

Public Ledger, May 1, 1860, page 1; October 13, 1853, page 18; October 12, 1870, page 1.

Philadelphia Inquirer, October 9, 1861, page 4; October 15, 1862; October 14, 1863,
  page 4; October 10, 1866; October 9, 1867, page 1; October 14, 1868, page 1; October 13, 1869; October 11, 1871, page 1; October 9, 1872; November 6, 1872;
  November 6, 1872, page 1; February 20, 1874; February 21, 1874; February 23,
  1874; November 4, 1874, page 1; November 3, 1875.

MISCELLANEOUS SOURCES FOR PENNSYLVANIA AND PHILADELPHIA

"From Harrisburg," *North American and United States Gazette,* February 8, 1851,
  issue 18,060, column F; March 8, 1851, issue 18,084, column F; March 28, 1851,
  issue 18,100, column F; April 19, 1852, issue 18,435, column E.

"Consolidation," *North American and United States Gazette,* August 29, 1853, issue
  18,876, column F.

"The Election To-Day," *North American and United States Gazette,* October 11, 1853.

"The Election and What It Settles," *North American and United States Gazette,* October 15, 1853, issue 18,917, column B.

"Local Affairs," *Public Ledger,* October 28, 1853, page 2.

"City Items," *North American and United States Gazette,* November 4, 1853, issue
  18,934, column I.

"Synopsis of the Bill for Consolidating the City and County into One City," *Public
  Ledger,* November 10, 1853, page 1.

"Consolidation," *Public Ledger,* November 21, 1853, page 2.

"City Items," *North American and United States Gazette,* November 23, 1853, page 1.

"Consolidation," *North American and United States Gazette,* November 28, 1853,
  issue 18,953, column A.

"The Consolidation Bill," *North American and United States Gazette,* December 30, 1853.

"Pennsylvania Legislature Harrisburg," *Public Ledger,* January 3, 1854, page 3.

"Consolidation," *North American and United States Gazette*, January 11, 1854, issue 18,990.

Full text of 1854 consolidation law: *Public Ledger*, February 1, 1854.

"The Municipal Election," *North American and United States Gazette*, May 24, 1854.

"The Election on Tuesday," *North American and United States Gazette*, May 30, 1854, issue 19,107, column C.

"National Aspect of Our Municipal Election," *North American and United States Gazette*, June 2, 1854.

"The Election Tomorrow," *Public Ledger*, June 5, 1854, page 2.

"The Election To-Day," *North American and United States Gazette*, May 1, 1855.

"Municipal Affairs," *North American and United States Gazette*, May 5, 1856.

"The Issues of May 1, 1860," *Philadelphia North American and United States Gazette*, April 24, 1860.

"The Election Yesterday," *Public Ledger*, October 10, 1860, page 2.

"Miscellaneous. The Spring Election to Be Abolished," *Philadelphia Inquirer*, December 31, 1860.

"The Change in the Municipal Election," *Philadelphia Inquirer*, March 12, 1861.

"House of Representatives," *Philadelphia Inquirer*, March 20, 1861.

"Legislative Acts or Legal Proceedings," *Philadelphia Inquirer*, March 29, 1861.

"Local Intelligence: The Constitutional Union Party and the Postponed Spring Election," *Philadelphia Inquirer*, April 4, 1861.

"Improper and Proper Legislation," *Philadelphia Inquirer*, April 4, 1861.

"The October Election," *Philadelphia Inquirer*, July 15, 1861.

"The October Election," *Philadelphia Inquirer*, July 31, 1861.

"No Half Way Reforms," *Philadelphia Inquirer*, August 23, 1861.

"Philadelphia and Suburbs, Constitutional Convention," *Philadelphia Inquirer*, January 16, 1873; January 17, 1873; January 21, 1873; January 22, 1873; February 27, 1873.

"The February Election," *Philadelphia Inquirer*, December 23, 1873.

"The New Constitution," *Philadelphia Inquirer*, December 29, 1873.

"Constitutional Convention," *Philadelphia Inquirer*, January 24, 1873, page 2.

Abram Douglas Harlan, *Pennsylvania Constitutional Convention 1872 and 1873: Its Members and Officers and the Result of their Labors*. Philadelphia: Inquirer Book and Job Print, 1873.

Thomas Raeburn White, Counsel for the Philadelphia Committee of Seventy and the Board of Registration Commissioners, "Separation of Elections," National Municipal League Proceedings, Providence, RI, 1907.

NATIONAL MUNICIPAL LEAGUE PROCEEDINGS

Proceedings of the National Conference for Good City Government, Held at Philadelphia, January 25–26, 1894.

Proceedings of the Minneapolis Conference, December 8–10, 1894.

Proceedings of the Cleveland Conference, May 29–31, 1895.

Proceedings of the Baltimore Conference, May 6–8, 1896.
Proceedings of the Louisville Conference, May 5–7, 1897.
Proceedings of the Indianapolis Conference, November 30–December 2, 1898.
Proceedings of the Columbus Conference, November 16–18, 1899.
Proceedings of the Milwaukee Conference, September 19–21, 1900.
Proceedings of the Rochester Conference, May 8–10, 1901.
Proceedings of the Boston Conference, May 7–9, 1902.
Proceedings of the Detroit Conference, April 22–24, 1903.
Proceedings of the Providence Conference, November 19–22, 1907.

Appendix B: Summary Statistics for Chapter 4

TABLE B1 **Summary statistics for table 4.2 and table 4.3**

	Mean	Median	SD	Min	Max	N
Legislative progress	1.261	0	1.815	0	5	203
Discretionary	0.133	0	0.340	0	1	203
November of even years	0.645	1	0.480	0	1	203
Specific government	0.049	0	0.217	0	1	203
% Democratic vote share	0.481	0.472	0.080	0.283	0.631	203

Appendix C: Sources of Election Timing Variation for the Eight-State Test, Chapter 5

ALABAMA

All Alabama school districts are coterminous with either cities or counties. County boards of education are elected at the same time as the county, state, and federal elections. City school board members are either appointed by the city council or city commission or elected. For this study, the Alabama Association of School Boards provided the election dates of all city school boards.

CALIFORNIA

Prior to 1988, all California school board elections were held in November of odd-numbered years, not concurrent with state or national elections. In 1986, however, the California legislature passed a law that allowed school districts and county boards of education to consolidate their elections with municipal, primary, or general elections, pending approval from their respective county boards of supervisors. Some school districts petitioned for the switch and were approved, some did not seek the change, and others petitioned but were rejected by their county boards.[1] For this study, I coded California school district elections as on-cycle or off-cycle using the California Elections Data Archive school district election files for 2000, 2001, 2002, and 2003. I excluded elections in which candidates ran for partial terms as well as any districts that did not hold elections during this four-year period.

GEORGIA

Georgia school districts are coterminous with either counties or cities. Prior to July 2001, all county school districts held elections in November of even-numbered years, at the same time as federal elections. Since July 2001, county school boards that hold nonpartisan elections have been allowed to hold elections during the federal primary election. Municipal school board elections are held in November of odd-numbered years, along with their parent municipalities.

INDIANA

As of 2003, school district elections in Indiana were either concurrent with primary elections or with general elections as a result of local district choices following the Reorganization Act during the mid-1960s. After the 1960s, school boards were allowed to change their election date (from primary to general or vice versa) if they allowed 120 days for community response, received approval from the Indiana Department of Education, and secured the approval of local voters in a referendum. Fifteen of the 290 districts in the state have appointed rather than elected boards. Note that Indiana districts are excluded from the main analysis in chapter 5 because they are all coded as on-cycle.

MINNESOTA

Prior to 1987, Minnesota school elections were held in May. In 1987, the state legislature passed a law that allowed local school boards to change their election dates to the first Tuesday after the first Monday in November. In 1992, the Minnesota Statutes were further amended to eliminate the May election date and to require school districts to hold school board elections in either November of even-numbered years or November of odd-numbered years.

Election dates and results for Minnesota school board elections prior to 2001 are not available at the state level. In 2001, as a pilot program, the Minnesota secretary of state started to report school district election results (including dates) from certain counties. This effort was expanded starting in 2006; school districts across the state were asked to report their election results to the secretary of state. I used the 2006 and 2007 election files from the secretary of state to determine whether the districts in the SASS data (from 2003) had on- or off-cycle election dates. There were forty-seven Minnesota districts in the SASS data that did not find matches in this list of districts that held school board elections in 2006–7. For those districts, I filled in election timing information using the 2002–5 pilot study information where possible.

I also used the 2008 election data from the secretary of state to code as on-cycle any districts that had elections in November 2008.

NORTH CAROLINA

The default election date for school districts in North Carolina is the federal primary election, but local laws can override that policy. Most districts that deviate from the federal primary election date consolidate with the federal general election in November of even-numbered years, but some districts choose dates that do not coincide with federal or statewide races. The North Carolina State Board of Elections provided the election dates of all North Carolina school boards.

SOUTH CAROLINA

There is no default date for school district elections in South Carolina. Elected school boards are found in seventy-eight of the eighty-five districts in the state. The South Carolina School Boards Association provided a list of school board election dates.

TENNESSEE

County school boards in Tennessee hold regular elections in August of even-numbered years at the time of the statewide primary election. There is no state law governing the timing of municipal school board elections; they have discretion to choose their own election dates. The Tennessee School Boards Association provided a listing of the election dates of Tennessee School Systems.

VIRGINIA

Virginia is divided into county school boards, city school boards, and town school boards. The state did not allow elected school boards until 1992. As of 1992, the voters of a county or city could hold a referendum to switch to an elected rather than an appointed school board. County districts with elected boards hold elections at the same time as the statewide general election in November of odd-numbered years. Municipal school districts hold elections concurrently with their respective municipalities, most of which are in May. The election schedules of both county and municipal school districts are available through the Virginia State Board of Elections.

Summary Statistics for Chapter 5

TABLE C1 **Summary statistics for table 5.1 and table 5.2**

	Mean	Median	SD	Min	Max	N
Bachelor's, no experience	10.338	10.294	0.138	10.041	10.864	665
Master's, 10 years	10.687	10.644	0.180	10.301	11.141	658
Highest step	10.972	10.976	0.190	10.374	11.401	665
Off-cycle	0.241	0	0.428	0	1	665
% Democrat	0.439	0.423	0.123	0.163	0.832	665
NEA-to-teacher ratio	0.775	0.849	0.365	0.004	1.770	643
Ln(Enrollment)	8.644	8.713	1.237	4.984	11.867	665
% Elderly	0.170	0.168	0.052	0.042	0.409	665
Ln(Median income)	10.715	10.685	0.271	9.902	11.688	665
City	0.150	0	0.358	0	1	665
Fringe	0.480	0	0.500	0	1	665
% Hispanic	0.146	0.032	0.227	0	1	665
% Black	0.185	0.080	0.231	0	0.997	665
% Asian	0.036	0.008	0.079	0	0.635	665
% Native American	0.018	0.003	0.080	0	1	665
% Revenue from state	0.568	0.580	0.138	0.115	0.850	665

TABLE C2 **Summary statistics for table 5.3**

	Mean	Median	SD	Min	Max	N
Avg. teacher salary	10.720	10.724	0.115	10.396	10.973	237
Superintendent salary	11.530	11.503	0.239	10.491	12.100	228
Off-cycle	0.257	0	0.438	0	1	237
% Democrat	0.463	0.452	0.098	0.208	0.921	235
Turnout	0.312	0.315	0.157	0.0003	1.003	230
Ln(Enrollment)	7.089	6.969	1.223	4.043	10.629	237
Ln(Median income)	10.787	10.746	0.236	9.902	11.481	235
% Rev. from state	0.746	0.756	0.065	0.539	0.880	236
City	0.038	0	0.192	0	1	237
Rural	0.620	1	0.486	0	1	237
Town	0.236	0	0.426	0	1	237
% Hispanic	0.043	0.019	0.063	0	0.381	237
% Black	0.024	0.010	0.048	0	0.413	237
% Asian	0.019	0.009	0.031	0	0.293	237
% Native American	0.041	0.007	0.128	0	0.999	237
Avg. teacher exper.	15.240	15.144	2.779	7.100	24.831	237
% New teachers	0.036	0.030	0.029	0	0.153	237

TABLE C3 **Summary statistics for table 5.4**

	Mean	Median	SD	Min	Max	N
Turnout, % of adults	0.103	0.071	0.095	0.018	0.548	110
Turnout, % of reg. voters	0.118	0.093	0.089	0.014	0.385	65
On-cycle	0.159	0	0.367	0	1	132

TABLE C4 **Summary statistics for table 5.5**

	Mean	Median	SD	Min	Max	N
% Salary growth, 2006–9	0.006	0.005	0.057	−0.328	0.733	916
Treatment group	0.190	0	0.392	0	1	916
Metro Status Code	2.487	3	0.598	1	3	916
Ln(Enrollment)	6.939	6.797	1.492	2.639	11.991	916
Ln(Median income)	10.835	10.816	0.246	9.929	12.186	916
% Hispanic	0.298	0.218	0.250	0	0.999	916
% Black	0.080	0.032	0.116	0	0.815	916
% Native American	0.005	0.003	0.011	0	0.256	916
Ln(Pretreatment salary)	10.677	10.673	0.075	10.449	10.934	916
Pretreatment growth	0.004	0.002	0.041	−0.171	0.252	916

TABLE C5 **Summary statistics for table 5.6**

	Mean	Median	SD	Min	Max	N
Average teacher salary	10.667	10.661	0.083	10.382	11.221	6418
General administration	6.236	6.172	0.599	4.759	9.862	5502
On-cycle	0.081	0	0.273	0	1	6419
Ln(Enrollment)	6.944	6.797	1.495	2.303	11.991	6419
Ln(Property value)	19.519	19.326	1.542	15.054	25.148	6408
Average years of experience	12.519	12.58	2.414	0	22.560	6418
% Native American	0.005	0.003	0.012	0	0.279	6419
% Asian	0.009	0.004	0.021	0	0.268	6419
% Black	0.079	0.032	0.115	0	0.869	6419
% Hispanic	0.306	0.227	0.250	0	1	6419
Union (Census, treatment only)	0.155	0	0.279	0	1	1204
Union (SASS)	0.596	0.625	0.268	0	1	2513

Appendix D: Summary Statistics for Chapter 6

TABLE D1 **Summary statistics for table 6.1**

	At-large elections					
	Mean	Median	SD	Min	Max	N
Turnout	0.461	0.476	0.165	0.017	0.886	1916
Presidential general	0.417	0	0.493	0	1	1916
Presidential primary	0.020	0	0.141	0	1	1916
Gubernatorial general	0.276	0	0.447	0	1	1916
Gubernatorial primary	0.023	0	0.151	0	1	1916
Other state primary	0.011	0	0.107	0	1	1916
Special state	0.033	0	0.180	0	1	1916
Mayoral race	0.227	0	0.419	0	1	1916
Council competition	2.360	2.000	1.062	0.286	11	1916
Ln(Population)	10.003	10.161	1.298	5.278	12.898	1904

(*continued*)

TABLE D1 *continued*

	At-large elections					
	Mean	Median	SD	Min	Max	N
Ln(Income)	9.977	9.917	0.506	8.796	11.640	1904
% Minority	0.332	0.275	0.244	0.023	0.996	1904
% 65 and over	0.122	0.111	0.064	0.033	0.864	1904
Charter city	0.242	0	0.428	0	1	1916

	District elections					
	Mean	Median	SD	Min	Max	N
Turnout	0.388	0.377	0.159	0.108	0.604	34
General	0.412	0	0.5	0	1	34
Primary	0.265	0	0.448	0	1	34
Ln(Population)	12.063	11.925	1.268	9.318	15.122	34
Ln(Income)	9.795	9.780	0.369	8.865	10.553	34
% Minority	0.546	0.499	0.227	0.081	0.995	34
% 65 and over	0.096	0.088	0.052	0.049	0.375	34
Charter city	0.912	1	0.288	0	1	34

TABLE D2 **Summary statistics for table 6.2 and table 6.3**

	Mean	Median	SD	Min	Max	N
Minimum salary	61,480	61,251	13,843	29,062	102,099	177
Maximum salary	77,132	76,307	17,168	37,099	127,185	177
Total wages	97,353	101,737	26,402	31,882	152,470	177
Health benefits	10,434	10,211	4,471	70	21,450	171
Off-cycle	0.311	0	0.464	0	1	177
Primary	0.079	0	0.271	0	1	177
History of nonconcurrence	0.379	0	1.658	0	10	177
Ln(Income per capita)	10.021	9.938	0.439	9.208	11.499	177
Ln(Population)	10.883	10.963	1.230	4.554	15.207	177
% in Poverty	0.125	0.116	0.068	0	0.331	177
% African American	0.046	0.024	0.062	0	0.403	177
% Hispanic	0.291	0.241	0.211	0.028	0.953	177
% 65 and over	0.117	0.110	0.042	0.055	0.331	177
LA County	0.147	0	0.355	0	1	177
Charter city	0.435	0	0.497	0	1	177

TABLE D3 **Summary statistics for table 6.4**

	Mean	Median	SD	Min	Max	N
Minimum salary	60,747	61,094	12,973	26,448	98,676	273
Maximum salary	76,433	76,519	16,257	32,965	139,776	273
Total wages	88,603	89,551	21,150	29,016	143,635	272
Health benefits	11,025	10,972	4,070	657	21,450	265

(*continued*)

TABLE D3 *continued*

	Mean	Median	SD	Min	Max	N
Off-cycle	0.278	0	0.449	0	1	273
Primary	0.062	0	0.242	0	1	273
History of nonconcurrence	0.531	0	1.97	0	12	273
Ln(Income per capita)	9.973	9.915	0.487	8.865	11.640	272
Ln(Population)	10.461	10.573	1.288	4.554	15.207	273
% in Poverty	0.131	0.116	0.079	0	0.368	272
% African American	0.041	0.019	0.062	0	0.471	272
% Hispanic	0.304	0.239	0.239	0.022	0.970	272
% 65 and over	0.118	0.107	0.051	0.038	0.375	272
LA County	0.143	0	0.351	0	1	273
Charter city	0.308	0	0.462	0	1	273
Ln(Violent crime)	1.242	1.292	0.795	−2.038	6.415	266
Ln(Property crime)	3.369	3.333	0.551	1.945	8.471	266

TABLE D4 **Summary statistics for table 6.5**

	Mean	Median	SD	Min	Max	N
Exp. on fire protection	4.846	4.965	0.801	1.154	6.824	293
Exp. on police protection	5.534	5.547	0.568	2.027	8.850	465
Exp. on salaries	5.755	5.810	0.751	3.245	8.645	466
Exp. on benefits	4.345	4.406	0.933	−0.531	7.455	458
Exp. on retirement	5.111	5.242	1.049	−2.491	8.512	423
Total operating exp.	6.965	6.931	0.593	5.569	9.635	466
% Compensation	0.473	0.493	0.171	0.070	0.992	466
Off-cycle	0.286	0	0.452	0	1	476
Primary	0.055	0	0.227	0	1	476
History of nonconcurrence	0.513	0	1.897	0	12	476
Ln(Income per capita)	9.971	9.898	0.531	8.796	11.640	472
Ln(Population)	10.157	10.264	1.394	5.366	15.206	475
% Poverty	0.133	0.116	0.083	0.013	0.445	472
% African American	0.039	0.016	0.059	0	0.471	472
% Hispanic	0.299	0.228	0.245	0.021	0.983	472
% 65 and over	0.121	0.110	0.066	0.033	0.864	472
LA County	0.181	0	0.385	0	1	476
Charter city	0.248	0	0.432	0	1	476

Notes

Chapter 1

1. These turnout figures (for countries outside the United States) are averages from lower house elections from 1960 to 1995. See Mark N. Franklin, "Electoral Participation," in *Controversies in Voting Behavior*, 4th ed., ed. Richard G. Niemi and Herbert F. Weisberg (Washington, DC: CQ Press, 2001).

2. US Census Bureau, 2012 Census of Governments: Organization Component Preliminary Estimates. *Preliminary Count of Local Governments by Type and State: 2012* (Washington, DC: US Census Bureau, 2013).

3. It is not obvious why fewer voters participate in subnational elections than in presidential elections. In countries like Japan, the opposite pattern holds. See, for example, Yusaku Horiuchi, *Institutions, Incentives, and Electoral Participation in Japan: Cross-Level and Cross-National Perspectives* (New York: RoutledgeCurzon, 2005). Based on the rational choice model of voting, one might actually expect turnout to be *higher* in subnational elections. Many national policy decisions affect the typical American only remotely, whereas state and local governments determine how much property tax he pays on his home, how well the local public schools educate his children, what businesses are allowed to exist in his neighborhood, and so on. An individual's vote is also more likely to be pivotal in a local race than in a presidential race. It is true that perhaps the costs of participating are higher in local elections: presidential elections feature well-known candidates, are covered extensively by the media, and deal with well-publicized issues, whereas gaining information about local elections is usually much more difficult. Still, altogether, it is far from obvious why turnout in local elections in the United States is lower than in national elections. I do not propose an explanation for this puzzle; I merely wish to establish it as a feature of the American political landscape today. Certain types of elections attract more voters to the polls than others. Even if we do not fully understand why this is so, we can take it as a given and use that empirical fact as a starting point for building and testing a theory of election timing.

4. For example, see Sidney Verba, Kay Lehman Schlozman, and Henry E. Brady, *Voice and Equality: Civic Voluntarism in American Politics* (Cambridge, MA: Harvard University Press, 1995).

5. Figures are from the websites of the Berkeley city clerk (http://www.cityof berkeley.info/), the Santa Clara County Registrar of Voters (http://www.sccvote .org/portal/site/rov), and the California secretary of state (http://www.sos.ca.gov/).

6. In 2010, Palo Alto's municipal elections were moved to November of even-numbered years.

7. These differences are not due to the fact that these were ballot measures, since there were ballot measures in the odd-numbered years as well.

8. Zoltan L. Hajnal, Paul G. Lewis, and Hugh Louch, *Municipal Elections in California: Turnout, Timing, and Competition* (San Francisco: Public Policy Institute of California, 2002). See also Zoltan L. Hajnal and Paul G. Lewis, "Municipal Institutions and Voter Turnout in Local Elections," *Urban Affairs Review* 38, no. 5 (2003): 645–68.

9. Curtis Wood, "Voter Turnout in City Elections," *Urban Affairs Review* 38, no. 2 (2002): 209–31.

10. Neal Caren, "Big City, Big Turnout? Participation in American Cities," *Journal of Urban Affairs* 29, no. 1 (2007): 31–46.

11. Zoltan L. Hajnal, *America's Uneven Democracy: Race, Turnout, and Representation in City Politics* (New York: Cambridge University Press, 2010), 159.

12. Wood, "Voter Turnout in City Elections," 225.

13. Frederick M. Hess, *School Boards at the Dawn of the 21st Century: Conditions and Challenges of District Governance* (Alexandria, VA: National School Boards Association, 2002).

14. See, for example, Samuel C. Patterson and Gregory A. Caldeira, "Getting Out the Vote: Participation in Gubernatorial Elections," *American Political Science Review* 77, no. 3 (1983): 675–89.

15. Gary C. Jacobson, *The Politics of Congressional Elections* (New York: Longman, 2001).

16. To take a prominent example from American politics research, it would not be much of an exaggeration to say that the vast literature on the US Congress is largely a literature about institutions—how the committee system, the filibuster, and rules that favor the majority party affect the legislative process, how and why those institutions form in the first place, and so forth. Many of the biggest research questions that have occupied the minds of comparative politics scholars over the years are questions about how institutions arise and how they shape social and political outcomes. This focus on political institutions is especially central to research on elections in the United States, which asks questions about the impact of direct primaries, campaign finance rules, nonpartisan elections, voter ID laws, voter registration laws, direct democracy—and the list goes on. It is fair to say that motivating a large swath of research in political science is the conviction that political institutions should matter and a belief that we need to understand institutions if we want to understand politics and government.

17. In 2012, however, the state government enacted a law that allowed school boards to move their elections to November. See, for example, Jeanette Rundquist, "Gov. Christie Signs Bill Changing School Board Elections, Budget Votes," *Star-Ledger*, January 17, 2012.

18. For example, see the website of a group called Residents for Efficient Special Districts at www.resd.info.

19. Christopher Berry tells the story of Nassau County, New York, which actually had to carry out a study to figure out when its special districts held elections. See Christopher R. Berry, *Imperfect Union: Representation and Taxation in Multi-Level Government* (New York: Cambridge University Press, 2009), 64.

20. There are also a few nonbolded cells labeled "N/A," which means the state does not have that category of government.

21. Alan S. Gerber and Donald P. Green, "The Effects of Canvassing, Phone Calls, and Direct Mail on Voter Turnout: A Field Experiment," *American Political Science Review* 94, no. 3 (2000): 653–63.

22. Some of the classics are: Robert Dahl, *Who Governs? Democracy and Power in an American City* (New Haven, CT: Yale University Press, 1961); David B. Truman, *The Governmental Process: Political Interests and Public Opinion* (New York: Knopf, 1951); E. E. Schattschneider, *The Semisovereign People: A Realist's View of Democracy in America* (Fort Worth, TX: Holt, Reinhart, and Winston, 1961); Theodore Lowi, *The End of Liberalism: Ideology, Policy, and the Crisis of Public Authority* (New York: W. W. Norton, 1969); Mancur Olson, *The Logic of Collective Action* (Cambridge, MA: Harvard University Press, 1965).

23. See, for example, Sarah F. Anzia and Terry M. Moe, "Public Sector Unions and the Costs of Government," working paper, Stanford University, Stanford, CA, 2012; Kathleen Bawn et al., "A Theory of Political Parties: Groups, Policy Demands and Nominations in American Politics," *Perspectives on Politics* 10, no. 3 (2012): 571–97; Jacob S. Hacker and Paul Pierson, "Winner-Take-All Politics: Public Policy, Political Organization, and the Precipitous Rise of Top Incomes in the United States," *Politics & Society* 38, no. 2 (2010): 152–204.

24. Robert Dahl, *Who Governs? Democracy and Power in an American City*, 100–102.

25. Joanne M. Miller and Jon A. Krosnick, "The Impact of Candidate Name Order on Election Outcomes," *Public Opinion Quarterly* 62, no. 3 (1998): 291–330.

Chapter 2

1. For a mix of perspectives, see Theda Skocpol and Morris P. Fiorina, eds., *Civic Engagement in American Democracy* (Washington, DC: Brookings Institution Press, 1999).

2. See, for example, Benjamin Highton and Raymond E. Wolfinger, "The Political Implications of Higher Turnout," *British Journal of Political Science* 31,

no. 1 (2001): 179–223; Raymond E. Wolfinger and Steven J. Rosenstone, *Who Votes?* (New Haven, CT: Yale University Press, 1980).

3. Zoltan L. Hajnal and Jessica L. Trounstine, "Where Turnout Matters: The Consequences of Uneven Turnout in City Politics," *Journal of Politics* 67, no. 2 (2005): 515–35.

4. Hajnal, *America's Uneven Democracy*.

5. Stephanie Dunne, W. Robert Reed, and James Wilbanks, "Endogenizing the Median Voter: Public Choice Goes to School," *Public Choice* 93 (1997): 99–118; Marc Meredith, "The Strategic Timing of Direct Democracy," *Economics and Politics* 21, no. 1 (2009): 159–77.

6. Charles R. Adrian, *Governing Urban America: Structure, Politics, and Administration* (New York: McGraw-Hill, 1955), 72.

7. Steven J. Rosenstone and John Mark Hansen, *Mobilization, Participation, and Democracy in America* (New York: Macmillan, 1993).

8. John H. Aldrich, "Rational Choice and Turnout," *American Journal of Political Science* 37, no. 1 (1993): 246–78.

9. Wolfinger and Rosenstone, *Who Votes?*, chap. 5.

10. Rosenstone and Hansen, *Mobilization, Participation, and Democracy in America*. See also Angus Campbell, Philip E. Converse, Warren E. Miller, and Donald E. Stokes, *The American Voter* (New York: John Wiley and Sons, 1960), chap. 5.

11. William A. Fischel, *The Homevoter Hypothesis: How Home Values Influence Local Government Taxation, School Finance, and Land-Use Policies* (Cambridge, MA: Harvard University Press, 2001); J. Eric Oliver, *Local Elections and the Politics of Small-Scale Democracy* (Princeton, NJ: Princeton University Press, 2012).

12. Dunne, Reed, and Wilbanks, "Endogenizing the Median Voter," 99–118.

13. Meredith, "The Strategic Timing of Direct Democracy," 159–77.

14. Terry M. Moe, "Political Control and the Power of the Agent," *Journal of Law, Economics, and Organization* 22, no. 1 (2006): 1–29.

15. Berry, *Imperfect Union*.

16. See, for example, Morris P. Fiorina, "Extreme Voices: A Dark Side of Civic Engagement," in *Civic Engagement in American Democracy*, ed. Theda Skocpol and Morris P. Fiorina (Washington, DC: Brookings Institution Press, 1999): 395–426.

17. See, for example, Terry M. Moe, *Special Interest: Teachers Unions and America's Public Schools* (Washington, DC: Brookings Institution, 2011).

18. Social Capital Community Survey, 2006 (computer file), http://www.roper center.uconn.edu/data_access/data/datasets/social_capital_community_survey _2006.html (Roper Center for Public Opinion Research Study USMISC2006-SOCCAP Version 2, Saguaro Seminar [producer], accessed December 2, 2012), 2006. Storrs, CT: The Roper Center for Public Opinion Research, University of Connecticut (distributor), 2009.

19. The SCCS asks respondents, "How interested are you in politics and national affairs?" There are four possible responses (other than "Don't Know" and "Refused") ranging from "Not at all interested" to "Very interested."

20. Of course, some policy stakeholders may not be members of interest groups, and they, too, should have greater presence in off-cycle elections. However, the more that people perceive that they have a stake in politics, the more likely it will be that they will overcome the collective action problem and organize. See Terry Moe, *The Organization of Interests* (Chicago: University of Chicago Press, 1980).

21. Adrian, *Governing Urban America*, 72.

22. This assumes that the group does not face organized competition, a point I discuss shortly.

23. Moreover, this example treats the interest group's ability to mobilize as fixed, whereas successfully mobilizing five hundred supportive voters—meaning persuading five hundred people to vote who otherwise would *not*—might be easier in off-cycle elections than in on-cycle elections. As Kevin Arceneaux and David Nickerson point out, in a high-salience election, many voters—especially high-propensity voters—are committed to participating even *without* being mobilized. In low-salience elections, by contrast, there are many more voters who can potentially be moved. If the people most likely to support an interest group are high-propensity voters, off-cycle election timing might make the task of nudging an additional five hundred supportive voters to the polls quite a bit easier. Thus not only does each successfully mobilized voter carry more weight when turnout is low, but a group's success rate in turning abstainers into voters may be higher in off-cycle elections as well. For a discussion of how the salience of elections affects the types of voters impacted by mobilization efforts, see Kevin Arceneaux and David W. Nickerson, "Who Is Mobilized to Vote? A Re-Analysis of 11 Field Experiments," *American Journal of Political Science* 53, no. 1 (2009): 1–16.

24. The mechanism could work in one of two ways: Either the group could be more successful in replacing incumbents with candidates friendlier to their favored policies in off-cycle elections, or a looming off-cycle election could make sitting elected officials more responsive to the interest group since the group will be more important to their reelection chances than it would be in an on-cycle election.

25. See, for example, Moe, *The Organization of Interests*.

26. James Q. Wilson, *Political Organizations* (Princeton, NJ: Princeton University Press, 1995), 331–37.

27. See, for example, Oliver, *Local Elections and the Politics of Small-Scale Democracy*.

28. Meredith, "The Strategic Timing of Direct Democracy," 159–77.

29. Felicia Sonmez, "The Fix: Timing of West Virginia Gubernatorial Election in Doubt," *Washington Post*, December 28, 2010.

30. Roy Salume, San Mateo County election inspector, e-mail message to author, September 2010.

31. I call the second type of voters *Presidential Voters* only because turnout tends to be highest during presidential elections. What I wish to emphasize is that these voters vote in a given election only when it is held at the same time as an-

other election the voters care more about—the primary reason that they make the trip to the polls.

32. This assumes the groups mobilize the same number of supporters in off-cycle and on-cycle elections. I return to this point shortly.

33. Steven Harmon, "California GOP Hard-Pressed to Dispute Law That Moves Initiatives to November Ballot," *San Jose Mercury News*, October 24, 2011.

34. See, for example, Elisabeth R. Gerber, *The Populist Paradox: Interest Group Influence and the Promise of Direct Legislation* (Princeton, NJ: Princeton University Press, 1999), 11.

35. See John Aldrich, *Why Parties? The Origin and Transformation of Political Parties in America* (Chicago: University of Chicago Press, 1995).

36. However, the distinction between political parties and interest groups is blurrier in multiparty systems, where political parties are frequently narrow in scope and small in size.

37. In fact, if political elites design parties according to their needs, as John Aldrich argues, parties are endogenous institutions that might not actually have "goals" independent of the elites who create and manage them. See Aldrich, *Why Parties?*

38. This chapter's first prediction—that interest group *members* will make up a greater proportion of the electorate in off-cycle elections because of the large stake they have in elections—has a looser connection to the analysis of political parties. Today, "membership" in a political party is not really the same thing as membership in an interest group: one can self-identify with the Democratic Party without being a member of it in the same sense as one is a member of AARP or a labor union. However, it is likely that partisans, and perhaps even strong partisans, make up a greater proportion of the electorate as turnout decreases. See, for example, James DeNardo, "Turnout and the Vote: The Joke's on the Democrats," *American Political Science Review* 74, no. 2 (1980): 406–20.

Chapter 3

1. Parts of this chapter were previously published in Sarah F. Anzia, "Partisan Power Play: The Origins of Local Election Timing in the United States," *Studies in American Political Development* 26, no. 1 (2012): 24–49, © Cambridge University Press. These parts are reprinted with permission.

2. See, for example, Keith Krehbiel, *Information and Legislative Organization* (Ann Arbor: University of Michigan Press, 1991), 29.

3. William H. Riker, "Implications from the Disequilibrium of Majority Rule for the Study of Institutions," *American Political Science Review* 74, no. 2 (1980): 445.

4. For examples of work that treats electoral institutions as endogenous, see, for example, Carles Boix, "Setting the Rules of the Game: The Choice of Electoral

Systems in Advanced Democracies," *American Political Science Review* 93, no. 3 (1999): 609–24; Thomas Cusack, Torben Iversen, and David Soskice, "Economic Interests and the Origins of Electoral Systems," *American Political Science Review* 101, no. 3 (2007): 373–91.

5. Dunne, Reed, and Wilbanks, "Endogenizing the Median Voter."

6. Meredith, "The Strategic Timing of Direct Democracy."

7. Steven P. Erie, "How the Urban West Was Won," *Urban Affairs Review* 27, no. 4 (1992): 519–54.

8. Contributors to a large literature in comparative politics have developed theories of how prime ministers make such decisions. Some scholars argue that governments wait until economic conditions are just right before they call elections. See, for example, Nathan Balke, "The Rational Timing of Parliamentary Elections," *Public Choice* 65 (1990): 201–16; Abdur R. Chowdhury, "Political Surfing over Economic Waves: Parliamentary Election Timing in India," *American Journal of Political Science* 37, no. 4 (1993): 1100–1118; Bernard Grofman and Peter van Roozendaal, "Toward a Theoretical Explanation of Premature Cabinet Termination," *European Journal of Political Research* 26 (1994): 155–70. Others show that incumbent parties use available policy instruments to construct favorable economic conditions just before the scheduled election. See Alberto Alesina, Nouriel Roubini, and Gerald Cohen, *Political Cycles and Macroeconomy* (Cambridge, MA: MIT Press, 1997); Masaru Kohno and Yoshitaka Nishizawa, "A Study of the Electoral Business Cycle in Japan: Elections and Government Spending on Public Construction," *Comparative Politics* 22, no. 2 (1990): 151–66. Alastair Smith points out the conceptual similarities between these two strategies and argues that early elections are a signal to voters that economic conditions are about to decline. See Alastair Smith, *Election Timing* (New York: Cambridge University Press, 2004).

9. Gary W. Cox, *Making Votes Count: Strategic Coordination in the World's Electoral Systems* (New York: Cambridge University Press, 1997).

10. Gabriel L. Negretto, "Choosing How to Choose Presidents: Parties, Military Rulers, and Presidential Elections in Latin America," *Journal of Politics* 68, no. 2 (2006): 421–33.

11. Philip J. Ethington, *The Public City: The Political Construction of Urban Life in San Francisco, 1850–1900* (New York: Cambridge University Press, 1994).

12. Erik J. Engstrom and Samuel Kernell, "Manufactured Responsiveness: The Impact of State Electoral Laws on Unified Party Control of the Presidency and House of Representatives, 1840–1940," *American Journal of Political Science* 49, no. 3 (2005): 531–49.

13. See Edward C. Banfield and James Q. Wilson, *City Politics* (Cambridge, MA: Harvard University Press, 1967); Richard Hofstadter, *The Age of Reform: From Bryan to F.D.R.* (New York: Alfred A. Knopf, 1956); Raymond E. Wolfinger and John Osgood Field, "Political Ethos and the Structure of City Government," *American Political Science Review* 60, no. 2 (1966): 306–26.

14. "Reasons for Spring Elections," *New York Times*, November 7, 1884, 4.

15. "Independence in Municipal Elections," *New York Times*, February 17, 1881, 4.

16. Amy Bridges, *Morning Glories: Municipal Reform in the Southwest* (Princeton, NJ: Princeton University Press, 1997), 16.

17. Bridges, *Morning Glories: Municipal Reform in the Southwest*. See also Amy Bridges and Richard Kronick, "Writing the Rules to Win the Game," *Urban Affairs Review* 34, no. 5 (1999): 691–706.

18. Jessica Trounstine, *Political Monopolies in American Cities* (Chicago: University of Chicago Press, 2008).

19. Frank J. Goodnow, *City Government in the United States* (New York: Century, 1908), 106.

20. Ethington's study of San Francisco is an exception; he discusses the importance of the city's election schedule for political parties' electoral success. See Ethington, *The Public City*.

21. See, for example, Aldrich, *Why Parties?*; David R. Mayhew, *Placing Parties in American Politics* (Princeton, NJ: Princeton University Press, 1986); Richard P. McCormick, *The Second American Party System* (Chapel Hill: University of North Carolina Press, 1966); Richard L. McCormick, *The Party Period and Public Policy* (New York: Oxford University Press, 1986).

22. John A. Fairlie, "Municipal Development in the United States," in *A Municipal Program: Report of a Committee of the National Municipal League* (London: Macmillan, 1900).

23. Richard F. Bensel, *The American Ballot Box in the Mid-Nineteenth Century* (New York: Cambridge University Press, 2004).

24. Undoubtedly, these would be approximations, since election timing could change the nature of party competition in the city, as I discuss below. Moreover, even the voters who consistently voted in local elections could change their votes for city candidates depending on when the elections were held.

25. Admittedly, it is difficult to separate organizational capacity from voter loyalty empirically. Increased voter loyalty likely strengthens a party's organization, just as a strong party organization can work to increase the number of voters loyal to the party. In theory, however, these are separable concepts. Voter loyalties in a city could be fixed at a given point in time, but party organizations may or may not have the resources and organization to encourage those individuals to vote in city elections.

26. Peter H. Argersinger, "A Place on the Ballot: Fusion Politics and Antifusion Laws," *American Historical Review* 85, no. 2 (1980): 287–306.

27. Amy Bridges, *A City in the Republic: Antebellum New York and the Origins of Machine Politics* (New York: Cambridge University Press, 1984), 140–41. See also "The Local Problem," *New York Times*, September 27, 1884, 4.

28. General law practices came into vogue in the late nineteenth century. See Nancy Burns and Gerald Gamm, "Creatures of the State: State Politics and Local

Government, 1871–1921," *Urban Affairs Review* 33, no. 1 (1997): 59–96; Gerald Gamm and Thad Kousser, "Broad Bills or Particularistic Policy? Historical Patterns in American State Legislatures," *American Political Science Review* 104, no. 1 (2010): 151–70; Jon C. Teaford, *The Unheralded Triumph: City Government in America, 1870–1900* (Baltimore: Johns Hopkins University Press, 1984).

29. These cities were also home to sizeable proportions of the populations of their states. See Campbell Gibson, "Population of the 100 Largest Cities and Other Urban Places in the United States: 1790–1990" (Washington, DC: US Bureau of the Census Population Division, 1998), table 11.

30. Steven P. Erie, *Rainbow's End: Irish-Americans and the Dilemmas of Urban Machine Politics, 1840–1985* (Berkeley: University of California Press, 1988), 2.

31. This is a critical preliminary step, for if today's large turnout gap between concurrent and nonconcurrent local elections did not exist during the nineteenth century, there may have been little to no difference between the composition of on-cycle and off-cycle electorates.

32. An exception, as discussed above, is Ethington, *The Public City*.

33. In particular, I rely heavily on Bridges, *A City in the Republic*; Erie, *Rainbow's End*; Ethington, *The Public City*; Peter McCaffery, *When Bosses Ruled Philadelphia* (University Park: Pennsylvania State University Press, 1993).

34. See appendix A. I attempted to use "official" election returns whenever possible, but oftentimes the official results were not reported in comprehensive fashion, and I had to rely on day-after reports of votes for candidates by ward. Even the official election statistics are not fully reliable, since there were far fewer election regulations in the nineteenth century than there are today.

35. See Bridges, *A City in the Republic*, 20, 81, 133. Bridges does not mention election timing in her discussion of figure 2 on page 20, but that figure makes it clear that turnout in city elections dipped below November turnout for the period in which city elections were held in April.

36. The Tammany Hall Democrats had a strong ward-based organization thanks to their history of mass party mobilization in New York City and a greater number of years in control of city patronage. With the exception of 1837 and 1838, when factionalism within the Democratic Party helped the Whigs to win the mayoralty, the Democrats had a consistent edge in city elections prior to the mid-1840s. They won especially large victories in elections in which nativist parties ran their own candidates and drained support from the Whigs. However, the Whigs consistently put up a strong opposition, commanding a large portion of the state government patronage that was available for distribution in the city. By the late 1840s, the Whigs competed with the Democrats on relatively even terms.

37. The Whigs might have had some incentive to move city elections to November in the mid-1840s in order to encourage the third-party nativists to fuse a ticket with them (since the nativists generally drained support from the Whigs), but the Democrats controlled the state legislature at that time.

38. The Democratic contingency in the Assembly was also divided. The fragmentation of the Democratic Party in state and national politics likely explains some of the strengthening of the Whig vote in November elections. See Bridges, *A City in the Republic*, 96–97.

39. "The New York Legislature," *Weekly Herald*, March 31, 1849, page 102, issue 13, column A.

40. "The New City Charter for the City of New York," *New York Herald*, April 3, 1849, column E.

41. "Election Returns: The General Result in the State," *Albany Evening Journal*, November 6, 1850, 2; *New York Herald*, November 6, 1850.

42. Local Democratic leaders tried to change city election timing back to April during the early 1850s, but these efforts were not taken up by the state legislature, which was either dominated by Whigs or split between the parties during this time period.

43. See, for example, Bridges, *A City in the Republic*, 34, 147.

44. To illustrate, in 1853, an election year in which there was no presidential or gubernatorial race on the ballot, the reformers managed to combine a ticket with the nativist Know Nothing party, and the fused ticket won a slight majority of the city's aldermanic seats. In 1854 and 1856, however, the Know Nothings had gubernatorial and presidential candidates at stake and feared that combining a local slate with the reformers would undermine their local party organization for state and national races. The reformers won only 26% and 5% of the vote, respectively, in those years. As Bridges explains, during nonpresidential years, "wealthy men could gather at a single meeting and support a reform candidate," whereas those same men were dedicated to their respective parties during presidential and gubernatorial years. See Bridges, *A City in the Republic*, 34–38, 140–43. See also "The Local Problem," *New York Times,* September 27, 1884, 4.

45. "Municipal Reform," *New York Daily Times*, March 7, 1853, 1; "City Reform at Albany," *New York Daily Times*, March 19, 1853, 1 and 4; "Proposed Amendment of the New-York City Charter," *New York Daily Times*, March 31, 1853, 3.

46. See M. R. Werner, *Tammany Hall* (New York: Doubleday, Doran, 1928), 79–80.

47. The revised charter made other changes to city government. For example, much of the authority over the city police was transferred from the city to the state government. "Important from Albany," *New York Daily Times*, March 3, 1857, 1; "State Affairs," *New York Daily Times*, March 27, 1857, 1.

48. The reformers' choice to promote December elections rather than the former April city election date was almost certainly calculated. In presidential and gubernatorial years, the springtime city vote had been viewed as an important indicator for how the parties would fare in the upcoming autumn state and national races, much like today's primaries. For a description of how this was also true in pre-1870s congressional elections, see Scott C. James, "Timing and Sequence in

Congressional Elections: Interstate Contagion and America's Nineteenth Century Scheduling Regime," *Studies in American Political Development* 21, no. 2 (2007): 1–22; Sarah M. Butler and Scott C. James, "Electoral Order and Political Participation: Election Scheduling, Calendar Position, and Antebellum Congressional Turnout," paper presented at the Annual Meeting of the Midwest Political Science Association, Chicago, IL, April 3–6, 2008.

49. "The Election Yesterday," *New York Times,* December 2, 1857, 4. However, Democratic candidates still won nearly half of the votes in the city even in that December election. It was thus the ability of the opposition to unite behind a single slate that led to its victory in 1857.

50. The city election in December 1862 did not feature a mayoral race. The highest citywide office on the ballot was city controller, a much sought-after office since it involved control of the city's funds. I examine this set of elections because they occurred a month apart, because each featured only a single Democratic candidate and a single Republican candidate, and because the data were available.

51. In two wards (the 1st and the 12th), turnout increased slightly, but the Democratic city controller still received a smaller percentage of the vote than the Democratic candidate for governor had received in those wards. In the single ward where the Democratic controller candidate fared better than the Democratic candidate for governor, turnout increased by over 30%.

52. Werner, *Tammany Hall*, 104.

53. Erie, *Rainbow's End*, 52.

54. It does not seem that this was an effect of New York City's off-cycle election isolation from pro-Republican national tides. The New York City vote share for Republican gubernatorial candidates was relatively steady throughout the Civil War and the years following it, except for 1864.

55. "Political," *New York Times*, May 15, 1870, 8.

56. "The State Legislature. Senate. Assembly. The City Charter," *New York Times*, February 3, 1870, 1; "The Newest Charter," *New York Times*, March 11, 1870, 2; "Albany," *New York Times*, February 11, 1870, 1.

57. "Albany," *New York Times,* April 6, 1870, 1; "Our New City Government," *New York Times*, April 13, 1870, 4.

58. "Albany," *New York Times*, March 31, 1870, 1.

59. "The Legislature and the City," *New York Times*, December 14, 1875, 4.

60. See, for example, "The Result of the Election," *New York Times*, May 18, 1870, 4.

61. "The Machine Ticket," *New York Times*, October 23, 1884, 4; "Defeated in the Senate," *New York Times*, March 25, 1885, 1; "The Elections Amendment," *New York Times*, April 18, 1885, 4; "Partisanship and City Government," *New York Times*, June 28, 1890, 4; "The Republicans and Tammany," *New York Times*, October 24, 1891, 4.

62. "Separate City Elections," *New York Times*, December 17, 1890, 4.

63. "The Platt Fight 'Up the State,'" *New York Times*, March 3, 1894, 4; "Bitter Talk against Platt," *New York Times*, July 27, 1894, 1.

64. "Non-Partisan Organization," *New York Times*, December 8, 1893, 4.

65. Delos F. Wilcox, "An Examination of the Proposed Municipal Program," in *A Municipal Program: Report of a Committee of the National Municipal League* (London: Macmillan, 1900); McCormick, *The Party Period and Public Policy*.

66. Erie, *Rainbow's End*, 97–99.

67. San Francisco Board of Supervisors, *San Francisco Municipal Reports for the Fiscal Year 1909–10, Ended June 30, 1910* (San Francisco: Neal Publishing, 1911).

68. See Erie, *Rainbow's End*, 27.

69. Ethington, *The Public City*, 166–67.

70. The leaders of the People's Party were committed to preserving the organization as a purely municipal party and resolved to stay out of the fray of state and national contests. In the mid-1850s, they agreed to support Republicans for state offices, and in turn, the new Republican Nominating Committee voted to endorse the People's candidates for San Francisco offices. See "Withdrawal of the Legislative Nominations by the People's Committee," *Daily Evening Bulletin*, October 20, 1856, issue 11, column B; "Our Opinion of the Duty of Reformers in the Municipal and Legislative Local Elections," *Daily Evening Bulletin*, October 29, 1856, issue 20, column A; "The Republican Bolters," *Daily Evening Bulletin*, October 11, 1856, issue 4, column A.

71. Debate over the Lecompton Constitution of Kansas split the Democrats at the national level, and the issue rose to the fore in San Francisco politics as well. The Lecompton and the Anti-Lecompton Democrats both nominated slates of candidates for state and city offices in 1858 and 1859, and the Anti-Lecompton Democrats siphoned off support from the People's Party. The Democratic split hurt the Republicans at the state level as well, and in 1859, the Republicans tried to fuse their ticket with the Anti-Lecompton Democrats. When the fusion attempt failed, the Anti-Lecompton party won enough votes in the city to hand almost the entire San Francisco delegation of the state legislature to the Lecompton Democrats. In the city races, the People's Party just barely squeaked out a victory. They won with less than a majority, which meant that if the Democrats somehow managed to combine their efforts in the city election the following year, they would almost certainly win. See "Election Returns—City and County of San Francisco," *Daily Evening Bulletin*, September 3, 1858, issue 126, column C; "Lessons of the Campaign," *Daily Evening Bulletin*, September 10, 1858, issue 133, column A.

72. While the Douglas Democrats held a plurality in the legislature, they were not hostile to the election timing change, and some even considered them to be supportive of the People's Party in the city. See Ethington, *The Public City*, 221.

73. See "Local and Political Elections," *Daily Evening Bulletin*, January 26, 1861, issue 93, column A. The same assemblyman, S. S. Tilton, had proposed the

election timing change a year earlier, but Lecompton Democrats had controlled the state legislature at the time, and the Lecompton Democrats were not interested in helping the People's Party. See, for example, "The New Municipal Election Bill for San Francisco," *Daily Evening Bulletin*, February 18, 1860, issue 112, column E.

74. However, Republicans only ran candidates for state offices and the People's Party only for local offices.

75. It is even possible that Douglas Democrats and Republicans in the legislature moved San Francisco elections to off-cycle to make it easier for them to fuse a ticket to run against the People's Party.

76. These two organizations did not combine their efforts in the fall state election of 1861, which suggests that they most likely would not have combined their municipal tickets if city elections had been held in the fall. "The New Fusion Ticket—Who Are the Candidates," *Daily Evening Bulletin*, May 15, 1861, issue 33, column C; "The Voter's Manual," *Daily Evening Bulletin*, May 20, 1861, issue 37, column D.

77. "The Combination Which Made the Mongrel Ticket," *Daily Evening Bulletin*, May 19, 1862, issue 36, column A.

78. Although, note that the People's Party had also won 57% of the vote in 1860 when it ran candidates under the combined label of People's/Republican/Bell.

79. Just as in New York, the spring election in San Francisco in 1864 took on a national tone in anticipation of the upcoming presidential election. The People's Party ran under the label of the People's Union Party and announced that it was "the choice of the true Union voters of the city." See "The Voter's Manual," *Daily Evening Bulletin*, May 16, 1864, page 5, issue 33, column D.

80. Ethington, *The Public City*, 196–98.

81. Previously, there had been years in which no state officers' terms expired but city elections were held.

82. Ethington, *The Public City*, 250–51.

83. Ethington argues that this change worked to the advantage of the major parties. Ethington, *The Public City*, 289–92. The Republican-dominated state legislature of 1880–82 had an opportunity to move city elections to off-cycle in order to discourage the turnout of the Presidential Voters who favored the Democrats, but at that time, the bigger threat came from third parties like the Workingmen's Party. Besides, the local delegation in the assembly was still strongly Democratic.

84. Ethington, *The Public City*, 342.

85. "The Question of Elections," *San Francisco Chronicle*, February 10, 1898, 5.

86. "New Charter Is Finished," *San Francisco Chronicle*, March 26, 1898, 7.

87. Ethington, *The Public City*, 342.

88. "City Items," *North American and United States Gazette*, November 23, 1853, 1.

89. Indeed, in the state legislature, representatives from the areas of Phila-delphia County outside of Philadelphia City were all Democrats, whereas the dele-gation from Philadelphia City was fully Whig. See, for example, "The Union of the City and the Districts in One Municipal City Corporation," *North American and United States Gazette*, October 31, 1849, issue 16,766, column G; "The Election and What It Settles," *North American and United States Gazette*, October 15, 1853, issue 18,917, column B.

90. "From Harrisburg," *North American and United States Gazette*, March 8, 1851, issue 18,084, column F; "From Harrisburg," *North American and United States Gazette*, March 28, 1851, issue 18,100, column F.

91. "From Harrisburg," *North American and United States Gazette*, April 19, 1852, issue 18,435, column E.

92. Ibid.

93. "Pennsylvania Legislature, Harrisburg," *Public Ledger*, February 3, 1854, 3. The measure not only extended the boundaries of the municipal government, tri-pling the population of the electorate, but also divided the city into twenty-three wards and altered the terms of the municipal officers. See "Synopsis of the Bill for Consolidating the City and County into One City," *Public Ledger*, November 10, 1853, 1. There was debate within the Committee on Consolidation about the change in election timing, but the specifics of that debate were not discussed in the local newspapers. "City Items," *North American and United States Gazette*, Novem-ber 23, 1853, 1. Off-cycle elections also facilitated Whig fusion with the nativists, and for two years after the new election schedule was instituted, the Whigs man-aged to stay in control of city government. "Election Results," *North American and United States Gazette*, June 7, 1854; "The Election," *North American and United States Gazette*, May 2, 1855.

94. If the Republicans had tried to shift city elections back to on-cycle during this period, they would have run up against either a fully Democratic or a divided state legislature.

95. "The Change in the Municipal Election," *Philadelphia Inquirer*, March 12, 1861; "House of Representatives," *Philadelphia Inquirer*, March 20, 1861.

96. "House of Representatives," *Philadelphia Inquirer*, March 20, 1861.

97. Ibid.

98. "Legislative Acts or Legal Proceedings," *Philadelphia Inquirer*, March 29, 1861.

99. "The Change in the Municipal Election," *Philadelphia Inquirer*, March 12, 1861.

100. "Local Intelligence: The Constitutional Union Party and the Postponed Spring Election," *Philadelphia Inquirer*, April 4, 1861.

101. "The October Election," *Philadelphia Inquirer*, July 31, 1861; "No Half Way Reforms," August 23, 1861.

102. McCaffery, *When Bosses Ruled Philadelphia*, 8–9. See also "Election Re-turns," *Philadelphia Inquirer*, October 14, 1863, 14.

103. See McCaffery, *When Bosses Ruled Philadelphia*, 53, 70, 141.

104. The original proposal was for city elections in March, but it was amended early in the debate so that elections would be held in February instead. Reformers complained that the state legislature passed many special bills that affected individual governments instead of legislation that applied uniformly to all local governments in the state. See Mahlon H. Hellerich, "The Origin of the Pennsylvania Constitutional Convention of 1873," *Pennsylvania History* 34, no. 2 (1967): 158–86.

105. "Philadelphia and Suburbs, Constitutional Convention," *Philadelphia Inquirer*, January 21, 1873.

106. *Philadelphia Inquirer*, January 24, 1873, 2. Many Republican delegates from other parts of the state supported the change to off-cycle city elections, but that is not surprising. There were likely areas of Pennsylvania in which Republicans benefited from off-cycle local elections, and the provision voted on by the delegates to the constitutional convention was to affect the election timing of *all* cities in the state.

107. McCaffery, *When Bosses Ruled Philadelphia*, 31.

108. Ethington, *The Public City*, 221; Negretto, "Choosing How to Choose Presidents."

109. See, for example, Trounstine, *Political Monopolies in American Cities*, 53–56.

110. Ethington, *The Public City*, 222–27.

111. See Trounstine's discussion of how a coalition can actually benefit from the institutions implemented by past coalitions. Trounstine, *Political Monopolies in American Cities*, 37.

112. Ernest S. Griffith, *A History of American City Government: The Conspicuous Failure, 1870–1900* (New York: Praeger, 1974), 212.

113. William E. Sackett, *Modern Battles of Trenton* (New York: Neale Publishing, 1914), 102.

114. Craig M. Brown and Charles N. Halaby, "Machine Politics in America, 1870–1945," *Journal of Interdisciplinary History* 17, no. 3 (1987): 587–612.

115. Frank Mann Stewart, *A Half Century of Municipal Reform* (Berkeley: University of California Press, 1950), 9.

116. Melvin G. Holli, "Urban Reform in the Progressive Era," in *The Progressive Era*, ed. Lewis L. Gould (Syracuse, NY: Syracuse University Press, 1974).

117. Griffith, *A History of American City Government*, 269.

118. If there were any cases in which a local reform organization wanted on-cycle elections and the National Municipal League advocated off-cycle election timing for the city, that would suggest the national league was pursuing something other than the electoral success of local reform groups. I do not know of any such cases, but I cannot know whether that is because no such cases exist or because I have not investigated a comprehensive set of cities.

119. See Griffith, *A History of American City Government*, 246–47.

120. Clarence E. Ridley and Orin F. Nolting, eds., *The Municipal Year Book 1940* (Chicago: International City Managers' Association, 1940), 29–60.

121. This number excludes thirty-eight cities that are missing data on election timing in 1986, two cases that are missing election timing information from 1940, and sixty-five cities that had annual November elections as of 1986.

122. It would be extremely tedious to determine whether each city election date was also the date of a state or national primary election (or even a state election not concurrent with a national election), and so I focus here on the date of national general elections. Since the 1986 survey asked respondents for both the date of their last regular election and their next regular election, I am able to drop any cities that had annual November elections as of 1986 (since they had a combination of on-cycle and off-cycle elections).

123. Delaware did not have any municipal governments that appeared in both ICMA datasets.

124. Initially, many state legislatures circumvented such bans on special legislation by devising complicated city classification systems based on population and then creating laws for specific classes of cities—which sometimes contained only a single city. See, for example, Teaford, *The Unheralded Triumph*, 93. However, by the 1890s and early 1900s, even those classification systems were eliminated, and state legislators were forced to govern cities within their boundaries in a uniform fashion.

125. Teaford, *The Unheralded Triumph*, 121–22.

126. Jerrold G. Rusk, "The Effect of the Australian Ballot Reform on Split Ticket Voting: 1876–1908," *American Political Science Review* 64, no. 4 (1970): 1220–38.

127. Elisabeth S. Clemens, *The People's Lobby: Organizational Innovation and the Rise of Interest Group Politics in the United States, 1890–1925* (Chicago: University of Chicago Press, 1997); Theodore J. Lowi, *The End of Liberalism: The Second Republic of the United States* (New York: W. W. Norton, 1979); McCormick, *The Party Period and Public Policy,* 302, 306–7.

128. Bridges, *Morning Glories*; Trounstine, *Political Monopolies in American Cities*.

129. Raymond E. Wolfinger, "Why Political Machines Have Not Withered Away and Other Revisionist Thoughts," *Journal of Politics* 34, no. 2 (1972): 395.

130. There are a few states that still allow fusion balloting, such as New York and Connecticut, but the practice is much less common than it was during the nineteenth century. See, for example, Alyssa Katz, "The Power of Fusion Politics," *The Nation*, September 12, 2005, http://www.thenation.com/article/power-fusion-politics, accessed November 14, 2012.

Chapter 4

1. Melissa M. Deckman, *School Board Battles: The Christian Right in Local Politics* (Washington, DC: Georgetown University Press, 2004).

2. Banfield and Wilson, *City Politics*, 87.

3. There are exceptions to this rule, however: state governments can sometimes create laws that only apply to a particular local government or a small subset of local governments.

4. Banfield and Wilson, *City Politics*, 87.

5. As I discuss later, election timing usually falls into what Kathleen Bawn and co-authors refer to as the "electoral blind spot." See Bawn et al., "A Theory of Political Parties: Groups, Policy Demands and Nominations in American Politics," 571–97.

6. On legislators' motivation to please constituents in their districts, see David R. Mayhew, *Congress: The Electoral Connection* (New Haven, CT: Yale University Press, 1974).

7. The nature of the relationship between interest groups and political parties is a subject of some debate. One theory posits that parties are created by elected officials for the purpose of helping them win reelection. By this account, interest groups provide important services to the parties but are not the reason that parties get organized in the first place. See Aldrich, *Why Parties?* Others, such as E. E. Schattschneider and, more recently, Bawn and coauthors, theorize that interest groups create parties to help them win majorities. See, for example, Schattschneider, *A Semisovereign People*, and Bawn et al., "A Theory of Political Parties: Groups, Policy Demands and Nominations in American Politics," 571–97.

8. This was an Internet survey of a nationally representative sample of one thousand people.

9. The order of the second and third sentences was randomized, so that some respondents saw the argument in favor of concurrent elections first. The response options were "Same day" and "Different day," which were also randomized.

10. This figure only includes American citizens and excludes the 20% of respondents who did not answer the question.

11. This is the result of an OLS regression in which the dependent variable is a binary indicator for preference for "Same day" local elections and the predictors are age of respondent, a binary indicator for whether the respondent is male, the respondent's educational attainment coded as a six-point scale (no high school, high school graduate, some college, two-year college degree, four-year college degree, postgraduate degree), and binary indicators for whether the respondent is African American or Hispanic.

12. The differences between Democrats and Republicans and Democrats and Independents are statistically significant at the 5% level in a two-sided test. Republicans and Independents are not significantly different. These results hold when I use OLS regression and control for age, sex, educational attainment, and race and ethnicity.

13. When I group moderates and conservatives together, a two-sided *t*-test rejects the null hypothesis of no difference between liberals and nonliberals at the 10% level.

14. Both would suggest that state elected officials shouldn't feel pressed to be responsive to voters, but the implications for representation are different. If voters do not care about the timing of elections, then they aren't necessarily badly represented by a government that maintains a system of off-cycle local elections. However, if voters *do* care about election timing and wish that the election schedule were different, a resistance to change by state government would indicate a breakdown in representation.

15. The differences between liberals and conservatives and liberals and moderates are statistically significant, but the differences between Republicans, Democrats, and Independents are not.

16. I focus on state legislatures because they are the most important decision makers when it comes to election timing. As I explained earlier, however, many state governments give their local governments discretion to choose their own election schedules. Moreover, many local governments with home rule can set their own election schedules. A comprehensive study of election timing choice would therefore have to look at decision making at both the state and local levels, but given the number of local governments in the United States, this would be an enormous task. Besides, even if local governments have control over their own election schedules, it is ultimately the state government that grants them that control. Thus by focusing on state legislatures, I make the task manageable and center my analysis on the most important political actors.

17. The database has been compiled over the years by NCSL researchers' searches of state legislatures' websites. The researcher in charge of this process explained that she used different strategies to search for the election bills, depending on the state. Some states index bills by topic, in which case she looked at the relevant categories. In others, she searched the pages for committees that had jurisdiction over elections. In yet others, she had to browse through lists of all introduced legislation or use text searches. Starting in 2011, however, the researchers used Statenet to track bills and then manually added any bills they became aware of later. Jennie Bowser, National Conference of State Legislatures, e-mail message to the author, December 13, 2011.

18. In addition to eliminating irrelevant bills, I had to eliminate one bill from Massachusetts because there was no information available on the bill (SB 354 from 2001).

19. The dataset includes a few bills that proposed consolidating all local elections on a single day. For simplicity's sake, I coded these bills as affecting county, municipal, school, and special district elections, even if one of those government types already had its elections on the proposed day.

20. In contrast, the only state that had a proposal to move their on-cycle state elections to the odd-numbered years during this time period was New Hampshire.

21. For example, for a bill that never even received a committee hearing, I code according to the provisions of the original introduced bill. For a bill that passed

one chamber but never received a committee hearing in the second, I code according to the text of the bill that passed the first chamber.

22. Jeffrey L. Barnett and Phillip M. Vidal, "State and Local Government Finances Summary: 2010" (Washington, DC: US Census Bureau, September 2012), 7.

23. Moe, "Political Control and the Power of the Agent," 1–29.

24. Terry M. Moe, "Teacher Unions and School Board Elections," in *Besieged: School Boards and the Future of Education Politics*, ed. William G. Howell (Washington, DC: Brookings Institution Press, 2005), 254–87.

25. Frederick M. Hess and David L. Leal, "School House Politics: Expenditures, Interests, and Competition in School Board Elections," in *Besieged: School Boards and the Future of Education Politics*, ed. William G. Howell (Washington, DC: Brookings Institution Press, 2005), 228–52.

26. Moe, "Teacher Unions and School Board Elections," 254–87.

27. Charlene K. Haar, *The Politics of the PTA* (Somerset, NJ: Transaction Publishers, 2002); Myron Lieberman, *The Teacher Unions* (New York: Free Press, 1997); Moe, "Teacher Unions and School Board Elections," 254–87.

28. Hess and Leal, "School House Politics," 228–52.

29. Moe, "Teacher Unions and School Board Elections," 254–87.

30. See, for example, Cox, *Making Votes Count.*

31. One way to distinguish between these two hypotheses about school board associations' positions on election timing bills would be to look at proposals to move school board elections to *off*-cycle: The first hypothesis would predict that school board associations would be opposed to such proposals, whereas the second hypothesis would predict that school board associations would favor them. However, I only have six cases of school board election timing bills that propose moving school elections to off-cycle, so my ability to carry out such a test is limited.

32. Wilson, *Political Organizations.*

33. See Moe, "Teacher Unions and School Board Elections," 254–87.

34. See Moe, *Special Interest*; Martin West, "Bargaining with Authority: The Political Origins of Public Sector Bargaining," paper presented at the Policy History Conference, St. Louis, MO, May 29–June 1, 2008.

35. Michigan House of Representatives, House Legislative Analysis Section, *Analysis of Senate Bills 438–444, 760, 1092, and 1202* (Lansing, MI, November 12, 2002), 1. Analysis available at http://www.michiganlegislature.org.

36. "Bills Would Reset School Elections," *Ann Arbor News*, June 23, 2003.

37. Michigan House of Representatives, House Legislative Analysis Section, *Analysis of Senate Bills 438–444, 760, 1092, and 1202* (Lansing, MI, November 12, 2002), 5. Analysis available at http://www.michiganlegislature.org.

38. Also, the default city election date was changed from November of even-numbered years to November of odd-numbered years.

39. State of Michigan Journal of the House of Representatives Number 54, 92nd Legislature, Regular Session of 2003, Lansing, MI (June 19, 2003): 931.

40. Brad Kadrich, "Schools Election Bills Headed to Governor," *Observer and Eccentric*, November 13, 2011.

41. Lori Yaklin, "Consolidate School Elections with General Elections," *Michigan Education Report*, August 15, 1999.

42. South Dakota Legislature, Seventy-Sixth Legislative Session, House Bill 1204, audio recording of floor debate in the House of Representatives, February 8, 2001, available online at http://legis.state.sd.us/sessions/2001/1204.htm.

43. South Dakota Legislature, Seventy-Sixth Legislative Session, House Bill 1204, audio recording of debate in the House State Affairs Committee, February 7, 2001, available online at http://legis.state.sd.us/sessions/2001/1204.htm.

44. South Dakota Legislature, Seventy-Sixth Legislative Session, House Bill 1204, audio recording of floor debate in the House of Representatives, February 8, 2001, available online at http://legis.state.sd.us/sessions/2001/1204.htm.

45. Ibid.

46. Ibid.

47. Ibid.

48. Montana, House Committee on State Administration, PDF Minutes, Exhibit #7, January 25, 2011, available online at http://data.opi.mt.gov/legbills/2011/Minutes/House/Exhibits/sth19a07.pdf, accessed February 11, 2012.

49. Montana, House Committee on State Administration, PDF Minutes, Exhibit #8, January 25, 2011, available online at http://data.opi.mt.gov/legbills/2011/Minutes/House/Exhibits/sth19a08.pdf, accessed February 11, 2012.

50. Montana, House Committee on State Administration, audio recording of hearing on January 25, 2011, available online at http://leg.mt.gov/css/bills/11BillCentric.asp?BillNumber=HB242, accessed February 11, 2012.

51. Ibid.

52. Ibid.

53. Ibid.

54. Hawaii has one statewide school district, and Alaska did not have any school board election consolidation bills from 2001 to 2011.

55. School districts in two of the states shaded light gray—Arizona and Louisiana—already had November of even-year elections as of 2001, but between 2001 and 2011, their state legislatures proposed consolidation of *all* local elections (or, in Louisiana's case, all state and local elections) in November. Since I coded such bills as affecting school districts (as well as counties, municipalities, and special districts), they are included in this analysis. However, none of my substantive conclusions change when I exclude those two bills.

56. The difference in means is statistically significant at the 10% level in a two-tailed test.

57. Since only a fraction of the 102 school bills received any kind of vote, the types of bills that made it to that stage—as well as the types of legislatures that advanced bills to that stage—might be those for which legislative advancement and

passage were more likely. This analysis therefore should not be interpreted as representative of what all possible votes would look like if state legislatures were randomly assigned to vote on a particular school election consolidation bill.

58. The set of twenty-eight bills excludes three bills from New Mexico that received committee votes but for which I do not have complete information about who voted for and against the bills. It also excludes one bill in South Dakota which had its election consolidation provision removed before it reached the committee vote. Lastly, I exclude one bill in Texas that involved only the election timing of school districts around Corpus Christi.

59. I dropped one vote cast by an independent legislator in New Mexico.

60. Specifically, this last bill proposed that every four years, February school board elections would be consolidated with presidential primaries.

61. HB 679, for example, which was voted down 38–57 in the lower chamber, had eighteen supportive Republican votes and twelve opposing Republican votes. The next year, HB 728 saw a similar bipartisan split, with nineteen out of the seventy-one "yes" votes coming from House Republicans and fourteen out of thirty-one "no" votes coming from House Republicans.

62. Here, to avoid mistaking partisanship on school issues for partisanship on municipal election timing, I only look at bills that propose changes to municipal election timing without changes to school election timing.

63. On the nine bills that made election consolidation discretionary for municipal governments, the final passage votes that were cast were all either unanimous or near unanimous in favor.

64. Specifically, in Colorado in 2001, the committee vote on a bill affecting town and special district elections featured four Republicans voting in favor, four Democrats voting in opposition, and a single Republican joining the Democrats. In Virginia in 2003, the House Committee on Privileges and Elections voted to kill a bill that would have required city elections to be held concurrently with either statewide or national elections, and six Democrats, ten Republicans, and one Independent voted for defeat while four Republicans and one Democrat voted to keep the bill alive.

65. This was Louisiana HB 1610 in 2003.

66. This was Utah SB 115 in 2004.

67. See, for example, Moe, *Special Interest*; Hacker and Pierson, "Winner-Take-All Politics," 152–204.

68. Banfield and Wilson, *City Politics*, 87.

Chapter 5

1. Parts of this chapter were previously published in two articles: Sarah F. Anzia, "Election Timing and the Electoral Influence of Interest Groups," *Journal*

of Politics 73, no. 2 (2011): 412–27, © 2011 Southern Political Science Association; Sarah F. Anzia, "The Election Timing Effect: Evidence from a Policy Intervention in Texas," *Quarterly Journal of Political Science* 7, no. 3 (2012): 209–48. The excerpts from the *Journal of Politics* article are reprinted with the permission of Cambridge University Press.

2. Moe, "Political Control and the Power of the Agent," 1–29; Moe, "Teacher Unions and School Board Elections," 254–87; Hess and Leal, "School House Politics," 228–52.

3. Albert Shanker, "A Reply to Myron Lieberman," *Phi Delta Kappan* (May 1979): 652–54.

4. US Census Bureau, Census of Governments, 2011 Public Employment and Payroll Data, Local Governments, United States Total (2011); Mark Dixon, "Public Education Finances: 2010" (Washington, DC: US Census Bureau, 2012), Current Spending of Public Elementary–Secondary School Systems by State: 2009–2010, Summary of Public Elementary–Secondary School System Finances by State: 2009–2010.

5. Sheila Murray, William Evans, and Robert Schwab find that 64.7% of the variance in per-pupil spending across school districts in the United States is explained by between-state differences. Sheila E. Murray, William N. Evans, and Robert M. Schwab, "Education-Finance Reform and the Distribution of Education Resources," *American Economic Review* 88, no. 4 (1998): 789–812.

6. The 2003–4 SASS used a stratified probability proportionate to size sample of the universe of 2001–2 NCES Common Core of Data (CCD) school districts that operated at least one school. Five thousand, four hundred thirty-seven public school districts were sampled in total, and the weighted response rate was 82.9%.

7. I exclude Alaska, Maine, Mississippi, and North Dakota because I could not find any central source of information on school district election timing. I also exclude South Dakota, since according to the primary election results the South Dakota secretary of state distributed, no school board elections were held during the statewide primary until 2008. I did not include Massachusetts because only its regional school districts that hold district-wide elections have elections in November of even-numbered years.

8. Hajnal, Lewis, and Louch, *Municipal Elections in California.*

9. Only three districts meet the latter condition. I exclude these districts because charter schools often operate according to different rules than regular public schools, including rules of how teacher salaries are determined. I also exclude districts that do not hold school board elections.

10. Moe, *Special Interest.*

11. Figures in parentheses are standard errors clustered by state.

12. District demographics have been used in the literature to measure education policy preferences: Michael Berkman and Eric Plutzer, for example, use demographics and General Social Survey data to impute school-district-level preferences for public education spending. See Michael B. Berkman and Eric Plutzer,

Ten Thousand Democracies: Politics and Public Opinion in America's School Districts (Washington, DC: Georgetown University Press, 2005).

13. Presidential vote shares are not readily available at the school district level for most states. Matching school districts to parent counties is unproblematic in the South, where many districts are coterminous with counties. In Minnesota and California, school districts usually do not follow county boundaries. Fortunately, for Minnesota, I am able to use precinct-level presidential vote share files from 2000 to create an accurate measure of presidential vote share at the school district level. I have used the Minnesota data to confirm that county-level vote share is a reasonable proxy for district-level vote share.

14. About 12% of teachers throughout the United States are organized in chapters of the AFT rather than the NEA, but they are predominantly in New York; Washington, DC; and Rhode Island, none of which are included in this analysis.

15. I am missing NEA data for ten of the school districts in the analysis. The ratio of NEA members to full-time equivalent teachers can be greater than 1 since part-time teachers, retired teachers, education support professionals, and students training to become teachers are eligible for NEA membership. For the results presented in table 5.2, I exclude twelve districts for which the NEA-to-teacher ratio is greater than 2 since the coefficient on that variable is sensitive to these outlying values. The coefficient on *Off-Cycle*, however, is not sensitive to the inclusion of these cases.

16. For a review, see Deborah Fletcher and Lawrence W. Kenny, "The Influence of the Elderly on School Spending in a Median Voter Framework," *Education Finance and Policy* 3, no. 3 (2008): 283–315.

17. See, for example, Eric Brunner and Ed Balsdon, "Intergenerational Conflict and the Political Economy of School Spending," *Journal of Urban Economics* 56, no. 2 (2004): 369–88; Cynthia Miller, "Demographics and Spending for Public Education: A Test of Interest Group Influence," *Economics of Education Review* 15, no. 2 (1996): 175–85; James M. Poterba, "Demographic Structure and the Political Economy of Public Education," *Journal of Policy Analysis and Management* 16, no. 1 (1997): 48–66.

18. Moe, *Special Interest.*

19. I calculate turnout by dividing the number of ballots cast in the race by the number of voters who were registered in the district as of 7:00 a.m. on the day of the election. Since most school districts allow voters to cast as many votes as there are available seats, I estimate the number of ballots cast by dividing the total votes cast by the number of seats up for election in each race.

20. One district with very high turnout is excluded from the figure for presentational purposes.

21. I lack median income data for two of the districts, and I exclude one district that has a logged average teacher salary that is below the first quartile by about 2.5 times the interquartile range.

22. Results are not shown. Specifically, when I include the NEA-to-teacher ratio in the model, the coefficient on *Off-Cycle* is still 0.02 and significant. Also, the coefficient on *Off-Cycle* changes only slightly when I use county-level Democratic vote share from 2004 as the measure of district ideology.

23. Debbi Weimer, *School Board Elections, Data Brief 5: September 2001* (East Lansing: Education Policy Center at Michigan State University, 2001).

24. Ann Allen and David N. Plank, "School Board Election Structure and Democratic Representation," *Educational Policy* 19 (2005): 519.

25. See, for example, Hajnal and Trounstine, "Where Turnout Matters," 515–35; Kim Quaile Hill and Jan E. Leighley, "The Policy Consequences of Class Bias in State Electorates," *American Journal of Political Science* 36, no. 2 (1992): 351–65; Kim Quaile Hill, Jan E. Leighley, and Angela Hinton-Andersson, "Lower Class Mobilization and Policy Linkage in the U.S. States," *American Journal of Political Science* 39, no. 1 (1995): 75–86.

26. Moe, "Political Control and the Power of the Agent," 1–29.

27. Nine districts do not have a superintendent salary on record.

28. Data come from the 2005–6 NCES CCD files. This figure represents the average salary of superintendents, deputy and assistant superintendents, and anyone with district-wide responsibilities such as district administrative assistants and business managers.

29. There may exist cases where teacher unions work to elect school board members whom they expect to hire a congenial superintendent—perhaps even a superintendent who is an ally of the unions. In this case, we might expect superintendent salary to also be tied to teacher union influence. The absence of effects of *Off-Cycle* and the turnout variables for superintendent salary suggests that this is not the case in the average district in Minnesota, even if it is true for some districts. The evidence that there is no salary advantage for district administrators reinforces this point.

30. Christopher R. Berry and Jacob E. Gersen, "Election Timing and Public Policy," *Quarterly Journal of Political Science* 6, no. 2 (2011): 103–35.

31. Party primaries and school tax and bond elections were exceptions to this rule.

32. Allyson H. Collins, senior attorney, Legal Services Division, Texas Association of School Boards, e-mail message to the author, December 3, 2008.

33. A few districts voluntarily moved their elections from May to November in spite of the fact that they could have retained their May election schedule. Also, the new law required a number of school districts to change the term lengths of their trustees in order to comply with the joint election requirement. HB 1 did not apply to any school district elections other than regular trustee elections. Even after 2006, districts were allowed to hold bond elections and proposition elections on either the May or November uniform date.

34. Allyson H. Collins and Melanie Best, "Elections Update," Texas Association of School Boards, Legal Division, Prepared for the TASB/TASA Convention, September 28–30, 2007.

35. Texas House of Representatives, House Committee on Elections, 79th Legislature Broadcast Archives, March 16, 2005, available online at http://www .house.state.tx.us/media/welcome.php. HB 733, which would have moved all bond elections in the state to November of even-numbered years, was considered by the committee on the same day. Many of the parties that testified against HB 733 were the same as those that testified against HB 855.

36. Ibid.

37. Ibid.

38. Texas State Senate, Senate Committee on Finance, Video/Audio Archives, 79th Session, May 1, 2006, available online at http://www.senate.state.tx.us/75r/senate/ commit/c540/c540.htm.

39. The 2008–9 school district boundaries shapefile is from the Texas Education Agency (TEA). The geographic information was collected by the GIS staff of the Research Division of the Texas Legislative Council. There are 1,032 independent school districts in Texas according to the TEA directory of school districts for 2008–9, but there are only 1,029 districts in the shapefile, and six of them are common school districts. Since the HB 1 elections rule did not explicitly apply to common school districts, I exclude them from the analysis. Therefore, with 1,023 independent school districts in the shapefile, I lack data on nine independent school districts. The shapefile for Texas municipalities comes from the Texas State Data Center and Office of the State Demographer, Texas 2009 TIGER/Line State Shapefiles, October 9, 2009, available online at http://txsdc.utsa.edu/txdata/. I removed all unincorporated places from that shapefile.

40. In addition, I read the individual local governance policies of ninety-eight school districts that I was unable to classify, seven of which stated that their elections are in November of even-numbered years. When I include those districts in the treatment group, the main results are unchanged. However, for the analysis here, I exclude those seven districts because I want the treatment group to only include districts that were forced to switch to November even-year elections (not those that voluntarily switched).

41. See TASB, 2010–11 TASB/TASA Teacher Report, available online at http:// www.tasb.org/services/hr_services/salary_surveys/documents/tchr_highlights _landing.pdf.

42. TASB conducts annual school district surveys that ask for detailed salary schedule information, but since only 60% to 70% of districts respond each year, those data cannot be combined into a complete panel. Even so, I have acquired three years of detailed salary survey data from TASB (2003, 2006, and 2009), and I use them in the robustness checks discussed in the following section.

43. The salary data include base salary only; monies from other programs such as the incentive programs created by HB 1 are excluded. TEA, Information Analysis Division, e-mail message to the author, October 29, 2010.

44. While incumbent defeat rates in school board elections tend to be low, they are higher than in US House races. See Christopher R. Berry and William G.

Howell, "Accountability and Local Elections: Rethinking Retrospective Voting," *Journal of Politics* 69, no. 3 (2007): 844–58. This suggests that sitting school board members often cannot safely ignore the policy pressure of organized groups in the electorate. Moreover, in California, Moe finds that teacher union endorsements are just as important to school board candidate success as incumbency. See Moe, "Political Control and the Power of the Agent," 1–29.

45. After HB 1 became law in 2006, it was unclear to officials in many affected districts whether they were required to change term lengths in order to comply with the joint elections rule. Between the summer of 2006 and the spring of 2007, many treatment districts simply rescheduled their May elections to November 2007, still an off-cycle election. To resolve the ambiguity, in April 2007, the Texas attorney general officially interpreted HB 1 as requiring school districts in the treatment group to reschedule their trustee elections for November 2008. (See Texas Attorney General Opinion GA-535, 2007.) That same month, the legislature passed SB 670, which allowed districts to change the term lengths of their trustees in order to comply with HB 1. Thus the implications of HB 1 were fully evident to school districts starting in the spring of 2007.

46. The denominator is the number of adults in the district as of the 2000 Census. Three of the thirty-one school districts in this dataset conduct school board elections by electoral district, and since I do not have the census figures broken down at the level of the school electoral district, I exclude those districts from the regression in column (1). Some districts that held at-large elections did not track the number of unique voters who participated in the school board elections, and in those cases, I estimated the number of ballots cast by dividing the total number of votes cast in the election by the number of positions up for election.

47. Specifically, only fourteen districts supplied the number of registered voters in the district for each election.

48. Data for both variables, as well as for the data on percent Hispanic, are from the CCD files from the NCES. Median family income is adjusted to 2009 dollars.

49. See Stephanie M. Martin, "Are Public School Teacher Salaries Paid Compensating Wage Differentials for Student Racial and Ethnic Characteristics?" *Education Economics* 18, no. 3 (2010): 349–70.

50. For all larger calipers that I tried, I did not achieve balance on either district enrollment or district median income.

51. Jasjeet S. Sekhon, "Multivariate and Propensity Score Matching Software with Automated Balance Optimization: The Matching Package for R," *Journal of Statistical Software* 42, no. 7 (2011): 1–52.

52. The number of control districts in this case is 742 instead of 743 because the TEA data are missing an average salary value for one district in 2006.

53. In order to achieve balance on the covariates here, I also have to match on pretreatment salary levels and growth. I use a caliper of 1.5 standard deviations for these variables.

54. See Nancy Burns, *The Formation of American Local Governments: Private Values in Public Institutions* (New York: Oxford University Press, 1994).

55. The teacher experience figures track how long a given teacher has been working for the Texas public school system, not the number of years he has been in a particular position.

56. Martin, "Are Public School Teacher Salaries Paid Compensating Wage Differentials for Student Racial and Ethnic Characteristics?" 349–70.

57. The number of observations in column (1) is 6,418 rather than 6,419 (917 districts x 7 years) due to missing average teacher salary data for one district in 2006. In addition, I am missing property values data for eleven district-years, which explains the number of observations in column (2).

58. The salary schedule data were provided by TASB for a subset of districts in 2003, 2006, and 2009.

59. The unionization rate equals the total number of instructional employees who were members of an employee organization divided by full-time equivalent instructional employees in 1987.

60. Moreover, there is one district that strongly influences the estimated coefficient on the interaction term. When I exclude that district from the analysis, the estimated coefficient on the interaction term drops from –0.013 to –0.008.

61. There are 359 districts in this model: 51 treatment districts and 308 control districts.

62. I do not have the TEA actual financial reports for the 2009–10 academic year; hence, I am missing a year of data in the results presented in column (6). However, when I replace the dependent variable with the budgeted amounts for all years—for which I have figures for 2009–10—the results do not change in any substantive sense.

63. Mark Dixon, "Public Education Finances: 2010" (Washington, DC: US Census Bureau, 2012), Current Spending of Public Elementary–Secondary School Systems by State: 2009–2010, Summary of Public Elementary–Secondary School System Finances by State: 2009–2010.

Chapter 6

1. Toni Mazzacane, "Voter Turnout Is Low in Capistrano," *Orange County Register*, April 14, 1988, 1.

2. Moe, *Special Interest*.

3. Moe, "Teacher Unions and School Board Elections," 254–87.

4. Berry, *Imperfect Union*, 51.

5. Hajnal, Lewis, and Louch, *Municipal Elections in California*.

6. This is the type of group that Berry envisions, which makes sense given that his focus is on the fiscal impacts of overlapping governments. See Berry, *Imperfect*

Union. However, not all interest groups pressure for a larger slice of the budget, and even the groups that *do* can operate as political allies rather than adversaries. Consider, for example, teacher unions and other public employee unions: teachers prioritize spending on teachers, and other school employees presumably prioritize spending on bus drivers, cafeteria workers, nurses, and librarians, but these groups usually aren't enemies in school elections. In fact, they often work together to promote greater overall spending on public schools.

7. The text of the argument against Measure A is from the League of Women Voters and Smart Voter.

8. For a discussion of the advantages of studying US local governments, see Jessica L. Trounstine, "All Politics Is Local: The Reemergence of the Study of City Politics," *Perspectives on Politics* 7, no. 3 (2009): 611–18.

9. US Census Bureau, Census of Governments, Preliminary Count of Local Governments by Type and State: 2012 (accessed March 28, 2013).

10. US Census Bureau, Census of Governments, Local Government Finances by Type of Government and State: 2006–7; State and Local Government Finances by Level of Government and by State: 2006–7.

11. US Census Bureau, Census of Governments, Summary of Public Employment and Payrolls by Type of Government: March 2007.

12. See, for example, the *Staff Report of the City of Lancaster, California* (Lancaster, CA, April 24, 2007), 2. The city was considering whether to consolidate its elections with the school board elections in November of odd-numbered years. The staff report from Geri K. Bryan, city clerk, explained, "Although it is not law, since 1981 the Board of Supervisors has consistently applied a policy of denying requests for consolidation with the Primary and General Elections (even-numbered years) due to a limited number of ballot positions and the risk of forcing concurrent elections."

13. The reason for this gap in the data is that Los Angeles County only provides information on city elections that are administered by the county. However, starting in 2004, Los Angeles County provided the CEDA with a calendar of all the elections held throughout the county—including those not administered by the county government—so that CEDA researchers could contact city clerks directly for any missing election information. Valory J. Logsdon, research analyst, Institute for Social Research, e-mail message to author, October 7, 2010.

14. For cities that hold either primary elections or runoffs in addition to the regular election, I coded their election timing according to the date of the general election. For any city in which the regular election date was not clear given the pattern of election dates in the CEDA data, I contacted the city clerk to confirm the city's election timing.

15. During the 1980s and 1990s, municipal governments in Orange County deserted the traditional off-cycle election schedule one by one in favor of elections consolidated with presidential and gubernatorial elections.

16. See, for example, Hajnal, Lewis, and Louch, *Municipal Elections in California*.

17. See, for example, Caren, "Big City, Big Turnout? Participation in American Cities," 31–46.

18. I drop the election results from 1995 to 1998 because I do not have information on the number of registered voters by city for those years.

19. I do not test for an effect of concurrence with school board elections because school districts are often not coterminous with city boundaries. Moreover, Hajnal, Lewis, and Louch do not find an effect on turnout of city election concurrence with school board elections. See Hajnal, Lewis, and Louch, *Municipal Elections in California*.

20. For each year, I used the registration files from either February or March.

21. As I explain below, the cities that hold elections by district all have staggered elections—for example, half of the districts are elected in one year and the other half are elected two years later—so I cannot simply add up the votes from each district in a given election to calculate the turnout rate.

22. J. Eric Oliver, *Democracy in Suburbia* (Princeton, NJ: Princeton University Press, 2001).

23. Figures on city population for each year come from the city program expenditures reports made available from the California Local Government Finance Almanac, the source for which are the Cities Annual Reports from the California state controller.

24. The demographic variables are constant within cities (with the exception of population), so I cannot estimate their coefficients in this model.

25. Most of the research along these lines characterizes business interests as critical to local politics and politicians for a variety of reasons. Clarence Stone, for example, argues that business leaders are important allies of city politicians because they have resources that are critical to politicians' electoral and policy goals. See Clarence N. Stone, *Regime Politics* (Lawrence: University Press of Kansas, 1989). As Paul Peterson explains, city governments have to compete with other governments for business development, hence the need for city hall to find allies in the business community. See Paul E. Peterson, *City Limits* (Chicago: University of Chicago Press, 1981).

26. Oliver, *Local Elections and the Politics of Small-Scale Democracy*.

27. Moe, "Teacher Unions and School Board Elections," 254–87.

28. US Census Bureau, *Annual Survey of Public Employment and Payroll*, 2011.

29. Moe, "Political Control and the Power of the Agent," 1–29.

30. Calculations made by Sarah Anzia and Terry Moe using data from the Current Population Survey, 2003–10.

31. Sarah F. Anzia and Terry M. Moe, "Public Sector Unions and the Costs of Government," working paper, Stanford University, Stanford, CA, 2012; Jeffrey Zax

and Casey Ichniowski, "The Effects of Public Sector Unionism on Pay, Employment, Department Budgets, and Municipal Expenditures," in *When Public Sector Workers Unionize*, ed. Richard B. Freeman and Casey Ichniowski (Chicago: University of Chicago Press, 1988), 323–64.

32. James T. Bennett and William P. Orzechowski, "The Voting Behavior of Bureaucrats: Some Empirical Evidence," *Public Choice* 41, no. 2 (1983): 271–83; Winston C. Bush and Arthur T. Denzau, "The Voting Behavior of Bureaucrats and Public Sector Growth," in *Budgets and Bureaucrats: The Sources of Government Growth*, ed. Thomas Borcherding (Durham, NC: Duke University Press, 1977); Elizabeth C. Corey and James C. Garand, "Are Government Employees More Likely to Vote? An Analysis of Turnout in the 1996 U.S. National Election," *Public Choice* 111 (2002): 259–83; Edward M. Gramlich and Daniel L. Rubinfeld, "Voting on Public Spending: Differences between Public Employees, Transfer Recipients, and Private Workers," *Journal of Policy Analysis and Management* 1, no. 4 (1982): 516–33.

33. Anzia and Moe, "Public Sector Unions and the Costs of Government"; Orly Ashenfelter, "The Effect of Unionization on Wages in the Public Sector: The Case of Firefighters," *Industrial and Labor Relations Review* 24, no. 2 (1971): 191–202; Stanley Benecki, "Municipal Expenditure Levels and Collective Bargaining," *Industrial Relations* 17, no. 2 (1978): 216–30; Richard B. Freeman and Robert G. Valletta, "The Effects of Public Sector Labor Laws on Labor Market Institutions and Outcomes," in *When Public Sector Workers Unionize*, ed. Richard B. Freeman and Casey Ichniowski (Chicago: University of Chicago Press, 1988), 81–106; Robert G. Valletta, "The Impact of Unionism on Municipal Expenditures and Revenues," *Industrial and Labor Relations Review* 42, no. 3 (1989): 430–42; Jeffrey S. Zax, "Employment and Local Public Sector Unions," *Industrial Relations* 28, no. 1 (1989): 21–31; Zax and Ichniowski, "The Effects of Public Sector Unionism on Pay, Employment, Department Budgets, and Municipal Expenditures," 323–64. Although, see Stephen J. Trejo, "Public Sector Unions and Municipal Employment," *Industrial and Labor Relations Review* 45, no. 1 (1991): 166–80.

34. Anzia and Moe, "Public Sector Unions and the Costs of Government."

35. Wilson, *Political Organizations*.

36. See Jack Stieber, *Public Employee Unionism: Structure, Growth, Policy* (Washington, DC: Brookings Institution Press, 1973); Zax and Ichniowski, "The Effects of Public Sector Unionism on Pay, Employment, Department Budgets, and Municipal Expenditures," 323–64; Timothy D. Chandler and Rafael Gely, "Protective Service Unions, Political Activities, and Bargaining Outcomes," *Journal of Public Administration Research and Theory* 5, no. 3 (1995): 295–318.

37. James L. Stern, "A Look Ahead at Public Employee Unionism," *Annals of the American Academy of Political and Social Science* 473 (1984): 174.

38. Many local police unions are affiliated with the Fraternal Order of Police or the International Union of Police Associations, but many are not.

39. Stern, "A Look Ahead at Public Employee Unionism," 175.

40. Anzia and Moe, "Public Sector Unions and the Costs of Government"; Chandler and Gely, "Protective Service Unions, Political Activities, and Bargaining Outcomes," 295–318.

41. Teaford, *The Unheralded Triumph*.

42. See ibid. As Teaford explains, firefighters had powerful allies in the fire insurance underwriters, who wanted the best possible firefighters and used their influence to ensure that fire departments were insulated from partisan politics. As a result, as early as the late 1800s, fire departments were staffed with professional firefighters who stayed in their jobs for many years. Police departments, by contrast, were some of the most politicized city departments of all. Because police departments were constantly being reshuffled and reorganized for political reasons, it took much longer for police to professionalize than firefighters.

43. This category includes wages, overtime, cash payments for vacation and sick leave, and bonuses. In the case that the employee had no wages subject to Medicare, the controller asked the local government respondent to calculate the appropriate amount.

44. There are additional cities that report having a fire department and fire protection employees, but they do not have regular, full-time firefighters. For example, some have fire battalion chiefs and fire captains but only volunteer or reserve firefighters, and these cities are excluded. I also exclude three cities whose median reported Medicare wages were less than the minimum firefighter salary.

45. As with firefighters, this excludes five cities in which the reported Medicare wages for police officers were less than the minimum salary for police officers.

46. In other words, it equals one for cities that switched to on-cycle elections in 1996 and thirteen if the city switched to on-cycle elections in 2008. It equals zero for cities that consistently held on-cycle elections since 1995, cities with off-cycle elections, and cities with elections concurrent with primaries.

47. It is not obvious that this set of control variables is warranted, but I would like to be able to reduce any concern that the effects presented above are spurious.

48. The crime data come from the Federal Bureau of Investigation, *Crime in the United States, 2008*, US Department of Justice (2009). Specifically, the variables used for the analysis are the logged number of violent crimes per thousand city residents in 2008 and the logged number of property crimes per thousand city residents in 2008. In order to keep cities with zero crimes in the analysis, I added one to the number of crimes before dividing by population and taking the log. I am missing the crime data for seven of the 273 cities in the dataset.

49. In results not shown, I also find some evidence that police officers tend to have more generous pension formulas in cities with off-cycle elections: Police officers in only 4% of off-cycle cities are eligible for less than 3% of salary multiplied by years of service, whereas the multiplier is less than 3% in 14% of on-cycle cities. (There isn't much variation in the pension formulas of California firefighters; almost all of them are eligible for 3% of their salary at age fifty, multiplied by their years of service.)

50. Cities with on-cycle elections but a history of nonconcurrent elections spend more on police officers' health benefits and on minimum salaries, but there is no significant effect for the other two compensation variables. Again, higher per capita income and lower poverty rates are associated with higher police officer salaries, as are charter city status and the percentage of residents who are Hispanic. In general, cities in Los Angeles County tend to compensate police officers less than cities outside of Los Angeles County. My main findings from table 6.4 are substantively the same when I exclude the crime statistics from the police compensation models (to make them comparable to the models from table 6.3), and also when I limit the sample to the set of cities used in table 6.3. The only notable difference is that *History of nonconcurrence* is a positive and significant predictor of total police wages when I limit the sample to the cities included in the firefighter compensation models, and its coefficient is insignificant in the model of minimum police salary when I exclude the crime variables.

51. I lose forty observations when I include the police unionization measure.

52. I limit the analysis to the cities that provide fire protection services and had positive fire protection expenditures in 2007 according to the state controller's financial reports.

53. The same is true when I include controls for the violent crime and property crime rates: the coefficients on the two election timing indicators are statistically insignificant.

54. See Jessica L. Trounstine, "Turnout and Incumbency in Local Elections," *Urban Affairs Review* 49, no. 2 (2013), 167–89.

55. Hajnal, *America's Uneven Democracy*, 157.

Chapter 7

1. Seymour Martin Lipset, *Political Man: The Social Bases of Politics* (Baltimore: Johns Hopkins University Press, 1981), 27.

2. Arend Lijphart, "Unequal Participation: Democracy's Unresolved Dilemma," *American Political Science Review* 91, no. 1 (1997): 1–14.

3. Hajnal, *America's Uneven Democracy*.

4. Eric Oliver and Shang Ha, for example, find that on average, the small group of voters that participates in off-cycle suburban elections is more knowledgeable about the issues at stake in those elections than the larger group of voters that participates in on-cycle suburban elections. J. Eric Oliver and Shang E. Ha, "Vote Choice in Suburban Elections," *American Political Science Review* 101, no. 3 (2007): 393–408.

5. Oliver, *Local Elections and the Politics of Small-Scale Democracy*, 84.

6. See, for example, Arthur Lupia, "Shortcuts versus Encyclopedias: Information and Voting Behavior in California Insurance Reform Elections," *American Political Science Review* 88, no. 1 (1994): 63–76; Samuel L. Popkin, "Information

Shortcuts and the Reasoning Voter," in *Information, Participation, and Choice*, ed. Bernard Grofman (Ann Arbor: University of Michigan Press, 1994), 17–35. Others are less optimistic, finding that low levels of political information among large numbers of voters result in election outcomes that differ from what they would have been if all voters were well informed. See, for example, Larry M. Bartels, "Uninformed Votes: Information Effects in Presidential Elections," *American Journal of Political Science* 40, no. 1 (1996): 194–230.

7. Lijphart, "Unequal Participation: Democracy's Unresolved Dilemma," 1–14.

8. On the turnout effects of voter ID laws and election day registration, see, for example, Kyle Dropp, "Voter ID Laws and Voter Turnout," working paper, Stanford University, Stanford, CA, 2012; Barry C. Burden and Jacob R. Neiheisel, "The Impact of Election Day Registration on Voter Turnout and Election Outcomes," *American Politics Research* 40, no. 4 (2012): 636–64.

9. Albert K. Karnig and B. Oliver Walter, "Decline in Municipal Voter Turnout: A Function of Changing Structure," *American Politics Quarterly* 11, no. 4 (1983): 491–505.

10. Popkin, "Information Shortcuts and the Reasoning Voter," 17–36.

11. Jack Citrin, Eric Schickler, and John Sides, "What If Everyone Voted? Simulating the Impact of Increased Turnout in Senate Elections," *American Political Science Review* 47, no. 1 (2003): 75–90; Highton and Wolfinger, "The Political Implications of Higher Turnout"; Wolfinger and Rosenstone, *Who Votes?*

12. Hajnal and Trounstine, "Where Turnout Matters."

13. For example, see Hill and Leighley, "The Policy Consequences of Class Bias in State Electorates," 351–65.

14. Oliver, *Local Elections and the Politics of Small-Scale Democracy*.

15. Hacker and Pierson, "Winner-Take-All Politics," 152–204.

16. Dahl, *Who Governs? Democracy and Power in an American City*; Truman, *The Governmental Process: Political Interests and Public Opinion*; Schattschneider, *The Semisovereign People: A Realist's View of Democracy in America*.

17. Dahl, *Who Governs? Democracy and Power in an American City*.

18. Schattschneider, *The Semisovereign People: A Realist's View of Democracy in America*.

19. Dahl, *Who Governs? Democracy and Power in an American City*, 279.

20. See Trounstine, *Political Monopolies in American Cities*.

21. Worth noting is that Dahl recognizes that his optimistic conclusion is dependent on widespread electoral participation. See Dahl, *Who Governs? Democracy and Power in an American City*, 100–102.

22. Bawn et al., "A Theory of Political Parties," 571–97.

23. Ibid., 571, 585.

24. Terry M. Moe, "The Politics of Bureaucratic Structure," in *Can the Government Govern?*, ed. John E. Chubb and Paul E. Peterson (Washington, DC: Brookings Institution, 1989), 268–69.

25. Krehbiel, *Information and Legislative Organization*, 29. See also Riker, "Implications from the Disequilibrium of Majority Rule for the Study of Institutions," 432–46.

26. As Hacker and Pierson explain, doing nothing is often a way that elected officials can satisfy interest groups without bringing it to the attention of voters that they are doing so. Hacker and Pierson, "Winner-Take-All Politics," 152–204.

27. See Wilson, *Political Organizations*, 331–37.

28. On the reciprocal relationship between institutions and interest groups, see Jack L. Walker, *Mobilizing Interest Groups in America: Patrons, Professions, and Social Movements* (Ann Arbor: University of Michigan Press, 1991).

29. See George Tsebelis, "Veto Players and Law Production in Parliamentary Democracies: An Empirical Analysis," *American Political Science Review* 93, no. 3 (1999): 591–608. See also Moe, *Special Interest*, chap. 9.

30. For more on this idea, see, for example, Moe, "The Politics of Bureaucratic Structure," and Trounstine, *Political Monopolies in American Cities*. Of course, enacting politicians can never be sure that the institutions that work for them in one period will continue to do so many years in the future. Chapter 3 showed that occasionally, political party leaders in the nineteenth century would move city elections to on-cycle only to have that choice work in favor of their rivals a few years later. Similarly, the Progressives locked in off-cycle elections across the country in hopes that that election schedule would weaken the urban machines, but in most of the big cities where urban machines were powerful at the end of the nineteenth century, episodes of machine government continued well into the twentieth century.

31. Dahl, *Who Governs? Democracy and Power in an American City*, 279.

Appendixes

1. Arthur J. Townley, Dwight P. Sweeny, and June H. Schmieder, "School Board Elections: A Study of Citizen Voting Patterns," *Urban Education* 29, no. 1 (1994): 50–62.

Index

Page numbers with a t *refer to a table; those with an* f *refer to a figure.*

AARP (American Association of Retired Persons), 20
Adrian, C., 17
African Americans: city elections and, 177, 190t, 191, 193t, 196t; Eight-State Test, 133t, 139t; Minnesota Test, 142t; poverty and, 189; school elections and, 133, 133t, 142, 156, 160, 162, 196t, 231t, 251n11; Texas Test, 157t, 161t
AFT (American Federation of Teachers), 128
Alabama, 131, 228
Aldrich, J., 19
American Association of Retired Persons (AARP), 20
American Federation of Teachers (AFT), 128
Arceneaux, K., 239n23
Arizona, 9, 116, 254n5
Arkansas, 7, 76, 89, 116, 129
Asians: Eight-State Test, 133, 139t; Minnesota Test, 142t; school elections and, 133, 160, 162, 231t; Texas Test, 161t

Banfield, E., 81, 85, 123, 125
Bawn, K., 86, 251n5
Berry, C., 20, 145, 168
blacks. *See* African Americans
Bridges, A., 42, 43, 50, 51, 68, 71
business groups: chambers of commerce, 34, 79, 181, 205; city elections and, 62–63, 263n25; economics and (*see* economics); off-cycle elections and, 21; organized groups and, 25, 79, 99, 181 (*see also* organized groups); People's Party and, 59; policies and, 25, 52, 169; political parties and, 34, 79 (*see also* political parties); professional groups, 21; school elections and, 99, 100, 119; unions and (*see* unions)

California, 228–229; Berkeley, 2, 19; CEDA and, 172–173, 175, 180; charter cities, 172; city elections and, 2, 19, 167–199, 174t, 178t (*see also* city elections; *specific cities, topics*); conservatives and, 33; consolidation proposals and, 172, 181; data sources for, 217–220 (*see also specific topics*); general law cities, 172; government employees and, 182; gubernatorial elections, 175; initiatives and, 33; interest groups and, 181–184 (*see also specific groups*); League of California Cities, 194–195; Local Government Compensation Reports, 185; Palo Alto, 2, 19, 236n6; presidential elections and, 175; San Francisco (*see* San Francisco); teacher unions, 99 (*see also* teacher unions); Torrance ballot measure, 170–171; turnout and, 173–181; unions and, 182 (*see also* unions; *specific types of elections, groups*). *See also specific cities, topics*
California Election Data Archive (CEDA), 172–173, 175
California Local Government Finance Almanac, 194

canvassing, 12, 27, 34, 41, 99
Caren, N., 2
CCD (Common Core of Data), 130
CCES (Cooperative Congressional Election
    Study), 87
CEDA (California Election Data Archive),
    172–173, 175
chambers of commerce, 34, 79, 181, 205
charities, 21
city elections: Australian ballot and, 78; in
    California 2, 19, 167–199, 174t, 178t (see
    also California); CEDA database and,
    172, 173, 175, 180; city spending, 194–198;
    competition in, 177, 180; consolidation
    and, 94f, 120, 167; constitutional conven-
    tions and, 77; Democrats and, 85 (see
    also Democrats); firefighters, 187f, 189t,
    192 (see also firefighters); home rule and,
    79; homeowners and, 207; ICMA sur-
    veys, 74–76; machines and (see urban
    machines); Moe study, 182; municipal
    employees and (see municipal employee
    unions; specific groups); national elec-
    tions and, 22, 41, 45, 50, 176 (see also
    national elections); in nineteenth century,
    11, 49–54 (see also specific cities); NML
    and (see National Municipal League);
    number of, 171; off-cycle elections, 7,
    50, 72, 74, 180, 197, 199, 201 (see also
    off-cycle elections; specific types, cities);
    on-cycle elections, 50, 74, 89 (see also on-
    cycle elections; specific types, cities); orga-
    nized groups and, 181–184, 194 (see also
    specific groups); Philadelphia (see Phila-
    delphia); police and (see police officers);
    political parties and, 49, 78, 79; presiden-
    tial elections and, 22; reforms and, 41, 42,
    43, 46, 73, 77, 78, 202, 213; renters and,
    207; Republicans and (see Republicans);
    San Francisco (see San Francisco); school
    elections and (see school elections); spe-
    cial districts and, 169; special legislation
    and, 77; state elections and, 41, 45, 49, 50,
    176 (see also state elections); state legis-
    lators and, 85; timing in, 49, 173–181;
    turnout and, 45, 144, 177, 180, 194, 198,
    201; unions and (see municipal employee
    unions; specific groups); urban machines
    and, 49, 69. See also local elections; spe-
    cific cities, groups, topics

City Politics (Banfield/Wilson), 81
Civil War period, 11, 65, 245n54
Common Core of Data (CCD), 130
comparative politics, 200
congressional elections: CCES and, 87; elec-
    torates and, 13, 251n6; institutional stud-
    ies and, 236n16; institutions and, 236n16;
    midterm, 1, 2, 3, 5, 31, 120, 204; policies
    and, 13; presidential elections and, 3, 37,
    60, 128, 175 (see also presidential elec-
    tions); reforms and, 244n48; school elec-
    tions and, 141; special elections, 204;
    studies of, 13, 25, 87; turnout, 3, 60, 141
    (see also turnout, low). See also specific
    states, topics
Connecticut, 72, 121, 250n130
conservatives, 89, 252n15; California and, 33;
    liberals and, 252n15 (see also liberals);
    on-cycle elections and, 88–89; Republi-
    cans (see Republicans); school elections
    and, 212; Tea Party groups, 110; turnout
    and, 89
Consistent Voters, 27–32, 49, 52, 68
consolidation proposals: in Arkansas, 116;
    in California, 172, 181; city salaries and,
    197; consolidation and, 121 (see also
    consolidation proposals); Democrats
    and, 120, 121t, 122f, 124, 129; Eight-State
    Test, 133, 133t; legislative progress, 92,
    95–100, 203; in Michigan, 103–105; in
    Montana, 109–111; municipal elections
    and, 120; in New Jersey, 116; nonschool
    elections, 122f; on-cycle elections (see
    on-cycle elections); organized groups
    and, 97–100 (see also organized groups);
    in Philadelphia, 64; political parties and,
    111–118, 120, 121f, 122, 122f; Repub-
    licans and, 111, 120, 121t, 124; school
    board elections and, 102–111, 124, 135;
    in South Dakota, 108–109; turnout and,
    122–123, 167, 200–201; Whigs and, 64
Cooperative Congressional Election Study
    (CCES), 87
Cox, G., 40, 42

Dahl, R., 14, 208, 209, 214
Database of Election Reform Legislation,
    90
democracy, 3, 12, 200–215. See also institu-
    tions; specific topics

Democrats, 46, 63, 243n36; city elections and (*see* city elections); consolidation and, 120, 121, 121t, 122, 122f, 129 (*see also* consolidation proposals); interest groups and, 34, 35 (*see also* organized groups); labor and, 34, 62; Lecompton Constitution and, 246n71; liberals and (*see* liberals); off-cycle timing and, 119; on-cycle elections and, 88, 123; Presidential Voters and, 53; public employee unions and, 101; Republicans and (*see* Republicans); school board elections and, 102, 105–107, 111–118, 117f, 124, 135; turnout and, 89, 118, 120 (*see also* turnout); Whigs and, 51. *See also* political parties; *types of elections, topics*
development, 20, 28–30, 170, 181–182, 205
Dunne, S., 19, 39

economics: business and (*see* business groups); downturn and, 159; incomes and (*see* incomes); municipal governments and, 170; organized groups and, 24–25, 241n8 (*see also* organized groups); timing and, 241n8; unions and (*see* unions). *See also specific topics*
Eight-State Test, 228–232. *See also specific groups, topics*
elderly, 20, 177, 190
electorates, 200; city elections (*see* city elections); composition of, 18–23, 204; Consistent Voters (*see* Consistent Voters); electoral blind spot, 210, 251n5; group effect and (*see* group effect); individual effect (*see* individual effect); information and (*see* information, voter); issues and (*see specific interest groups, topics*); loyalty and, 242n25; median voter and, 208; mobilization of (*see* mobilization); off-cycle timing and, 23, 87, 200, 202 (*see also* off-cycle elections); on-cycle elections (*see* on-cycle elections); organized groups and (*see* organized groups); preferences and, 82, 201, 206, 207, 210; Presidential Voters (*see* Presidential Voters); registration and, 1; representativeness and, 206–210, 252n14; school elections (*see* school elections); state government and, 87–90; turnout and, 16, 19, 200, 201, 202, 207. *See also*

specific groups, types of elections, topics
Engstrom, E., 40
Erie, S., 39, 50
Ethington, P., 40, 42, 43, 50, 67
ethnic groups, 177, 189, 191

factionalism, 27; Democrats and, 56, 57, 58, 243n36; parties and, 46, 48, 76; Republicans and, 67; Union Party and, 61; Whigs and, 521
farm groups, 21, 25
firefighters, 182, 184–198, 203; city elections and, 187f, 189t; city model and, 190t; commissioners and, 5; compensation, 184–194, 187f, 189t, 190t; IAFF, 184; insurance and, 265n42; off-cycle elections and, 189t, 192, 194, 199; police and, 184–198; timing and, 189t
Fischel, W., 19
fusion balloting, 250n130

general-purpose governments, 169
Georgia, 114, 130, 131, 134, 229
Gerber, A., 12
Gersen, J., 145
Goodnow, F. J., 44
Gore, A., 112
Green, D., 12
group effect, 28, 168–170; individual effect and (*see* individual effect); mobilization and, 22; municipal employee unions and, 205; off-cycle elections and, 22, 26; organized groups and, 84; teacher unions and, 205
gubernatorial elections, 3; in California, 180; CEDA and, 175; city elections and, 2, 48, 51, 54, 60, 180, 188, 191; Civil War period, 188, 245n54; Know Nothings and, 244n44; in New York, 57; in Pennsylvania, 225; presidential elections and, 3; school elections and, 165; Texas and, 147; turnout and, 56, 60. *See also* state elections; *specific states*

Hacker, J., 208
Hajnal. Z., 2, 16, 198, 207
Hansen, J. M., 18
Heise, K., 106
Hess, F., 99

Hispanics: city elections, 177, 189, 190t, 191, 193t, 196t, 266n50; Eight-State Test, 133, 133t; Minnesota Test, 142t; school elections, 139t, 155, 155t, 156, 157t, 160, 162, 231t, 232t, 234t, 251n11; Texas Test, 157, 161t
home rule, 77, 79, 213
homeowners, 19, 207

IAFF (International Association of Fire Fighters), 184
ICMA (International City/County Management Association) survey, 74–76
immigrants: Democrats and, 55, 68; electorates, 41; off-cycle elections and, 68; reformers and, 42. *See also specific groups*
incomes: city elections and, 177, 179t; electorates and, 144, 177; firefighters and, 191; high-income voters, 144; measurement of, 132, 160, 260n48; poverty and, 191; teacher salaries, 134, 154–158, 160
Independents, 88, 89, 252n15
Indiana, 76, 116, 229
individual effect, 28; group effect and (*see* group effect); municipal employee unions and, 205; off-cycle elections and, 22–25, 26, 27, 32; organized groups and, 21, 25, 27, 84; teacher unions and, 205; voters and, 22
information, voter, 41; off-cycle elections and, 123, 201–202; organized interest groups and, 21, 211; parties and, 206; reform and, 70; school elections and, 104, 105, 106, 148; turnout and, 201, 207; voter education and, 123
institutions: congressional studies and, 236n16; interest groups and, 212; National Municipal League and, 41, 71; parties and, 69, 268n30; reform movement and, 42, 43; research on, 3, 212, 236n16; stability of, 13, 38, 212–213
interest groups. *See* organized groups
International Association of Fire Fighters (IAFF), 184
International City/County Management Association (ICMA) survey, 74–76
Italy, 1

Japan, 235n3

Kansas, 246n71
Kentucky, 7, 9, 89, 171
Kernell, S., 40
Know Nothing party, 53, 244n44
Kolmogorov-Smirnov (K-S) test, 156
Krehbiel, K., 212

labor unions. *See* unions
League of California Cities, 194–195
Leal, D., 99
least squares model (OLS), 96, 251n11, 251n12
Lewis and Clark Conservatives, 110
Lewis, P., 2
liberals, 88, 89, 251n13, 252n15
Lijphart, A., 200–201
Lipset, S. M., 200
local elections: city elections (*see* city elections); county elections, 94f; interest groups and, 20, 25–26; machines and (*see* urban machines); national elections and, 37, 45, 46, 57; National Municipal League and (*see* National Municipal League); off-cycle scheduling, 10–13, 42, 73, 76; parties and, 45, 47–48, 49, 59, 65; presidential elections and, 37, 57; Progressives and, 41–42; research on, 25; school elections (*see* school elections); state elections and, 37, 45, 46; turnout and, 16, 19, 235n3. *See also specific cities, types of elections, groups*
Louch, H., 2
Louisiana, 7, 92, 95, 121
Lowi, T., 14

machines, political. *See* urban machines
McCaffery, P., 50
Medicaid, 20
Medicare, 20
Meredith, M., 20, 39
Mexico, 205
Michigan, 9, 83, 103–108, 116
Minnesota, 69, 140–143, 229–230
minority groups, 177, 180. *See also specific groups*
Mississippi, 7, 92, 95, 120
mobilization, 22; canvassing and, 12, 27, 34, 41, 99; Democrats and, 101; group effect

and, 18, 22, 24; individual effects, 13, 31; local elections and, 73–78; machines and, 79; off-cycle elections and, 4, 12, 21, 26, 28, 163; organized groups and, 4, 21, 22, 211 (*see also* organized groups); political parties and, 84, 86; teachers and, 163, 166; turnout and, 19, 21 (*see also specific types of elections*); types of, 12, 21; voters and, 13

Moe, T., 20, 98, 182, 183, 211

Montana, 83, 102, 109–111, 116

municipal employee unions, 99, 101, 182, 183; city elections and (*see* city elections; *specific cities, states, groups*); city spending, 197 (*see also specific groups*); firefighters and (*see* firefighters); group effect and, 205; individual effect and, 205; off-cycle elections and, 197; police (*see* police officers); teachers and (*see* teacher unions)

Municipal Year Book (1940), 74

Napoli, W., 108

National Center for Education Statistics (NCES), 130

National Conference of State Legislatures (NCSL) Database on Election Reform Legislation, 90, 91

National Education Association (NEA), 128, 136

national elections: congressional elections (*see* congressional elections); consolidation and (*see* consolidation proposals); presidential elections (*see* presidential elections)

National Municipal League, 41, 44, 49, 69–72, 249n118; off-cycle elections and, 69, 71, 72; political parties and, 71; Progressives and, 49 (*see also* Progressives); urban machines and, 69–72

National Rifle Association (NRA), 34

Native Americans: city elections, 177; Eight-State Test, 133, 133t, 139t; school elections, 142t, 156, 157t, 158t, 160, 162, 231t, 232t; Texas Test, 157t

NCES (National Center for Education Statistics), 130

NCSL (National Conference of State Legislatures) Database on Election Reform Legislation, 90, 91

NEA (National Education Association), 128, 136

Nebraska, 7, 76

Negretto, G., 40, 42, 43, 67

neighborhood associations, 20

New Jersey, 92; complex schedule, 5; consolidation bills, 95; Democrats and, 120; off-cycle elections and, 7, 39; on-cycle elections and, 69, 95, 130; Republicans and, 69; school board elections, 111, 116

New York, 7, 44, 220–225

New York City, 52; Consistent Voters, 52; Democrats in, 51, 52, 54, 55, 55f, 56; first reform movement, 52; intraparty factionalism, 56; National Municipal League and, 49; in nineteenth century, 44, 51–59; off-cycle elections, 58, 63; on-cycle elections, 68, 69; organized groups and, 11; parties and, 42; Presidential Voters, 52; reformers and, 58, 59, 67, 70; Republicans and, 57, 58; Tammany Hall, 49, 55, 56, 58; turnout in, 51, 52, 53, 53f, 54; Whigs and, 52, 69

Nickerson, D., 239n23

North Carolina, 92, 130, 131, 230

NRA (National Rifle Association), 34

nurses, 182, 261n6

off-cycle elections: city elections and (*see* city elections); costs/benefits and, 24; countervailing forces, 29; Democrats and, 119; effects of, 126–166; electorate and, 19, 23, 198, 202 (*see also* electorates); factionalism and (*see* factionalism); group effect and, 22, 26 (*see also* group effect); homeowners and, 19; immigrants and, 68 (*see also specific groups*); individual effect and, 23–24, 25, 26, 27 (*see also* individual effect); information and (*see* information, voter); interest groups and (*see* organized groups); lower classes and, 68; machines and (*see* urban machines); minority voters and, 17; mobilization and (*see* mobilization); municipal elections and (*see* city elections); National Municipal League and, 71, 72 (*see also* National Municipal League); organized groups and (*see* organized groups); policy and, 20, 32, 36, 207 (*see also* policies; *specific groups,*

off-cycle elections (*continued*)
topics); political parties and (*see specific parties*); presidential elections and (*see* presidential elections); Progressives and (*see* Progressives); reasons for, 16; reformers and, 72; representation and, 206 (*see also* electorates); Republicans and, 34, 56–57; school elections and (*see* school elections); as stealth elections, 81; turnout and, 22, 31, 51, 89, 144, 198, 200, 201 (*see also specific types of elections*; turnout, low); unions and (*see* unions). *See also specific types of elections, cities, states, groups, topics*

Oliver, E., 19, 170, 182, 201, 207

OLS. *See* least squares model

Olson, M., 14

on-cycle elections: Civil War and, 65; conservatives and, 88–89; Democrats and, 123–124; liberals and, 88–89; off-cycle elections and (*see* off-cycle elections); organized groups and, 17–18, 22, 24, 32, 170, 239n23, 239n24 (*see also* organized groups); policy and, 36, 206–207 (*see also* policies); political parties and, 45, 48, 210 (*see also* political parties); presidential elections and (*see* presidential elections); reformers and, 69–76; representation and, 206; Republicans and, 88, 90, 101, 118, 123, 149, 210, 247n83, 249n106; research methods and, 127–128, 159–164, 187–189; salaries and, 191–197, 265n49, 266n50 (*see also specific groups*); school board elections, 101 (*see also* school elections); second-order elections, 201; state legislatures and, 90–97; turnout and, 24, 31, 122–123, 152–153, 202; voter education, 123, 201, 266n4; voter stake and, 19, 20, 24, 84. *See also specific types of elections, states, cities, groups, topics*

ordinal logit model, 96

Oregon, 7, 76

organized groups, 14; business groups and (*see* business groups); California and, 181–184 (*see also* California; *specific groups*); city elections and (*see* city elections); competition and, 18, 24–28, 119, 169, 170, 199; Consistent Voters and, 28–32; consolidation and, 97–100, 122

(*see also* consolidation proposals); costs/benefits and, 25, 26; cross-sectional analysis, 127; decision makers and, 82; definition of, 18; economic interests and, 25; effects of, 14; electorate and, 4, 82 (*see also* electorates; *specific groups, types of elections*); government size and, 170; group effect and, 27–28, 84 (*see also* group effect); importance of, 14; incentives of, 201; individual effect and, 13, 21, 25, 27, 84 (*see also* individual effect); information and, 21 (*see also* information, voter); institutions and, 13, 38, 125, 212 (*see also* institutions); lobbying, 33; machines (*see* urban machines); mobilization and, 239n23 (*see* mobilization); municipal government and, 170; off-cycle elections and, 14, 15, 17, 19, 22, 33–34, 84, 169, 202, 204, 207, 240n38 (*see also* off-cycle elections); on-cycle elections, 4, 32, 84 (*see also* on-cycle elections); organizational capacity, 27–28; pluralists and, 14, 208, 210; policy and, 14, 23–24, 82, 169, 207 (*see also* policies; *specific issues, topics*); political parties and, 18, 82, 251n7 (*see also* political parties); power of, 17; Presidential Voters and, 28–32; representation and, 208 (*see also* electorates); school elections and, 98, 123, 168 (*see also* school elections); stakes of, in elections, 19, 20, 21, 24, 84; state legislators and, 85, 86, 89, 100; success of, 125; survey experiments and, 13; timing and, 15–19, 23–32, 81–125, 199, 202, 204, 207, 240n38; turnout and, 17, 110, 123, 209 (*see also* turnout, low); twenty-first century and, 81–125; types of, 169; unions (*see* unions); voting research and, 13. *See also specific categories, groups, issues*

parent-teacher associations, 99

Pennsylvania, 7, 77, 225–226. *See also* Philadelphia

People's Party, 59–61, 246n70, 246n71

Peterson, B., 107

Philadelphia, 44; data sources for, 225–227; Democrats in, 64; nineteenth century, 63–67; reform movement and, 66, 70; Republicans and, 64, 65, 249n106; Second Party American System, 63; urban machines and, 49–54, 67; Whigs and, 64, 68

Pierson, P., 208

Platt, T. C., 58

pluralists, 14, 208, 210

police officers, 182, 184–194; benefits and, 186; city elections and, 184–198, 187f, 193t; city spending and, 195; compensation, 186, 187, 187f, 192, 193, 193t, 194; firefighters and, 184–198; off-cycle elections and, 193, 194, 199, 265n49; policy interests, 185; political competition and, 184, 185; unions, 182, 184, 194, 204, 264n38

policies: city elections and, 198 (*see also* city elections); interest groups and, 4, 14, 23, 25, 181; school elections and, 100 (*see also* school elections); timing and, 11, 23–32, 206, 207, 239; turnout and, 16, 36, 206–207; voter information and, 201, 210, 213; voter representation and, 16–19, 201–210, 252n14 (*see also* electorates). *See also specific groups, elections, topics*

political parties: business groups and, 34, 79; centralized machine, 47; city elections and (*see* city elections; *specific cities, groups*); Democrats (*see* Democrats); factionalism (*see* factionalism); functions of, 33, 82, 210; fusion and, 47, 48, 79; interest groups and, 14, 18, 33–34, 35, 82, 86, 169, 209, 210, 240n36, 240n38, 251n7 (*see also* organized groups); machines and (*see* urban machines); membership in, 240n38 (*see also specific parties*); National Municipal League and, 41, 44, 70, 71, 249n118; New York, 51–52 (*see also* New York); in nineteenth century, 37–80; number of, 40; off-cycle elections, 36 (*see* off-cycle elections; *specific parties*); on-cycle elections and, 40, 45, 48, 210 (*see* on-cycle elections; *specific parties*); People's Party (*see* People's Party); policy and, 34, 35; presidential elections and, 40, 47, 49; Progressives and, 41, 42, 70, 71, 78, 79 (*see also* Progressives); Republicans (*see* Republicans); San Francisco, 59 (*see also* San Francisco); Second American Party System,

46, 50; straight-ticket voting, 47; strength of, 82, 83, 85, 86; Third American Party System, 46, 69; third-party efforts and, 48, 62, 251n12; timing and, 11, 15, 32–35, 45, 76, 213; turnout and, 72, 89, 119 (*see also* turnout, low); in twenty-first century, 83–84; urban machines and, 43, 44, 47, 69, 71, 79; voter loyalty, 242n25; zero-sum competition, 34. *See also specific groups, parties, topics*

presidential elections, 1, 12; coattail effect, 40; congressional elections and, 37; Democrats and, 247n83; group effect and, 27; gubernatorial elections and, 3; history of, 40; local elections and, 2, 3, 22, 37, 47, 53, 54, 60, 62, 72, 89, 176–181, 235n1; loyalty and, 68; Presidential Voters and, 27–32, 47, 52, 68, 239n31; public opinion, turnout and, 90, 203; school elections and, 147; state elections and, 120; turnout and, 1, 12, 60, 178–180, 235n3; Whigs and, 52, 69

Presidential Voters, 27–32, 47, 52, 68, 239n31

pressure group system, 209

Progressives: National Municipal League and, 49 (*see also* National Municipal League); off-cycle timing and, 41–44, 70–76, 78, 79, 84, 203; organized groups and, 79, 84; political parties and, 41, 42, 70, 78, 79; reforms and, 41, 43, 46, 73, 77, 202, 203, 213

public school employees, 99, 100, 106, 111. *See also* teacher unions

public utilities, 39

rational choice model, 235n3

Reed, W. R., 19, 39

referendums, 39, 40

religious groups, 21, 91, 100

renters, homeowners and, 207

representativeness, 16, 19, 201–204, 206–210, 252n14. *See also* electorates

Republicans: California initiatives and, 33; consolidation and, 114, 116, 120, 121t (*see also* consolidation proposals); Democrats and (*see* Democrats); factionalism and, 67; interest groups and, 18, 34, 82 (*see also* organized groups); Know Nothings and, 53, 244n44; low turnout and, 89, 106, 118, 119, 120;

Republicans (*continued*)
  off-cycle elections and, 34, 56–57 (*see also* off-cycle elections); on-cycle elections and, 88, 90, 101, 118, 123, 124, 149, 210, 247n83, 249n106 (*see also* on-cycle elections); Philadelphia, 63–67; reformers and, 68; San Francisco, 59–63; school elections and, 101–114, 115f, 116, 117f, 124, 135, 148; state legislators and, 114, 123; Texas, 148; Third American Party System, 46; third parties and, 48, 62, 251n12; urban machines and, 49, 58, 67, 68
Rhode Island, 7, 76
Rhoden, L., 108
Riker, W., 38
Rosenstone, S., 18

SASS (Schools and Staffing Survey), 130
San Francisco, 44, 60t; city charter, 63, 78; data sources for, 217–220; Democrats, 49–50, 63; machines and, 49–54, 63, 65; nineteenth century and, 40, 59–63; People's Party, 59–60, 61; Reform Ballot Act and, 62; reform organizations, 70; Registry Act, 68; Republicans, 63; timing and, 59–63, 60t, 69, 78; Union Party, 61, 68, 69; Whigs, 59; Workingmen's Party, 62
Schattschneider, E. E., 14, 208, 209, 210
school elections, 7–8, 14–15, 20, 83, 100, 116; city elections and, 109–110 (*see also* city elections); consolidation bills, 94f, 112f, 113f, 114, 124; data collection for, 6, 130; Democrats and, 102, 105, 106, 107, 111, 113, 114, 115f, 116, 117f, 124, 135; district characteristics, 132–133, 152–165; district superintendent, 144–145; Eight-State Test, 129–139; elderly voters and, 136–139; general-purpose government, 168; group activity in, 100; internal variation in, 129–130; in Michigan, 108; in Minnesota, 140–143; Minnesota Test, 137, 140–145; minority groups, 160, 162; in Montana, 109; municipal elections and, 9; national elections and, 111; NEA members, 136; off-cycle, 39, 98, 100, 106, 131–145; omitted variable bias, 130; on-cycle elections and, 101, 115f, 117f, 152–165; organized groups and, 123, 168 (*see also specific groups*); party reversals and, 118–119; Republicans and, 101, 102, 104,

106, 107, 108, 109, 111, 113, 114, 115f, 116, 117f, 124, 135; school board associations and, 100, 106; in South Dakota, 106; state legislators and, 98–102, 101, 111; teacher unions and (*see* teacher unions); Texas Test, 145–165; timing and, 126–166; turnout and, 103, 137, 140–145, 167; urban districts, 153–155. *See also specific cities, states*
Schools and Staffing Survey (SASS), 130
Second American Party System, 46
Semisovereign People, The (Schattschneider), 14–15, 208
seniors, 20, 177, 190
Shanker, A., 128
Social Capital Community Survey (SCCS) 2006, 20
Social Security, 20
social welfare organizations, 21
South Carolina, 130, 131, 230
South Dakota, 7, 83, 102, 106–109, 111, 116, 126, 256n7
state elections: consolidation and, 94, 94f (*see also* consolidation proposals); gubernatorial (*see* gubernatorial elections); local elections and, 37, 49; in Mississippi, 120; school elections and, 111 (*see also* school elections). *See also specific states*
straight-ticket voting, 47
survey experiments, 13
Sweden, 1
Switzerland, 1, 205

Tammany Hall, 49, 55, 58, 59, 243n36
tax protest, 100
Tea Party, 110
teacher unions, 12, 99, 110, 128–129, 258n29; administrators and, 145; AFT and, 128; Census of Government and, 163; collective bargaining, 128; compensation and, 128, 129, 131–134, 135, 262n6; competition and, 170; district superintendent and, 144, 258n29; fringe benefits and, 163; group effect and, 205; health insurance and, 163; individual effect and, 205; Minnesota Test, 143, 144; mobilization and, 99, 136, 166; in Montana, 110; NEA and, 128; off-cycle elections and, 129, 131, 135–137, 149, 166; on-cycle

elections and, 128, 148, 149; school elections and, 99, 118, 135, 166, 168, 203 (*see also* school elections); senior teachers and, 134; TASB and, 148; Texas Test, 154, 154t; treatment effect and, 154
Teaford, J., 77, 185
Tennessee, 230
Texas, 92, 116, 130, 145–165, 255n61, 259n39
Third American Party System, 46, 69
third party groups, 40, 46, 48, 62, 243n37
Trounstine, J., 16, 42, 43, 68, 71, 207
Truman, D., 14, 208
turnout, low: Democrats and, 55; firefighters and, 194; homeowners and, 19; Independents and, 89; interest groups and, 110; machines and, 55, 72, 79; off-cycle elections and, 54, 71, 89, 199, 202, 203, 204 (*see also* off-cycle elections); outside U.S., 205; political parties and, 51, 71, 72, 79, 118; representation and, 16, 19, 201, 202, 205, 207; Republicans and, 89, 106, 118, 119, 120
Tweed, W. M., 55, 56

unions: in California, 182; Democrats and, 34, 62; electorates and, 21; firefighters (*see* firefighters); government employ-
ees, 182; machines and (*see* urban machines); municipal employees (*see* municipal employee unions); on-cycle elections, 185; organized groups and (*see* organized groups); police (*see* police officers); policies and, 25; teacher unions and (*see* teacher unions)
urban machines: low turnout and, 72, 79; off-cycle elections and, 268n30; political parties and, 43, 70; Progressives and, 41; Tammany Hall, 55, 243n36
Utah, 121

Van Norman, T., 107
Virginia, 7, 95, 230
voters. *See* electorates

West Virginia, 93
Whigs, 46, 51–53, 64, 243n36
Who Governs? (Dahl), 14–15, 208, 209
Wick, H., 107
Wilbanks, J., 19, 39
Wilson, J. Q., 25, 81, 85, 123, 125, 212
Wisconsin, 7, 93
Wolfinger, R., 79
Wood, C., 2
Wyoming, 10, 76

2377447